LUXURY IND
FASHION

Materializing Culture

Series Editors: Paul Gilroy and Daniel Miller

LUXURY INDIAN FASHION

A Social Critique

Tereza Kuldova

Bloomsbury Academic
An imprint of Bloomsbury Publishing Plc

B L O O M S B U R Y
LONDON · OXFORD · NEW YORK · NEW DELHI · SYDNEY

Bloomsbury Academic

An imprint of Bloomsbury Publishing Plc

50 Bedford Square	1385 Broadway
London	New York
WC1B 3DP	NY 10018
UK	USA

www.bloomsbury.com

BLOOMSBURY and the Diana logo are trademarks of Bloomsbury Publishing Plc

First published 2016
Paperback edition first published 2017

© Tereza Kuldova, 2016

Tereza Kuldova has asserted her right under the Copyright, Designs and Patents Act, 1988, to be identified as Author of this work.

British Library Cataloguing-in-Publication Data

A catalogue record for this book is available from the British Library.

ISBN: HB: 978-1-4742-2092-7
PB: 978-1-3500-4949-9
ePDF: 978-1-4742-2094-1
ePub: 978-1-4742-2093-4

Library of Congress Cataloging-in-Publication Data

Kuldova, Tereza, author.
Luxury Indian fashion : a social critique / by Tereza Kuldova.
pages cm. – (Materializing culture)
Includes bibliographical references.

ISBN 978-1-4742-2092-7 (hardback) – ISBN 978-1-4742-2094-1 (ePDF) – ISBN 978-1-4742-2093-4 (ePub) 1. Fashion design–India. 2. Elite (Social sciences)–India. 3. India–Social life and customs. I. Title.
TT504.6.I4K85 2016
746.9'20954–dc23
2015033454

Series: Materializing Culture

Typeset by RefineCatch Limited, Bungay, Suffolk

For Robert

CONTENTS

ILLUSTRATIONS

ACKNOWLEDGEMENTS

*L*uxury Indian Fashion: A Social Critique echoes numerous encounters with those who have invited me to enter their public as well as intimate worlds in the field and with those who critically engaged with my writing. I am extremely grateful for the guidance, discussions and friendship with Lucknow's most esteemed bookseller, Ram Advani, whose bookshop in the old Mayfair building, in Lucknow, is a well-known meeting place of both international and local academics; a space of true inspiration. I owe deep gratitude to all my interlocutors, both in Lucknow and New Delhi, who opened my eyes to new experiences, thoughts and lifeworlds and who are to remain largely anonymous. Furthermore, this book would not be possible without the support of my colleagues and friends at the University of Oslo, in particular Øivind Fuglerud, Thomas Hylland Eriksen, Kjersti Larsen, Arne Røkkum, Arne A. Perminow, Anders E. Rasmussen, Unni Wikan, Pamela G. Price, Claus Peter Zoller, Keir Martin, Arild E. Ruud, Veronique Pouillard, and Ellen Semb. Outside the Norwegian borders, I have benefited from warm support of and conversations with Robert Pfaller, Rane Willerslev, Marion Wettstein, Caroline Osella, Rachel Dwyer, Awani Kant Deo, Sanjay Srivastava, Clare Wilkinson-Weber, Melia Belli, Aalok Khandekar and Paolo Favero. I would also like to acknowledge the HERA funded post-doctoral fellowship that enabled me to finish this manuscript, as well as the contributions of all involved in the project *Enterprise of Culture: International Structures and Connections in the Fashion Industry since 1945*. Last but not least, I thank all the photographers, Lill-Ann Chepstow-Lusty for her images and lasting friendship, Arash Taheri for daring to briefly enter my field sites, Vijit Gupta for his beautiful cover image, and Kirsten Helgeland and Adnan Icagic for documenting Fashion India, an ethnographic exhibition that I curated at the Historical Museum in Oslo.

Certain parts of Chapter 1 have previously appeared in 'The Maharaja Style': Royal Chic, Heritage Luxury and the Nomadic Elites', in: *Fashion India: Spectacular Capitalism* (Kuldova, Tereza, ed.), pp. 51–72, Oslo: Akademika Publishing, 2013. A few parts of Chapter 4 have previously appeared in 'Designing the Illusion of India's Future Superpowerdom: Of the Rise of Neo-Aristocracy, Hindutva and Philanthrocapitalism', *The Unfamiliar: An Anthropological Journal*, 4(1): 15–22,

2014. Parts of Chapter 5 have appeared earlier in 'Laughing at Luxury: Mocking Fashion Designers', in: *Fashion India: Spectacular Capitalism* (Kuldova, Tereza, ed.), pp. 167–194, Oslo: Akademika Publishing, 2013. Parts of Chapter 6 have previously appeared in 'Fashionable Erotic Masquerades: Of Brides, Gods and Vamps in India', *Critical Studies in Fashion and Beauty*, 3(1): 69–86, 2012. I thank all the publishers for their kind permissions to reuse parts of this previously published material.

INTRODUCTION

Radhika entered a coffee shop in the Emporio luxury mall in Vasant Kunj, an upmarket residential area of South West Delhi; her heels click-clacking louder against the marble floor than usual. She sunk deep into a soft armchair, yelled at the waiter, ordered a latte and looking at me shivering with urgency, said: 'We have to call up Aman, ASAP'. 'Ok, sure, but what's going on?' 'Abhi's father is about to expire, totally out of the blue, but it's a sure thing. They are giving him max five days. Abhi's mom is out of her mind, and Aisha has enough to do supporting Abhi. All that pressure, he will have to take over the companies, arrange the cremation.' 'Sorry to hear that, but why do you need Aman, a fashion designer?' 'Seriously? We must turn this funeral into an event. It is a golden chance for all of us!' Dreaming herself away, she again emphasized 'golden'; gold being the ultimate purifying substance in the Indian universe, connected to auspiciousness and immortality of the lineage, to wealth, power and fame, and in psychoanalytical terms to faeces, waste, and shit (Laporte 2000). Indeed Patrizia Calefato has a point when noting that 'luxury fever becomes total delirium when our eternal rest is at stake' (Calefato 2014: 48), a statement that pushes us towards an inquiry into the perplexing connection between luxury and death, waste, and pollution. Cremation diamonds, anyone?

'Hello-o-o, MJ was a big shot, the self-made industrialist. Nobody will forget this funeral, I swear. Abhi will become the new MJ and they will have to take him seriously.' 'So the idea is to turn this funeral into a PR stunt?' 'Exactly! We are talking at least 13 days packed with rituals, offerings, mingling, and high-profile visitors. It will be stunning and lavish, emotions running high. We have to get going, call up Aman right now, we must get hold of his white embroidered *saris*, *salwar suits*, *kurtas*, table cloths, and decorations, whatever he has. I stock only colourful *chikan* and bridal couture. We need the white on white classics. That is the thing to wear for a funeral, high quality, delicate and traditional, understated luxury and yet royal. They will shift MJ home from the hospital tomorrow evening. We have to style the house – flowers, incense, pillows, sheets, curtains, even soaps. After he expires we need to cover the mirrors with the embroidered cloth, also we have to fix the food catering. I was thinking custom-made white chocolate truffles in shapes of gods, and crystal decorations. We need to make a list of guests, fix a

celebrity priest. Oh, maybe we could showcase MJ's art collection at the occasion.'
I already feel overwhelmed, thinking about MJ still fighting on the deathbed.
'Radhika, I know you are superb at designing stunning weddings, but are you sure
about applying the same logic to a funeral? What about the mourning and ritual
pollution?' 'Oh come on, times are changing, funeral or wedding, it is all about
mingling and business. Who comes to your funeral will soon be as important as
who comes to your wedding. Besides, people should be blown away by the event
and say: "MJ expired in style." We should celebrate him, it is just the soul leaving
the body, after all if everything is beautiful around, it will go so much smoother for
the soul, isn't it?' She laughs at the thought and continues, 'I swear, design funeral
is the music of tomorrow. The greatness of the man reflected in the greatness of his
funeral.' Radhika went on. The phantasmatic image that she painted in front of us
was a montage of an exotic calmness of a Thai spa, like those in five-star hotels,
retouched by ambient music of sacred Hindu chants, all set in MJ's neo-baroque
farmhouse akin to a royal palace with lush gardens decorated with even more
white flowers. Even in death and mourning there is no escaping the logic of
ambient theatrical stage sets, the logic that dominates fashion shows and elite
events. Affective spaces and experience design are the current *mantra* of fashion
design and marketing. Forget direct advertising, this is the era of self-effacement of
the advertiser (Serazio 2013), of invisible consumer governance that tries to seduce
our unconscious and capture and direct our desires. It operates through affective
ambient design and emotionally charged ritualized spectacles carefully staged
within such theatrical spaces. As Frédéric Lordon argued, manipulation of affects
capable of inducing an aligned desire is the perennial goal of power and of all
institutions of capture (Lordon 2014). Such a strategy of power relies on inducing
joyful affects and amorous passions towards the master and his desire, be the
master a boss, a brand or public opinion. As a result, it creates men and women
who passionately embrace the master desire, even if it were their own servitude.

A few hours later, we sit in Aman's studio in South Delhi, discussing the idea of
a designer funeral. Aman is overexcited, burning with sudden creative passion.
Having designed trousseaus and weddings far too many times in his career and
having been forced to do the neo-royal opulent bling time and again in order to
stay in business, he now sees an opportunity to show off the designs he loves the
most, that is the sober, multi-layered but airy attires decorated with delicate white
on white traditional *chikan* embroidery from Lucknow. For any luxury connoisseur,
chikan embroidery evokes the indulgent worlds of the Nawabi rulers of Awadh,
synonymous with cultural refinement and Indo-Persian style and the city of
Lucknow that once used to be called the Venice of the Orient, Shiraz-i-Hind or the
Constantinople of India and has built its reputation as a fashion centre of
languorous grace. Aman loved the popular local tale of the extravagant nawabs
who commissioned artisans working under their patronage to embroider such
elaborate and delicate *chikan kurtas* on muslin that they took two years to make,

only to be worn once (see Chapter 2). These pieces are said to have been so delicate that after a single use they simply dissolved, bringing luxury and waste together yet again. Traditional white on white *chikan* has an ambiguous status. On the one hand it is the utmost royal-like luxury that takes months to produce, making the women embroiderers progressively blind; on the other hand its whiteness is symbolic both of mourning and widowhood and of purity and knowledge. It is almost as if its proximity to death increases its seductive appeal.

Nine days later MJ expired, to use the popular Hinglish idiom. He died in style, indeed. Radhika made Aman and his workers run around the house and the garden, decorating it to minute detail. The official funeral theme was White Lotus, signifying purity, truth and divinity as much as proud patriotism (lotus is the national flower). In all bathrooms, white soaps were placed on porcelain lotuses, in all rooms, the air was permeated by a smell of sandalwood, flowers, and oil lamps; an enormous statue of a marble Ganesh, MJ's mate in business whom he worshipped every morning, appeared in the entry hall; a stunning crystal chandelier replaced the old inconspicuous lamp, and an excess of bright arranged flowers and candles in crystal and golden holders of different sizes and shapes lit up the villa. A few days after MJ's cremation, Radhika was showcasing his art collection to the visitors interested in speaking to the son, the heir of the business. Aman was taking care of the dresses of the family members and close friends. Aisha was seen running around in a chiffon *chikan anarkali* dress wearing pale make-up, while Abhi sported light blue jeans and a long *chikan kurta*. Radhika and Aman managed to turn the funeral into a lavish commemoration and a demonstration of prestige, wealth and power during which the business elite had a chance to mingle and discuss future deals. A real drama of emotion, inheritance and power played out in the home turned into a theatrical stage set, where all the actors knew quite well how to play their parts and maintain the family honour as well as business ties. Aesthetics and fashion are clearly an important ingredient of what Abner Cohen calls power mystique. Power mystique to him is 'not just an ideological formula, but is also a way of life, manifesting itself in patterns of symbolic behaviour that can be observed and verified. The ideology is objectified, developed, and maintained by an elaborate body of symbols and dramatic performances' (Cohen 1981: 2–3).

In the lotus world: luxury and mud, high and low

White Lotus, the theme of the funeral that has transported us into the world of fashion designers and the South Delhi business elite, is a fitting metaphor for the key motif of this book. It is also a fitting metaphor for the ethnographic journey in which this work is grounded and for its analytical angle. Like the lotus, the beauties of Indian fashion and heritage luxury cannot be conceived without their juxtaposition, without the mud from which they grow and that brings them to life. *At the core of luxury lie painful expropriations. The question might arise: is that maybe precisely what the luxury shopaholic's pleasure derives from?*

India is often portrayed as a land of contrasts, of parallel worlds. It is the land of the rich and the poor, formal and informal economy, materialism and spiritualism, civilization and backwardness, and so on. Not only political ideologues, but academics too are often guilty as charged of (re)producing these bifurcated worlds of the 'new' India versus the 'real' India, one symbolic of modernity and future, the other of tradition and past. And so we read that once we exit the exceptional gated spaces of Gurgaon's world-class amenities, we are '"back in India" as it were' (Kalyan 2011). The new and world class is portrayed as deterritorialized and as distinctively non-Indian, a world set apart, one that provides a 'totalizing experience that makes interaction with the surrounding environment redundant and unnecessary' (Kalyan 2011: 39). It is often said that those living in these gated luxury spaces aspire to live 'as though one were rich and lived in New York, London, Paris, Frankfurt or Amsterdam' (Mani 2008: 53). But is this really so? I suspect that these statements tell us more about the authors than the subject at hand. Anthropological research on elites in South Asia, on the very rich, on those with political ties, black money and lavish lifestyles, is practically non-existent. It is revealing that the only way in which monied elites are represented is by being swallowed into the abstract global and turned into the phantom of neo-liberal globalization, into abstractions such as forces of global capital and therefore into an explanation rather than an object of study. Maybe anthropologists do not want to get their hands really dirty. The old trope of virtuous poverty is still with us; very often it seems that writing about the poor, weak, oppressed and marginalized is still as a noble and morally superior quest, along with giving the poor a voice or empowering them. However, with the changes in political economy that India has seen in the last two decades, this research bias has been criticized. The last decade has seen a boom of a new research agenda, this time focusing on the great rising Indian middle class, on the study of the salaried white collar workers swayed by consumer culture. Governmental employees are the stars of this research, followed by call centre workers, aspiring young men and middle class housewives. Their consumption habits and moralities are placed under the scrutiny of the academic (Brosius 2010, Donner 2011, Favero 2005, Gupta 2008, Liechty 2003, Upadhya 2008, Varma 1998, Nielsen and Waldrop 2014). While this might be a crude oversimplification of the current diverse research efforts, it is at the same time a telling categorization that captures the main trends. What is startling here is the utmost exclusion of the capitalist class and the constant need for its textual purification by way of abstraction, that is, a process of moving away, of eliminating all unnecessary dirt (think abstract art).

Dominique Laporte's exhilarating and provocative *History of Shit* might throw some light on this exclusion and the need to purify the rich even in theory (Laporte

2000). Laporte confronts us with the crucial role of the management of human waste and privatization of shit for the constitution of modern individual subjectivity, organization of our cities, development of capitalism and emergence of the nation-state. In the process of which, the state obsessed with sanitization – recall the campaign of India's current Prime Minister Narendra Modi prior to the Indian elections of 2014 and his slogan 'toilets first, temples later' – has become the ultimate purifier. As Laporte notes,

> the State is understood as pure and inviolable, as capable of purifying the most repulsive things – even money – through the touch of its divine hand. Money, therefore, is pure insofar as it belongs to the State; so are, by association, those experts who are summoned to serve it. . . . the site of power must distance itself from shit. So as not to stall the accumulation of wealth, mercantilism must be consigned to the private sphere. . . . It is essential that the private be absolutely and unequivocally aligned with shit.
>
> **LAPORTE** 2000: 40–42

The distinction between private and public was, according to Laporte, established during the sixteenth century also as a distinction between bad money and good money, the private turning into a space of primitive accumulation of money, of hoarding one's shit. As crude as it may sound at first, one is tempted to say that this legacy goes on. The realms of private business and capital are often portrayed as dirty. We find the same logic in Hindu thought that is obsessed with questions of purity and pollution pertaining to the caste system and patterns of hierarchical organization of society. It is no coincidence that the caste of *baniyas*, the moneylenders and businessmen, and also the caste to which some of India's richest individuals belong, from Mukesh Ambani, Lakshmi Mittal, Gautam Adani, K.M. Birla, to Savitri Jindal, is due to its remarkable ability to hoard money portrayed as dirty, untrustworthy, wicked, and as lacking in honour. It is said that the *baniyas* do not perform honour killings, since they have no honour. Repeatedly, I have been told by my *brahmin* friends and others not to trust a *baniya*, since their mercantile mindset, I was told, is 'dirty and dangerous'. We will develop and elaborate on these points below, but now suffice it to ask: do not academics, receiving their money from the state, money that is purified by the state, share this caste prejudice? Is it not why they prefer to study the 'pure' poor or the governmental servants? Do they fear the shit of private money spilling over their pages? Why else the need to turn the flesh and blood of the rich into an abstracted and purified global force or neo-liberalism? Maybe, this pervasive exclusion of the rich global elites from anthropology is driven by the same sort of disgust academia feels towards corporate-funded research.

Similarly, fashion has been for a great portion of history considered a far too frivolous subject in academia, approached only with utmost care, precisely due to its connection with the rich (fashion history is a different matter as the time that has passed allows for the necessary purifying and ennobling distance to emerge). Only in the past decade have fashion studies emerged as a respected discipline. In the case of the study of fashion and clothing in India, we see again clearly what the permissible topics of inquiry are. While high fashion and moneyed elites are a non-existent subject, crafts and textile traditions along with the impoverished craftspeople steal the academic scene (Venkatesan 2009; Wilkinson-Weber 1999; Mohsini 2011; Tyabji and Das 2007; Tarlo 1996; Crill 2006). Clothing, textiles and craft are the decent subjects, while fashion and luxury are obviously still an academic taboo. But we are becoming better at breaking it (Calefato 2014; Entwistle 2009); the recent emergence of critical luxury studies only confirms this (Armitage and Roberts 2015). However, within fashion studies we see another split emerging. Those studying fashion refuse to be associated with those studying craft. At a recent fashion conference, a colleague of mine made this clear. After her talk in which she mentioned craft innovation several times, she exclaimed: 'I just really hope the audience did not think that I am one of those craft losers and do-gooders!' Academia is no value-free universe. It is driven by parallel dynamics to the one into which we are about to dive – the dynamics of high and low, of the luxurious and the dirty, the valuable and worthless and their recurrent collapses into each other. Initially, we posed the question: *if at the core of luxury lie painful expropriations might it be that this is precisely what the luxury shopaholic's pleasure and power derive from?* In order to address this question, we need to bring together that which is so desperately being kept apart, in academic theory, and in practice – namely craft and fashion. We also have to ask, why are they being kept apart? Is it merely their proximity and dependency on each other that demands this pervasive production of distance? Or is there more to this? What kind of real effects does this production of distance have on the ground? How does it translate into power and reproduction of ideology?

Connecting fashion and craft

One thing is central for our considerations here. The unique selling point (USP) of Indian luxury fashion and heritage luxury is craft. The same craft that appears only within the academically permissible contexts, such as in relation to the nation state, grass-root movements, non-governmental organizations and governmental schemes, and art history. The fact that hundreds of thousands of craftspeople and artisans are more or less directly linked to transnational luxury industries and that Indian fashion designers systematically portray themselves as craft revivalists, and benevolent patrons of diverse craft traditions, is wilfully ignored, as are the actual relations between the rich and the poor. The exploitation of craft, both material and ideological, has intensified during the last decade; we will look at the causes later (see Chapter 1), now suffice it to say that we are facing a new fashion trend in the elite segment. This trend consists of a combination of heritage luxury, i.e. 'royal chic' (Kuldova 2013a, 2013b) marked by a revival of feudal aesthetics inspired by pre-colonial Indian grandeur (Figure 0.1), and ethical fashion that goes well together with both the aesthetics and ideology of neo-feudalism and the neo-imperial ambitions of the elite India. In contrast to fashion as we know it today from the Western fashion centres, where value derives predominantly from the immaterial, from the brand and the designer name, while the products are marked by an emphasis on cut, detail, often simplicity, in India we see a far stronger emphasis on the value of the material, on the handmade fabrics as much as the opulent ornamentation and its meticulous production by the artisans. This emphasis on the material value itself is subject to dominant ideologies that the designers themselves effectively (re) produce through their own brand mythologies. Craftspeople are indispensable for two reasons. First, in their abstract, purified form, they collectively stand for Indian heritage and the past, materializing Indianness itself, the intangible commodity par excellence. Second, their impoverishment is key to the construction of an image of 'ethical and socially responsible business' and as such, impoverishment is precisely the condition that must be perpetuated. This in turn transforms the designers and the elite consumers not only into benevolent patrons imagined along the lines of the royal patrons of arts and crafts of the bygone era, but also keepers of tradition and guarantors of its continuation – at least, so they say. The elite fashion segment is strongly marked by the emergence of 'philanthrocapitalism' (Bishop and Green 2008) that has fairly recently infected the Indian business and political elite. The field of Indian fashion clearly shows that its success in India is predicated upon a neo-feudal, elitist and hierarchical sentiment. The so-called ethical neo-feudal fashion embodies the power of the elite to subject, to create dependency and to perpetuate poverty and status quo. Craft also guarantees uniqueness, while standing behind other buzzwords of the industry like 'eternal', 'royal', 'timeless', 'ornamentalist', 'heritage', 'fusion' and 'tradition'. Interview any designer in India and he or she will not omit one of them; or read any fashion magazine or press release of India's leading designers like Arjun Khanna, Tarun Tahiliani, JJ Valaya, Ritu Kumar or Rohit Bal. Their ornamentalist heritage luxury pieces, inspired by pre-colonial royal courts, are designed to convey old-world charm that is in many ways anti-modern and anti-democratic and does not care either for political correctness or for female emancipation (Kuldova 2013c). It cares for power and prestige; it aims to recreate hierarchy, aesthetically stunning gender divisions, strong kingly figures and national retro-futuristic fantasies of India's golden age. Philanthropy and ethical consumption, as a distinctly elitist pastime, revolve around carefully designed theatrical bestowals of benevolence. They are about power to subject, about visible displays of inequality. A Marathi poet, Covindaraj, wrote in 1919 that Hindu society is made up of men 'who bow their head to the kicks from above, who simultaneously give a kick below, never thinking to resist the one or refrain from the other' (cited in Dundes 1997: 4).

FIGURE 0.1 Backstage at India Couture Week 2014, collection by Rohit Bal
Image courtesy: Nitin Patel Photography.

Indian heritage luxury depends on the meticulous labour of thousands, and as we will see throughout this book, also on the continuation of their impoverishment. The so-called ethical fashion far too often reproduces conditions it claims to elevate; nowhere is this more visible to an anthropologist than in the emerging Indian luxury fashion, where designers catering to the local elites still do work intensely with craftspeople. The lotus, the beauty and luxury always depends for its existence on mud, dirt and poverty, and so it needs to (re)produce it. Luxury depends on sacrifice. Think of the fabulous tales of luxury, the tales of eyes going blind embroidering, or of Tibetan antelopes slaughtered for fleece for the legendary *shahtoosh* ring shawls, a symbol of power whose value has only increased since the trade has been illegalized (Nowell 2004).

Fieldworking across luxury and dirt

The white lotus will take us on a journey across landscapes of dirt and luxury, as we will follow the material and immaterial production of *chikan* embroidery (Figure 0.2), from the villages surrounding Lucknow to the wealthy elite mourning in style in South Delhi. Unlike most anthropological studies devoted to descriptions of semi-homogenous segments of people and their lifeworlds, this book explores the relations and mutual production of people from diverse backgrounds tied together at various stages through the production and consumption of this luxury embroidery and the

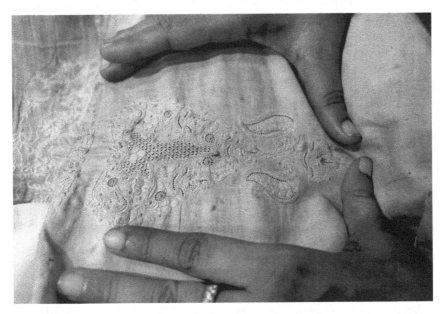

FIGURE 0.2 *Chikan* embroidery detail, a ninety-year-old piece from a private collection
Image courtesy: Tereza Kuldova.

role of marketing, and theatrical rituals. Following a commodity (Appadurai 2008; Kopytoff 2008) like luxury *chikan* meant accompanying designers on their trips to the Lucknow artisans, working with each independently, as well as with their clients. This tactic goes under the name of work-shadowing (Dwyer and Jackson 2003: 270) and it has proven invaluable since it in practice translated into an understanding of the intense connections between the worlds that are so desperately being kept apart by different players, at the same time as throwing light on how they are systematically produced as separate. Between 2008 and 2013 I spent roughly two and half years in India during long and short visits and worked with craftspeople, designers, and business elite, while living in different places in Lucknow and South Delhi, from Greater Kailash I, Greater Kailash II, Jangpura, Sadiq Nagar, Hauz Khas to the more peripheral gated community in Noida, not to mention all the temporary hotels. As often as I was chatting with printers in the old city, embroiderers in the villages, washermen on riverbanks, dyers in their workshops, I was talking to designers in their studios and their clients in farmhouses. As often as I was attending village weddings and fairs, I was visiting art and fashion exhibitions in luxury hotels and private parties. In order to understand the world of luxury and of India's rich, we need to understand how this world and its opposite are produced and sustained. As Shamus Rahman Khan pointed out in his study of privilege in America's elite St. Paul's college, if we are to understand the increase in inequality, 'we must know more about the wealthy, as well as the institutions that are important for their production and maintenance' (Khan 2010: 5). Fashion, as the realm of cultural production, is precisely one of such institutions where the aesthetic both gives shape to and reflects dominant ideological tendencies. It is therefore not enough to follow only the material production and to understand the relational dynamics that pertains to it, but we must also step into the broader ideological narratives and affective fantasies that push people to act. Luxury Indian fashion is where local 'vernacular economies' (Jain 2007) meet and weave with neo-liberal structures and strictures, where the informal blends with the formal and where new regimes of organization of labour are imposed. Only when we understand these processes in relation to ideological beliefs and fantasies, can we understand how 'power over human bodies and the transformation of bodies into precious commodities' become 'the conditions of the new luxury of the globalized world' (Calefato 2014: 72).

Fantasy of superpowerdom: ideology and utopia

In his explorations into the relationship between aesthetic structure, gothic architecture, and a structure of thought, medieval philosophy, Erwin Panofsky has shown how the aesthetic often mirrors and reinforces the ideologies of the given time; peculiarities of architectonical style for instance become tangible equivalents to philosophical ideas (Panofsky 1976). In India, cultural production, from Bollywood movies, street art to the fashion ramps, is intensely tied to the political and the cinematic, imaginary and mythological shapes the melodramas of real life (Mankekar 1998; Appadurai 1995; Dwyer and Pinney 2003). Therefore, understanding the dynamic relation between aesthetic production and ideology, fantasy and utopia has to go hand in hand with our explorations of the relations of production. If we are to make sense of the indispensable role of fashion designers in policing and maintaining class boundaries, while strategically representing the greatness of India at large, we must understand the ideological, phantasmatic and utopian dimensions of this form of cultural production.

The metaphor of white lotus can guide us even here. Not only does lotus signify nobility, while growing from the mud, it is also enshrined in the Indian constitution as the national flower of India. In Hindu mythology the centre of the universe is believed to be the lotus flower on which Brahma, the creator of the world, sat arising from the navel of Vishnu. In the last decade, Indian luxury fashion has become likewise a matter of constructing, displaying and furthering ideas of Indianness and the nation with all their intense political pathos. Designing elites goes hand in hand with designing the nation, both firmly grounded in contemporary ideological currents, while painting utopian fantasies of the future (Kuldova 2014). The more Indian fashion capitalizes on craft that has been central to Indian nationalist narratives since the Independence movement, recall Gandhi and his *khadi*, the deeper it inserts itself into current ideologies of national belonging, patriotism, and imagined India within the global space. In ways that we shall explore, elitist Indian fashion design feeds directly, more or less consciously, into the current peculiar merger of Hindu nationalism, neo-liberalism and philanthrocapitalism, all of which work remarkably well together.

Frederik Jameson has insisted that when studying cultural artefacts, we must analyse both the ideological ways in which fantasies are represented and materialized, as well as the social or even utopian hope that they contain and the conflicts that they attempt to resolve, even when they do so through ideological containment (Jameson 1979). Similarly, Ernst Bloch attempted to discern the dynamics of the ideological and utopian dimensions of fashion, art and popular culture, claiming that hope, utopian visions of a better life and unrealized potentialities latent in the present, permeate cultural production, at the same time as the same cultural production tends to reproduce the hegemonic ideologies of the day (Bloch 2000). In fact, following Bloch, we could even claim that designing is a utopian process (Howells 2014). Bollywood movies might be the best example we have from India of hegemonic ideologies walking hand in hand with emancipatory utopian visions and wishful images of the future. But the same also goes for designing fashion in India. Fashion design translates into designing of both the material and ideological stuff of Indianness and eliteness on the stage of the contemporary world.

Keyword: Indianness

Indianness is the buzzword of contemporary Indian fashion design. These days, all Indian designers know that if they do not attempt to capture the *essence* of being Indian in one way or another in their designs they are likely to be out of business. Therefore, even the most extravagant and artistic designs often claim to express that mysterious quality of Indianness. William Mazzarella has written in depth about the necessity of crafting this quality of Indianness vis-à-vis the local, international and the global in Indian advertising and marketing industries (Mazzarella 2006). However, there has been a marked change in the branding of Indianness in the last decade; namely, a progressive strengthening of the perceived Indian element over the global (Figure 0.3). Rather than wanting to be part of the globality in an Indian way, the globe is today to be conquered by proud Indians on their own terms, the global is to be submerged, possessed, swallowed into, rather than admired and aspired to. And so, the more blatantly obvious this displayed Indianness is, most often taking the form of heavy embellishments, craftwork and hand-woven cloth, the better. While the general popularity of traditional garments is nothing new to India, within the context of the fashion industry that emerged as a serious enterprise first after the neo-liberal reforms of the 1990s, heavily influenced by Western fashion centres, this is a fairly recent phenomenon, dating back roughly to the 2008 financial crisis. As India emerged victorious out of what was perceived to be a global crisis, the emphasis on the strength of India and Indianness has acquired new significance. The elites that used to look up to the West were suddenly struck by the following revelation. In words of one of my interlocutors, a CEO of a multinational company in New Delhi: 'We have something that the West lacks, we have our heritage, our traditions, our Indian entrepreneurial spirit; our strength lies in our Indianness. We can possess the West, we can buy Dior or Gucci, but the West can never have what we have. . . . We have that little extra that will turn the world's tables'. This reimagined Indianness is consciously directed at the (often invisible) global audience; it is the very leverage against the failing West and its crushing markets; it is the articulation of a 'positional superiority' over the West (Nader 1989: 326). Paradoxically, while working with Indian designers and their clientele, it became pressingly obvious that this celebrated Indianness is precisely what the Indian elite appear to lack. Once, a designer fittingly pointed this out to me, 'our market is created by the lack, the void, by that which people desperately desire and want to be, but which they know they are not. . . . They come to us with the hope that we can fill this void and that we can transform them to what they believe they should be.' Other designers mixed into their English statements Hindi words such as *adhurapan* (incompleteness), or *khalipan* (vacuum, emptiness) and took it as their mission to fill this void, a void they identified, helped to manufacture, and pretended to cure. This sense of lack they attempted to fill matched the pervasive obsession of my elite interlocutors with 'being Indian at the

FIGURE 0.3 Detail of Sahara Ganj Mall in Lucknow
Image courtesy: Tereza Kuldova.

core', as they used to say, 'you have to be Indian first'. To the elites, largely perceived by the majority of India's population as westoxicated, morally corrupt and driven by pure self-interest (Gupta 2007), staging of their Indianness became even more important, even if it were behind closed doors, directed at an invisible Other. The high investments into repetitive staging of Indianness signify the lack of this elusive and continually escaping essence.

The costumes that these designers produce play with aesthetic referents of the pre-colonial Indian elite aiming to visually reconstruct India's greatness by citing (Nakassis 2013) and re-inscribing (Cameron and Palan 2004) the symbolic and material worlds of the maharajas, nawabs and Mughal rulers and projecting them into the future, into India's anticipated future (and present) as a global economic power, thus creating an aesthetics of power and wealth. What is at stake in Indian elite fashion is not only the negotiation of the position of these elites, as distinctively Indian elites within a global space, but also the idea of nation itself. The essence of Indianness and the current strength and potency of India is imagined to reside in India's heritage; an increasingly popular concept among the elites. This heritage needs to be flaunted, celebrated and personally cherished. Again, the artisans belonging to India's second largest sector of the economy that employs over 54 million people are essential for the elite's project of filling the lack in their hearts. At the same time, however, their bodies perceived as polluting have to be sanitized from the materiality of their products; the artisans have to be turned into an abstraction, into heritage, into a symbol standing for the nation and tradition. They have to be projected in their bodily materiality into the past and in their idealized abstractedness into the glorious future. Only in such a sanitized form can they become effective in the construction of this national narrative.

Theatrical spectacles of heritage luxury go hand in hand with the rise of Hindu nationalism and the dominance of the muscular right wing. It is no coincidence that the princes of bygone eras, famously labelled as effeminate by the British colonial rule and proclaimed weak and ill by colonial psychiatry because of their habits of self-abuse (masturbation) among other things, have been today redesigned as strong muscular kings (see Chapter 7). The recent boom of both menswear and the fitness industry across India has to be read in terms of the desire of the subjects to participate in the phantasm of the nation's power (Kuldova 2010). The new Hindu nationalist and right wing Prime Minister Narendra Modi, a self-proclaimed muscular self-made man, priding himself on his 56-inch chest, oscillates between being Brand India's new CEO and India's king, thus skilfully merging rhetoric of meritocracy with neo-feudal aesthetics and strategies of power. The revival of kingly models of Indian political culture (Price 1989) that finds its expression in current production of elite Indian fashion designers, and is equally visible in populist right wing politics, was fittingly captured in a remark by Anil Ambani, the chairman of the Reliance Group, one of India's largest business conglomerates. Ambani called Narendra Modi the 'king among kings', one who will turn India into a superpower backed by the benevolent neo-aristocracy, the business elite riding on a wave of CSR (corporate social responsibility) and philanthropy, who has been supporting this king's rise to power. Elite Indian business, politics and fashion are all equally pervaded and seduced by a belief in India's future inevitable superpowerdom. A belief that is repetitively cited, acted out and materialized, and yet it is never clear who and if anyone really believes in it. Let us look more closely at this illusory belief and its structure, only to unpack it in more detail throughout the book.

What is striking about this widespread belief in India's greatness, past and future, is that literally none of my interlocutors, be they designers, businessmen or even artisans, really believe in it. They all knew, some indeed better than others, that the reality looks radically different, and so would the future, and yet they still acted as if they did not know. And so the businessmen would invest their capital in real estate projects deemed never to look as seductive as on the promotional images, making profit on the virtuality of this fantasy. At the same time, they also derived great pleasure and pride from their acts of belief in India's greatness and power. We could identify this illusion as an 'illusion without owners', to use Robert Pfaller's concept (Pfaller 2014), an illusion that no one really believes in, and yet one that is for that matter no less powerful and no less capable of structuring reality. Even popular books of non-fiction writers and economic ideologues regularly perpetuate this shared illusion, often starting with a sober summing up of the pervasive ills of Indian society. First they talk of poverty, ecological crisis, caste discrimination, communal violence, lack of quality education, a dysfunctional health care system, but then they quickly move on to a discussion of the booming IT industry, the emergence of billionaires, scientists and professionals, and so on (Kamdar 2007; Das 2000; Rai and Simon 2007; Thussu 2013). As Pfaller points out,

> not every utopia must then exist in the form of a 'confession' – with convicted followers who know what they believe in or wish for. Instead, a utopia can also be present as an 'illusion of the other', in the form of an 'as though' materialized in diverse practices and objects, which no one has to believe in consciously or with conviction. Like the tricks at a magic show or politeness, such utopias could also exist as fictions held by groups or even entire societies, without any individual ever coming into question as the owner of such an illusion.
>
> **PFALLER** 2014: 46

The utopian visions of India's future greatness consist precisely of such a shared illusion that has at its heart a convergence of imagined economy and (re)invented tradition. Indian fashion designers are in a business of designing elites and neo-imperial atmospheres of power that provide the material and aesthetic form to the ruling ideologies of the day, from Hindu nationalism, to philanthrocapitalism, while designing utopias that 'not only offer an arresting vision of future possibilities, but because they tend to be written in the past narrative tense, also imply that their depiction of the good life, an ideal world, is eminently attainable. The future is past' (Brown and MacLaren 1998: 279).

Designer funerals, commodification of death brought to the next level, are an expression of the capitalist age in India. The funeral home is modelled like a stage set for a theatrical fashion show, designed to create an ambient space, an affective space. The funeral is in perfect alignment with contemporary marketing strategies that deliberately seek to manipulate our affects (neuromarketing, sensory branding and so on), and capture our power to act; strategies that seek to align our desires with the master desire of the brand, or in this case with the family staging the theatrical funeral home. The theatrical funeral, as we shall see, fits perfectly well within the current paradigm of marketing, or 'ambient governance', which points to strategies of capture and invisible consumer governance through affective ambient design and ritualistic spectacles framed within a brand mythology. If the designer funeral is so obviously infused with contemporary ideologies, explicitly mimicking strategies of capture that we observe in the commercial and political spheres, is there anything at all that might be potentially emancipatory about it? There might be something after all. Due to the polluting nature of female tears, funerals are commonly men's business, as women are excluded from the cremation grounds. Women tend to be pushed into invisibility during such occasions. However, in staging this spectacle of a funeral home, Radhika has stolen the show on the domestic grounds and created a new legitimate area for herself and other women, while creating a new niche market for Aman and aesthetically representing and strengthening the wealth and power of the family's patriarchs, dead and living. In this case, the emancipatory element touches upon the personal rather than the structural; something that we will delve into later in this book (see Chapter 6).

Plan of the book

By way of introduction we have touched upon the most pertinent issues to be investigated, outlining our two main concerns. First, the dynamics of the mutual interdependence of fashion and craft, and thereby of the capital owners and the workforce, and second, the point of contact between aesthetics, ideology, fantasy and utopia and the role of the elites in maintaining established social order and investing in the appearance of prestige and the signs of symbolic capital, and wealth. Chapter 1 brings us into the world of the Indian fashion industry and analyses the currently dominant trend of neo-aristocratic aesthetics, reading this trend as a part of larger sociopolitical developments and of reorientations of the economy towards new economic centres of the world, such as the Middle East, Russia or Singapore and as a key to understanding the utmost desire of the elite, namely mastering time and space through conspicuous displays of status and wealth. It walks the reader through three key rituals. First, the interactions between designers and their clients in the studios, where they 'celebrate Indianness' together. Second, the fashion show as an emotionally charged ritualized spectacle and third, the elite wedding. Throughout, it is argued that Indianness can be delegated onto the garment, and the wearer thus relieved from its social and moral pressures. Chapter 2 links the role of imagined economy in India's visions of its superpowerdom to the commodification of heritage by zooming on the complex material and ideological production of the 'traditional' *chikan* embroidery from Lucknow, following it from the local to the cosmopolitan contexts. It traces the movement of this embroidery, popular with India's leading designers, from the local networks of its material production by specialized and largely impoverished craftspeople (e.g. printers, embroiderers, dyers), to its immaterial, that is, ideological production by the designers and elevation from the local to the national, and its transformation into a source of pride and Indianness staged for the imagined global Other. Chapter 3 turns to the tense relations between design and craft. Developing further the case of *chikan* embroidery, as it moves from villages to fashion boutiques, the chapter analyses the ways in which material labour is artificially separated from immaterial labour. It shows how the designers' narratives about creativity, innovation and artistic genius systematically push craftspeople into invisibility, inferiority and passivity, and deny their creativity, individuality and agency and how the designers' authoritative discourses and acts sanitize heritage luxury from the polluting bodies of the craftspeople, at once celebrated as emblems of national traditions and despised for their poverty and low classness. It is argued that only in their sanitized form can these luxurious garments be consumed by the elite and the hierarchies effectively reproduced. Chapter 4 further develops the theme of power relations between design and craft and between the rich and the poor. Many designers working with craftspeople also run non-governmental organizations to 'empower' these workers, while cultivating the rhetoric of ethical business and philanthropy, offering their customers good conscience in addition to luxurious clothing. Such NGOs and trusts become effective tools of co-option of the village workforce into the capitalist system and reproduce the existing power relations rather than unsettling them. This trend is connected to the larger context of both national and global proliferation of ethical business and corporate philanthropy that takes over the state responsibility, from education to social security, and places it into private hands. Chapter 5 returns to the villages surrounding Lucknow, where women embroider the luxurious fabrics for the elites while being patronized by the designers, their NGOs and discourses of 'ethical business'. Recognizing the destructive power of such efforts and the potential violence inherent in benevolence, the craftswomen often use irony and laughter when confronted with patronizing discourses that position them as vulnerable, poor and in constant need of rescue. This chapter shows how they mock the designers and with them the urban way of life, defending their right to be lazy and to define their own virtues, while reminding the designers that it is not they who are dependent on him, but that it is the designer who would be a nobody without them and their skill. Chapter 6 moves away from the village into the world of elite women, and looks at their own ways to resist and carve out a space in public life, paradoxically enough often by taking on a charitable cause of the poor, turning the vulnerable craftswomen into the vehicle of their own emancipation, while developing their 'erotic capital'. Carving a space for themselves in the business world or public life, while being good and moral wives is problematic. The chapter shows how in order to be both moral and sexy, the women displace their morality onto an external social cause and often speak on the behalf of the poor, and especially the 'vulnerable' women and create various initiatives in their name. The charitable cause of the poor and vulnerable woman thus proves indispensable to the empowerment of the elite wife and her emancipation from the domestic sphere. Chapter 7 turns back to the initial questions of aesthetics, power and Indianness, only this time by recasting them as questions of anxious and insecure masculinity, and the role of the alcohol industry and fashion in shaping the aesthetics and ideology of elite masculinities. It investigates the role played by the 'rhetoric of muscularity' in relation to the threat of effeminacy, stemming from indulgence in luxury and consumption. The chapter shows how in order to counteract this threat, men appropriate symbols of low class machismo and incorporate them in the elitist aesthetic, in a similar way in which they use 'dirty' substances, such as alcohol and cigarettes in order to virilize their bodies. The chapter goes on to connect these processes both to the shifts in the political field and the heavy sponsorship of fashion events by the alcohol industry, and whisky brands in particular. It concludes with a discussion of total environments and ambient governance. The Conclusion sums up the relation between luxury and reproduction of the social order and inequality, questions that underlie all the present chapters.

1 NEO-FEUDAL ORNAMENTALISM AND ELITIST FANTASIES

After days spent in Delhi's designer studios, it became apparent that all encounters taking place inside these spaces were highly repetitive, ritualized, and therefore also predictable. These interactions had an echo-chamber-like quality; same expressions on everyone's lips and rehearsed scripts rarely broken. The question was: how do these fashion rituals, these patterned social interactions that reproduce beliefs and aesthetic expressions, fit within larger socio-economic and political contexts. What role do they play in relation to (re)production of social order and what illusions do they fuel and maintain? Or, if these interactions within studios were to be understood as ritualized actions, actions that are 'embodied, enacted, spatially rooted, temporarily bounded, prescribed, formalized, and repeated' (Grimes 2011: 13), then what purpose did they serve?

We have already noted that Indianness is the buzzword among contemporary Indian fashion designers (Mazzarella 2006), whose 'artistic nationalism' (Ciotti 2012) is increasingly becoming one with elite identity (Figure 1.1). As it turned out, rituals performed in designer studios could be understood only through their relation to such elitist nationalism. Clearly, these rituals were perfectly choreographed (Hewitt 2005) and curated instances through which the ideology of Indian exceptionalism and India's future global superpowerdom was played out and (re)produced, all the while providing the elite with a neo-feudal aesthetic of distinction, prestige and belonging. But how did this work in practice? In order to answer this question, let us now look at three rituals of different scale and yet of near-identical logic: (1) interactions in the designer studio, (2) JJ Valaya's fashion show and (3) an elite wedding in order to prepare ground for our future explorations.

FIGURE 1.1 Front *lehenga* design by Sabyasachi Mukherjee, a piece that was on exhibit at the Historical Museum in Oslo, during the *Fashion India: Spectacular Capitalism* exhibition curated by the author

Image courtesy: Kirsten Helgeland.

Ritual I: celebrating Indianness in a designer studio

The stage (play-sphere): Designer studios across North India share a number of family resemblances, such as luxurious interiors including statues of gods (often multi-faith symbolism), antiques, Venetian mirrors, art works, book collections, throne-like chairs, crystal chandeliers, mannequins, the smell of incense, curated artefacts from all over the world, suggestive music and so on (Figure 1.2). Brought together, the ecstasies of these design elements produced a particular 'affective atmosphere' (Böhme 1993, 2010). This atmosphere is clearly intersubjective and sets the studio apart from the ordinary, turning it into a ritual space, into a 'web of sensation' (Gagliardi 1990: 18) in which customers became trapped the moment they enter. With few exceptions, almost all clients described their visits to the designer studios in terms of being transported into a different world. The studios, like gated luxury boutiques, are clearly delineated and set apart from the everyday; as such, studios, too, function as stages for rituals in which collective affects, irreducible to individual bodies, emerge (Anderson 2009). The designer studio, being a stage, is also a space of play and play-acting, a secret space of play for making and crafting of the highly crafted and curated public image. As such, studios are spaces of 'sacred seriousness' (Huizinga 1955) marked by an 'extreme involvement and celebratory affect that is initiated by play' (Pfaller 2014: 76).

The actors: Raghav, a fashion designer in his mid-thirties from a family of landowners-cum-businessmen from Haryana. His father used to be the head of the village *panchayat* before his death; Raghav did an MBA and briefly flirted with fashion design when he decided to pour his family cash into turning himself into a designer. Working against the stereotype of the bling loving, crude and tasteless Punjabis, Raghav marketed himself as the connoisseur of crafts, heritage and as a style *guru*, much like the majority of the leading designers. His studio is surrounded by an air of secrecy; he strategically chooses whom to allow onto his sacred grounds. Anjali, a daughter of an industrialist in her early thirties; a new customer about to be initiated into the ritual play.

The plot (function: ideotypical): 'She'll be here in ten minutes, it'll be her first *darshan*', Raghav enlightened me. 'Are you playing a *guru*?', I laugh. 'This is serious, please don't giggle like this'. *Darshan* translates as sight or vision and is commonly used to describe Hindu worship, the act of seeing and being seen by a deity, an exchange of vision between the deity and the devotee. However, it is not only a matter of seeing, it is also about touching, smelling and hearing, a material and sensuous practice intended to connect the devotee to the spiritual (Eck 1998). Today, *darshan*, this 'sacred viewing' is being sought even from politicians, activists (think Anna Hazare), Bollywood celebrities, or fashion designers. Raghav too claimed to have a transformative power, something that was enthusiastically confirmed by his regulars, who talked of their need to *see* him in order to feel well,

FIGURE 1.2 Outside the designer boutique of Nitiya Bajaj in Shahpur Jat, New Delhi
Image courtesy: Arash Taheri.

as they considered him 'soothing, knowledgeable, empowering'. One of his clients even called him the 'remover of obstacles', thus likening him to the god Ganesha. Akin to the divine or not, the designer emanated authority and power, enhanced by the affective power of the theatrical stage, the studio.

Anjali entered the studio and even before she sat down, she managed to complain about the traffic in Delhi, the pollution, heat and all that noise. In the middle of her rant, Raghav stopped her and gestured that she should take a deep breath and relax. 'Rants, aggression and complaints are not allowed inside the studio, now it is time to calm down, feel at peace and enjoy', he said, establishing the rules of the game. A few hours later, she will feel rejuvenated and relaxed. But let's not jump in time. Raghav scrutinized Anjali from head to toe, loudly passing his judgement: 'you are too westoxicated, look at you, we need to fix that my dear'. Her Louis Vuitton bag and jeans were the obvious triggers, he considered them 'so 2000'. 'It is time to celebrate India, reconnect with your roots and work the traditional magic'. After an intense silent pause and an exchange of ambiguous gazes, he continued, 'can't you see, there is no magic in a LV'. After another pause, with a raised finger, he finished her sentence before she even began: 'it is imperative to project the image of a powerful and proud India'. The strong and stubborn Anjali was within minutes turned into a submissive woman, just the way Raghav liked his customers; he could not stand the women arguing back and 'being difficult' – their 'default setup' as he called it, therefore he developed his affective strategies of aligning their desire with his master-desire (Lordon 2014). Once Anjali became 'receptive', as he called it, he began his lecture on India's craft traditions, pulling out encyclopaedic books on Indian textiles and his own collection of antique sample pieces, mixing in stories of *begums*, painting a fantasy world of Indian opulence. Anjali got lost touching all the exquisite museum-like pieces in Raghav's collection and demanded more. Raghav's 'commercially inflected nationalism' (Bhachu 2004: 75) was doing its magic as Anjali was becoming increasingly sentimental and nostalgic. Raghav proposed that she tried on one of his recent creations, a *rani* pink *lehenga*, heavily embroidered in gold metal wire, with Swarovski crystals matched by a very modest long sleeved blouse with a light contrasting *dupatta*. When Anjali emerged from the changing room, he held her shoulders from the back, and looking into the large golden mirror, he whispered into her ear, 'look at you – the perfect Indian beauty'. Anjali's face suddenly changed, she looked demure, obedient and she began moving slowly with her gaze lowered. She knew exactly how to embody the ideal of the Indian woman and transform herself instantly; after all, she has rehearsed it in front of her relatives many times before (see Chapter 6). But this time, this time she was truly moved. Considering herself tough, independent and successful in the male dominated business world, it came to her as a surprise that within the affective atmosphere of the studio she suddenly fell for the seductive trappings of patriarchal ideology. Observing this from distance, I was reminded that 'subjects carry on doing the symbolic performances of ideological ceremonies ... because they engender a partial satisfaction, what Žižek terms "surplus enjoyment"; there is an unconscious enjoyment in subjection, in yielding and obeying – and being seen yielding and obeying – to the rules of ideology' (Gook 2011: 18). Anjali enjoyed succumbing to the ideal and was running around the studio from one mirror to another, contemplating herself in different poses of modesty, utterly enchanted. These powerful and affective national mythologies that came alive in the ritual play-sphere of the studio enabled Raghav to harness Anjali's power to act, and with it her capital. She walked away with her *rani* pink *lehenga*, an aesthetic object that, as we shall see later when we follow Anjali to a wedding, not only does the ideological work, but also is Indian for her and believes in the greatness of the nation on her behalf betraying a structure of interpassivity (Pfaller 2014, 2003, Žižek 1989). But let us first return to our initial question: how does this ritual of celebrating Indianness in the designer studio fit within the larger socio-economic landscape?

'We are high on ourselves': retro-futuristic utopias

In August 2000, the first fashion week in India took place, the Lakmé India Fashion Week. Under the patronage of the Fashion Design Council of India (est. 1998) it featured, among others, the first generation of designers educated at the National Institute of Fashion Technology (NIFT) in Delhi (est. 1986). The event was modelled upon similar events in the fashion capitals of the West, and the designers too, educated as they were in design and technology, focused largely on Western silhouettes, with limited amounts of embroidery and other traditional Indian decorative ornaments. As one of them recalled, 'we just did not want to be stamped as Indian designers, and be equated with embroideries and senseless bling; we wanted to show that we too have what the international buyer wants'. Among the designers, who graduated from NIFT, was also Ritu Beri, today a star designer. Beri's first Indian fashion week collection was all about classical Western silhouettes and limited ornament. She wanted to create something sexy and exciting for her generation. Those days were all about liberating Indian women from heavy layers of fabrics, about revealing and daring to show some skin, spicing things up, as Rina Dhaka pointed out to me during our interview. Then a shift happened, roughly after the financial crisis of 2008. In 2013, the same Ritu Beri presented at the PCJ Delhi Couture Week an over-the-top, extravagant, heavy, multi-layered, ornamentalist, excessive, and directly outlandish collection called 'Punjabi Rock & Roll', a collection that covered women from head to toe, inspired by a proud return to tradition and to her Punjabi roots. The white simple ramp of the initial fashion weeks was also gone, now it was all about theatrical stage sets and collaborations with other artists, such as in this case the Punjabi singer Jassi and the classical singer Sunanda Sharma. This shift could not be more revealing. The attitudes have changed. Today designers are proudly Indian (Figure 1.3). Being stamped as Indian is no longer a bad thing; on the contrary, India has become one of the world's largest luxury markets, and now it is the Western luxury brands that desperately try to penetrate this market. Even the Indian designers realized that the Indian market is their best shot, as the Mumbai-based designer Wendell Rodricks writes in his biography, 'we concentrated on the business in India, which is far more lucrative. Many other designers tried their luck at foreign fairs and learnt the same lesson. The Indian market is so large that it is best to try and exploit its vast potential' (Rodricks 2012: 297). Indian elites with their hunger for bridal and party fashions are the biggest market for the Indian designers, and the rest – they can just get inspired, as one of the designers said 'now they are running after us'. While the early 2000s were marked by Indo-Western or fusion garments, where Indianness had to be undercommunicated, the 2010s are the exact reverse; Indianness was overcommunicated and Western elements served only to express the idea of possessing the West, thrown in together with elements of other cultures, they stood for a good neo-imperial mix. Heritage luxury has become an inevitable part of the power mystique of the elites. At the same time their critique of imitating the West has become a staple the designers' discourse. Running after the West has become to the elite oh so middle class. Among the business elites, the West was increasingly perceived as a failure, in both moral and economic terms; the flow of investment shifted towards localities such as Dubai, Abu Dhabi, Saudi Arabia, Morocco, Turkey, China, Singapore, Russia, Korea, Thailand, Bali, Japan, Colombia, and Brazil. India's increasing confidence and the celebrated utopia of its future superpowerdom, now fuelled to new heights by the iconic Narendra Modi, has become a powerful economic force. Designers providing the aesthetics of this utopia sought patronage of Indian elites and Middle Eastern royals – dressing Hollywood celebrities was still good for the reputation and popularization of simple ready to wear collections aimed at (upper) middle classes, but it was not where the hard cash was. The tables have turned, at least for the elites 'high on Indianness'. Sophie Maxwell captured the same sentiment when noting that Karl Lagerfeld's 'Parisian ateliers' copying of Indian embroidery and craftsmanship rather than the other way, show the shifting influence from west to east and a growing reverence by global creative leaders' (Maxwell 2012: 35). And so while Western critics have argued that Chanel's collection ('Paris/Bombay 2011/12') was a case of cultural theft, the dominant West yet again exploiting the marginalized Other, and while praising the 'culturally sensitive' Hermès' *sari* collection from 2011 (Scott 2012), the interpretations on the ground differed. Upon questioning, several designers and their clients claimed in unison that Lagerfeld's act of appropriation of Indian

FIGURE 1.3 Backstage at India Couture Week 2014, collection by Manish Malhotra
Image Courtesy: Nitin Patel Photography.

aesthetics signified a shift in the global order, India being the trendsetter, the country with 'actual heritage' – there was no trace of victimhood; being a weak Other was out of question. And when it came to Hermès, Sabyasachi Mukherjee was heard saying that Indians who bought those *saris* should be ashamed of themselves, while Deepika Govind was angry and called it obnoxious (Narayan 2012). One client remarked, 'when you go to Hong Kong you find a huge fake Hermès market, who wants anything that can be so easily copied? Hermès is not real luxury, it's for posers.' No traces of elusions to the logic of cultural theft, and as for cultural sensitivity – a mere branding excuse on the part of Hermès. The initial popularity of Western luxury brands is also wearing off among the elites, as brands alone cannot serve as a source of distinction, especially the more they are being embraced by upper middle class buyers. Louis Vuitton, as Shefalee Vasudev, former editor of India's *Marie Claire*, also pointed out, 'once loved as a luxury brand by aristocracies, its democratization has distanced the classes from it. Most Indian designers, too, seem underwhelmed by the LV logo on bags, saying it looks jarring with embellished Indian couture.... Those who hankered after LV bags now don't want to be seen wearing them' (Vasudev 2012: 62).

Similarly to ideas like 'cultural theft', or 'cultural sensitivity', the concept of 'self-Orientalization' (Geczy 2013) has become the dominant lens through which fashion studies scholars understand the 'appropriation of one's own exotic culture' in high-end fashion. Jones and Leshkowich even suggest that 'wearing traditional dress can be seen as trendy, modern, or fashionable precisely because it is a self-Orientalizing move that often involves a distanced gaze or nostalgia' (Jones and Leshkowich 2003: 31) and that 'self-Orientalizing and internal Orientalizing have become widespread and viable techniques for attempting to acquire material and discursive power' (Jones and Leshkowich 2003: 36). Within this discourse, the only way for India to be valuable and fashionable is by way of succumbing to the Orientalist gaze it throws at itself. And so it is claimed that Indian 'designers internalize the Oriental gaze' (Nagrath 2003: 362) and that they 'make fashion choices that are primarily based on the way that global fashion system operates, which includes following trends that involve seeing one's own tradition as unique and exotic' (Nagrath 2003: 366). Not only do such simplistic explanations conceal more than they reveal, but, as one designer rightly pointed out, they perpetuate the idea that the British invented India, thus echoing Wendy Doniger for whom such theories act as if:

before the British got there, there was nothing south of Himalayas but a black hole... and then the British came and sat in a circle, holding hands, eyes tightly shut, chanting a *mantra* ('Rule Britannia'), until, like Athena from the head of Zeus... India popped up on the map,... full grown, complete with the word for Hinduism and the *Laws of Manu*.

DONIGER 1999: 944

Self-Orientalization arguments notoriously homogenize places like India, preventing us from understanding certain developments and fantasies as class-specific and multiply localized.

Raghav's studio, as we saw, is an enclosed space, designed in contra-distinction to the world out there, a ritual space, but also a profoundly utopian space, where fantasies of power and belonging can be enacted and mythologies of inevitable future superpowerdom, of tables turning, are affectively incorporated into the elite bodies. It is here that we have to look for the meaning of the neo-feudal aesthetics, not in any imaginary self-Orientalization. Neo-feudal ornamentalist aesthetics belongs to the utopian, the transformatory that embodies social hopes. Dressing up contains the utopian potential of transformation into an ideal self. Most designers appeal to this transformatory power when selling their utopian dreams of perfection, joy and class. The utopian potential of advertising, as Ernst Bloch observed, invests commodities with magical qualities (Bloch 2000). It is not a coincidence that all high-end fashion events, farmhouses, five-star hotels and luxury shopping malls, are gated. They are 'islands of sanity, security and peace', as one of my Indian friends called them. Separated from the everyday by a visible boundary, they are profoundly utopian spaces where past greatness merges with unlimited world luxuries and the inevitable future conquest of the world by the Indian elite. As John Carey remarked, 'paradises, like utopias, tend to be on islands. This may be because they suggest seclusion and purity. But it has also been pointed out that the human foetus is an island. So the island-paradise may reflect man's longing for the protective fluid that once surrounded him' (Carey 1999). To the elite bodies that move from one gated space to another, transported by luxury cars, observing the dusty, polluted, impoverished, and sweaty outside through the darkened window, luxury spaces function as protective fluid; they are an echo-chamber where the same ideas resonate time and again, intensified, amplified. In the capital city, the city of rulers, these designed utopian islands of luxury resonate with their factish (Latour 2010) *mantras* magnified by the collective effervescence of rituals: Indianness, heritage, rate of growth, cosmopolitanism, economic boom, rootedness, modern aristocracy, prestige, sovereignty and separation from and control of the rest. Like all utopias, these places are surgically clean, purged of any dirt and yet, built on dirt. The role of these utopian spaces is (1) to reproduce at all cost the feudal logic of rulers and subjects in face of democratization and social changes, such as the rise of the Dalits and other backward castes to political power, and (2) to nurture the dominant mythologies of spectacular capitalism, such as the myth of the self-made man, a meritocratic hero and to peculiarly merge it with neo-feudal aesthetics, as the old rich seek meritocratic legitimations of their wealth, while the new rich feed off the aesthetics of hereditary wealth to claim their position among the rulers. Rituals like the one in Raghav's studio perpetuate the divide, police the class boundaries and train newcomers like Anjali. Let us now proceed by way of another illuminating and paradigmatic ritual: JJ Valaya's fashion shows.

Ritual II: JJ Valaya's fashion shows

For his *Azrak* collection inspired by the Ottoman Empire and showcased at the Bridal Fashion Week 2012, JJ Valaya created a lavish stage set. It featured replicas of a lively Turkish *bazaar* with chandeliers glittering above it, balconies and domes as the backdrop, belly dancers moving through the scenery and aerial dances performed by gymnasts on fabric trails. While the models walked the ramp like royalty, the stage was decorated by fake *bazaar* people, by impoverished embroiderers and craft sellers impersonated by theatre students. This theatrical stage set was a perfect visual metaphor for the logic of fashion with its dependency on and reproduction of the low. Like other top designers for the rich, Valaya's shows are a powerful ritualistic spectacle of elitist distinction steeped in embellishment, ornamentation, texture, detailing, and craft, pregnant with uncontrollable references to the past and aristocracy that transgresses any imagined boundaries of time and space. As Valaya's mission statement proclaims, he is determined to show to the world the new India, resplendent with an aura of blue-blooded elegance, innovative craftsmanship and modern sensibilities. For his show one year later, *The Maharaja of Madrid*, Valaya placed on the stage a huge white replica of a Spanish battleship, hinting at India's conquest of the world. The show culminated with the showstoppers and movie actors Kabir Bedi, known among other things for his role as Shah Jehan, impersonating the phantasmatic Maharaja of Madrid and Kangana Ranaut as the maharaja's daughter and the bride to be. Kabir walked the ramp proudly, with a touch of royal pomp, beckoning his subjects to follow, inciting the ovation of the audience. Inspired by Spanish nobility, the collection combined elements, such as Spanish headgears, with heavy Indian royal style. Valaya also did away with the first row and replaced it with a lounge with tables covered in wine and cheese, the intention being to make everyone feel special (indeed except for the photographers and bloggers who have to squeeze on uncomfortable seats, stand and sit on the ground). The audience was bedazzled, clapping and shouting, emotions running high. Valaya induced joyful passions in the audiences and ignited their desire not only for his clothes but also for power, and consequently presented himself as the very solution to this desire, thus aligning successfully their desire with his master-desire (Lordon 2014). The neo-feudal aesthetic set within the narrative framework of the conquest of the world by the few at the top has provided the necessary direction to the induced joyful affects. The audience was pushed to imagine themselves in the place of the models, buy the clothes and, more importantly, buy into the mythology.

Such spectacles cannot be grasped through the framework of self-Orientalization and auto-exotization. Instead, such theatrical spectacles need to be understood as part of the struggle against democratization and abolition of feudal structures. The feudal desire to maintain firm hierarchies, and class and caste differences, governs Indian high fashion. Therefore, in order to make sense of these theatrical rituals that so successfully move the affects of the elites, it is crucial to shift perspective here – from the counterproductive Orientalism to the more illuminating Ornamentalism. David Cannadine argues in his book *Ornamentalism* (Cannadine 2002) that the British Empire was not exclusively about race, about the distinction between the superior West and the inferior Orient, but even more significantly about hierarchy, one that cuts across any division between West and its Other. This argument is significant in today's age of dramatically increasing inequality. It is imperative to shift the focus back to the simple fact that the high/low divide was something shared across the West/East distinction. The British were enamoured by what they imagined as traditional India precisely because they could mirror in it their own class-based social structure. India still possessed something that they saw as disappearing in the West, the West which they perceived as falling prey to democratic vulgarity. India had the traditional elite and admirably firm social hierarchy. One wonders if this is precisely the little extra so painfully celebrated in designer studios and fashion shows. Is this what is wrapped up in the notion of 'heritage'? Being so enamoured with hierarchy, the British failed to acknowledge the emergence of the urban, educated, nationalist and modernizing middle classes. Contemporary elites still scorn the middle classes as unimportant and hypocritically moralistic westoxicated aspirants. Cannadine thus points out that 'depending on context and circumstances, both white and dark-skinned peoples of the empire were seen as superior; or alternatively as inferior' (Cannadine 2002: 124). In other words, the English gentlemen had more in common with an Indian maharaja than an East End costermonger. British rulers found it amusing that low class white settlers had an unprecedented difficulty grasping the fact that aristocratic breeding cut across any imagined racial boundaries. The empire was united through its hierarchy, which positioned the chiefly, kingly and royal elite across the empire, against the 'inferior' subjects – what greatly mattered was social status and position. The empire, not unlike the spectacles of Indian haute couture catering to the new 'nomadic royals' as Valaya calls his customers, was

> about antiquity and anachronism, tradition and honour, order and subordination; about glory and chivalry, horses and elephants, knights and peers, processions and ceremony, plumed hats and ermine robes; about chiefs and emirs, sultans and nawabs, viceroys and proconsuls; about thrones and crowns, dominion and hierarchy, ostentation and ornamentalism.
>
> **CANNADINE** 2002: 126

The Independence of 1947 was the triumph of the middle-classes and urban-based radicals, so detested by the Raj. 'The matchless splendours of viceroyalty, in New Delhi, and at Simla, vanished ... the whole ceremonial carapace of durbars and state elephants and loyal toasts and Empire day was swept away', the rulers of the native states 'lost their freedom and independence, and eventually in 1971, their revenues and their titles, in this brave new world of post-imperial egalitarianism' (Cannadine 2002: 156). But the princes consigned to the dustbin of history have now re-emerged, turning their palaces into five-star luxury heritage hotels, themselves turning into businessmen, others into socialites, fashion designers, industrialists, or politicians – recall Gayatri Devi, who happened to be once named by *Vogue* among the ten most beautiful women in the world – thus retaining their power. Simultaneously, the progressive liberalization of the Indian economy since the 1990s enabled the emergence of a newly monied business elite that now seeks an equal place at the top. It is telling that JJ Valaya is patronized by the Royal house of Jaipur, Glenfiddich whisky, Middle Eastern royal families and a number of prominent self-made businessmen and industrialists.

Mastering time and space

Rituals like Valaya's fashion shows that play with notions of conquest, by evoking the Spanish or Ottomans and projecting their exploits on the canvas of contemporary and future India, and rituals like those inside Raghav's studio are first and foremost about mastering time and space. Valaya's Home of the Traveller label confirms this hunch, as it features interior decorations hand-picked by the designer himself during his travels, each piece dated, hand-made, unique, evoking ancient dynasties. Valaya's luxury store reminds us of a museum, where antique, unique and imperially charged objects from all over the globe – from India, Siam, and Turkey to Russia – are displayed. The items sold there, even though placed within the space of his enormous luxury store, are in principle unbrandable and unmarked. They are perfect for the nomadic royalty for whom fashion houses like Chanel, Louis Vuitton, or Dior no longer represent real luxury and exclusivity. Real luxury to them lies in things that defy any association with mass production, industrialization, democratization and modernization. Even couture from these fashion houses is viewed with suspicion. The taste for rare and beautiful objects from all over the world is nothing new among the elites. We find it everywhere, from the court of Louis XIV to Indian princes. Like in today's Indian elite worlds, the court of Louis XIV was marked by social instability within the courtly society with people moving in and out of favour. In such a setting, as Chandra Mukerji points out,

> collection was not just an aesthetically sanctioned excuse for hoarding. Objects collected in a household were put to work in the world of status just as capital was put to work in the world of business. Collector's items were used to claim and negotiate social rank ... Conspicuous consumption was an important and elaborated practice for nobles as well as the bourgeois in the period. Social rank was problematic for all members of the elite in this period of restratification.
>
> **MUKERJI** 1990: 655

Discussing the lavishly crafted gardens of the elites, Mukerji argues that these gardens 'could be seen as collector's maps, marking the international reach of the trading systems that reached their owners' (Mukerji 1990: 657). Collecting and exhibiting precious objects in one's home was directly connected to mastering of time and space. Rolls Royce and Cartier are likewise an integral part of Indian heritage luxury. Rather than about imitating the British, Indian heritage luxury has been and still is about mastering of the transnational space of power. Customized automobiles, the great passion of the maharajas, are a case in point. They are epitomized by the famous Throne Car embellished in brocade, silk and silver made in 1911 for Mahbub Ali Khan, Nizam VI of Hyderabad, the wealthiest man of his time. Even today this car serves as a source of pride for the Hyderabad elite. Mavendra Singh Barwani, an erstwhile royal, representative of Cartier in India as a curator for Concours d'Elegance and the co-author of *The Automobiles of Maharajas*, points out that India is the probably the only country in the world, where culture and climate as much as religion are reflected in the automobile – luxury cars were vehicles of mastering of social space and of natural forces:

> Nowhere else in the world were luxury cars put to uses as varied as ceremonial processions, tours of the state, during weddings, for hunting or for women secluded in *purdah* and on occasion, even as conveyors of garbage! Special cars and contoured bodies were fabricated by the manufacturers or coachbuilders to the specification of royalty, often catering to their incredible eccentricities. For the Maharajas, luxury motorcars became the symbols of prosperity, power and prestige.
>
> **SINGH** and **DWIVEDI** 2010: 6

Contemporary elite fashion is likewise marked by a cacophonic montage of incongruous elements from past and present, of diverse geographical origins and eccentric tastes – the way elite luxury has always been. As with any montage, it has to be assessed as an excess that can never be traced to its individual components; montage is not the sum of single components (Willerslev and Suhr 2014). Therefore any search for origins, authenticity, any dissection into traditional, modern, cultural theft and so on, becomes futile and meaningless. Mastering time and space transgresses and defies the logic of origin, even when stemming from it; as such it is profoundly utopian and phantasmatic. What would we achieve by dissecting the living room of the famous designer duo Abu Jani and Sandeep Khoshla?

> A corner of their living room in Mittal Park, Mumbai, is like an artist's shrine. In this small private alcove, a Jain mandala appears next to a massive carved anthropomorphic Shiv *linga*. These are overseen by *dua* mirrors – common to Muslim and Sufi shrines, with verses of the Koran carved on them, as benediction to the devoted. Cheek by jowl, carved wooden *gandharva* musicians in high

relief appear to fly off the wall, their elegant winged bodies pinned back in dynamic flight. A Buddha, resplendent and silent in contemplation, sits framed by a massive silver door, bearing carved scenes from 'Ram Darbar', the coronation of the Hindu mythical king Ram. Home, shrine, temple, mosque, bazaar, all occupying levels within the same space, mingle in this oneness of faiths.

JANI and KHOSLA 2012: 9

Maybe it is more fruitful to think of such montages in a way akin to Jacque Ranciere's reflection on Balzac's famous depiction of an antique shop in *The Wild Ass's Skin*:

The shop was indeed a mixture of worlds and ages.... The mixture of the curiosity shop made all objects and images equal. Further, it made each object a poetic element, a sensitive form that is a fabric of signs as well. All these objects wore a history on their body. They were woven of signs that summarized an era and a form of civilization. And their random gathering made a huge poem, each verse of which carried the infinite virtuality of new stories, unfolding those signs in new contexts. It was the encyclopaedia of all the times and all the worlds.

RANCIERE and CORCORAN 2010: 162

Valaya commented on his collection as follows: 'It's an assortment of motifs and it's almost impossible to start identifying each one of them' (Caroli 2012) – and we should probably take his word for it. The understated luxury of Western elites is the opposite of desirable. 'We are over the top; we are all about excess. The maharajas did everything in style and so do we!' as Sandeep Khoshla proclaimed (Jani and Khosla 2012). Utopian islands of plenty come to mind. Their goal: demystification of the notion of Western exceptionality and superiority (Mahbubani 2009), a reclaiming of India both as an economic and a soft global power. The ritualistic spectacles taking place on these utopian islands put normative pressures on the participants; they demand certain behaviours, restrict others and set limits to what can be said. Certain ideas and people are expelled from these luxury utopian islands – only the chosen few, accepted largely on grounds of their wealth, are present, and they have to act as prescribed. It is impossible to count the instances when on the way home from an elite fashion event, women suddenly felt relief – for instance, they could finally say that they hated the designs they praised after the show, and so on. First when off the island, they could claim their distance from it and acknowledge the artificiality of the ritual space. They emphasized to me that they merely acted as if they really cared or liked certain things, or really bought into the luxury products and the whole ideology of superpowerdom. Yet they enjoyed it, possibly even more precisely because they claimed this distance. The power of the fashion show as a ritual practice and the enjoyment derived from it lie not only in the resulting enhancement of self-esteem following the participation, but more importantly in the acting as if. I often caught the same women wearing the designs they distanced themselves from for a wedding or a party weeks later. No matter how much these women cynically claimed their distance towards their elitist pleasures, they not only (re)produced them, but also fell for them; they fell for their own act – like Anjali did. Cynicism does not prevent the strategies of capture from being effective.

Collective effervescence and directing affects

Theatrical fashion rituals of the Valaya kind are not only driven by the ornamentalist logic of elite distinction, but also by the commercial logic of experience design. Experience design strategically aims at manipulating consumers' affects and their subconscious – think sensory branding, neuromarketing and so on (Lindstrom 2009). All of these ambient elitist spaces, built as theatrical stage sets, are saturated with more or less visible brand messages. They invite people to participate in the mythologies of eliteness, to co-create these environments and to invest them with their power to act. One thing is the deliberate production of ambient affective atmospheres and spaces, aimed at arousing joyful affects, another thing is how people collectively move within such spaces. It is namely in the collective movement that one embraces the embedded ideologies and brand mythologies. It is here that the importance of staged events comes to the fore. The profit-oriented organizers aim at an ecstatic state of shared excitement, one that can align people's affects with the master-desire of the brands. They aim at creating an event akin to a sacred ritual celebration that makes people move together. It can be argued that such events aim at producing, to use the good old Durkheimian notion, 'collective effervescence' (Durkheim 1965), that is, an alignment of the affective states that produce a sense of belonging in the participants, a social glue – a 'fusion of particular sentiments into one common sentiment' (Durkheim 1965: 262). Mediation in this case becomes not only a matter of directing affect and aligning the desire of the consumers with the master-desire of the brand, but also as an increasingly invisible direction of collective affects – an effective disciplining measure. Theatrical stage, ritual spectacle, and memorable experiences – those are the commercial tools used to move people's affects and to harness their power to act. But what makes people move together, collectively? Affects understood as unbound energy or intensity can certainly push us to act, however the question is in what direction they push us, and to what effect. As Yves Citton argues, affects can become effective only when integrated into a narrative structure or a story line that can make sense of our experiences and structure our future paths of action – 'we feel in and through stories' (Citton 2010: 64). And we could add – through ritualized action that provides similarly structured and patterned frameworks. As already Durkheim pointed out, ritual is essential in the making and remaking of society because it exercises profound force and influence over its participants. Narratives and rituals, as much as affects, have to be therefore understood on a collective basis, existing outside our own individual subjectivity, while having their own epidemiology. Fashion brands attempt to provide such ready-made myths, narratives and ritual structures that serve as attractors for action or mobilization within an ambient space. Therefore, vast amounts of social labour go not only into developing ambient spaces, designed to induce positive effects, but also into creating mythical narratives framing these environments and into developing ritual practices that take place within such spaces. Framing, wording and editing are as crucial here as is ritualized action – the silence before the fashion show, the male voice resonating in the hall: 'please take your seats as we are now about to commence the show, out of respect to designers we urge you to silence your mobile phones, guests are also requested not to use flash or professional cameras' and so on, dancers or musicians, the first model, claps, snaps, the showstopper, the parade, the designer kissed by the showstopper, the ecstatic finale, ovations, admiration, thanks. All this is repetitive, carefully structured, timed and rehearsed.

Valaya, like other designers, aims at creating a 'lovemark', not a mere brand. Lovemarks (Roberts 2004) aim at tapping into people's dreams by creating mythical narratives that encourage empathy, passion and commitment; they aim at being loved and respected beyond reason; they aim at producing loyal followers. Lovemarks capitalize on the Durkheimian insight that social knowledge and belonging are born and strengthened in the collective effervescence of ritual enactment. And the uncanny element? While consumers are being fed the idea of brand distinction, of each designer being a unique and independent creative genius with an original set of ideas, comparative empirical material tells us otherwise. Valaya is not the exception, he is the rule. The reality is one of collaborating brands that enforce each other's power rather than competing. Together they push the same elitist utopian mythology with only minor differences. Designers have often emphasized to me that coming together enriches everyone; capital accumulates through inclusion, not through exclusion as we are far too often led to believe. Part of this collaboration is pushing the same mythology to the same segment of clients.

The illusion of India's future superpowerdom materializes not only in fashion design, but also in the actions of the architects of utopia par excellence, the planners of and investors in India's future smart cities for the worthy citizens, the new rich and upper middle class. But the masses of the poor who build these cities, these utopian islands, are expelled (Sassen 2014) – from imagination, from belonging to a nation, and from the state's responsibilities. The newly elected right-wing government has already in its budget allotted start-up money for 100 smart cities of the future, envisioned along the lines of the yet non-existent utopian city of Dholera planned in Gujarat, a city resembling Shanghai, double the size of Mumbai, running on renewable energy, a special investment region, no crowds, pollution, excessive noise, and a new age international airport to secure smooth penetration of international capital. This megalomaniac construction project promises to deliver the magical 9 per cent rate of growth, or so its political and corporate ideologues claim. Today, there is only a vast land with a bunch of skyscrapers under construction close to the coastline that is being eaten up by the rising sea at the rate of 1cm a day. This land is populated by roughly 40,000 farmers, the future dispossessed slum dwellers, as typical of such construction projects (Roy 2014). They protest in vain. Instead of providing clean water, health care and social services within the already existing cities, the state, much like the business people, is determined to capitalize on phantasmatic virtualities and promises. During the election campaign, merely due to the anticipation of Modi's victory with his promise of further pro-business reforms, the stock of Reliance Industries has gained 20 per cent even before Modi was really elected, while Adani Enterprises, of the billionaire and devoted supporter of Modi, Gautam Adani, jumped 60 per cent from April to May 2014. This is the real power of carefully designed and staged illusion.

Ritual III: wedding spectacle

Rituals are powerful and effective because they are staged. Anjali was moved and touched by the patriotic sentiment enacted in the studio precisely due to the staged character of the encounter within a particularly suitable gated affective atmosphere. The fact that 'the psychic intensity produced during play ... is greater than the extent of affect that appears otherwise in life' (Pfaller 2014: 74), became also fairly obvious when I met Anjali a month later at a wedding in Jaipur, where she was wearing Raghav's creation. Weddings are likewise staged affairs of largely staged emotions, following prescribed rites and ritualized practices, with appropriate demeanour. Weddings are also the biggest market for Indian designers. During weddings elite Indianness is staged most intensely and the personal and family image matters most when business deals are sealed during the celebrations (Figure 1.4). High on emotion and drama, wedding plays/rituals have recognized cultural functions; this means that they are bound with notions of duty and obligation (Huizinga 1955). This makes them a different sort of play to the one behind the closed door of the secretive designer studio, where the intensity of emotion connected to the illusion can be freely played out and one can more easily fool oneself into believing that he/she really believes. But back to Anjali. The moment she escapes from the wedding stage, where she acts as the demure Indian woman dressed up in tradition from head to toe, and runs out through the back

FIGURE 1.4 At an elite wedding
Image courtesy: Arash Taheri.

entry to the parking lot, the weight of enacting ideal Indian womanhood falls off
her shoulders. In the parking lot, a group of men is drinking, smoking and telling
dirty jokes; they welcome her with a cheer. She laughs and begins mocking both
the uncomfortable costume she is wearing and the whole business of pretending to
be a modest and traditional woman, touching feet of all the elders and so on. She
begins her rant: 'I am fucking fed up of touching feet of all these oldies, most of
them are bloody corrupt illiterates. Give me a smoke dude, else I fucking die, for
real.' Anjali's transgressive smoke, especially for her being a non-smoker, was
precisely the necessary act of distantiation. Anjali also occasionally made remarks
about Raghav outside his studio, such as 'he talks a lot of crap', in order to make
sure that I understand that she knows that he does it all for money, still, she would
be paying him in *lakhs* and feel rejuvenated.

All these ritual plays reproduce the utopian mythologies or illusions that no
one seems to really believe in. And yet, these illusions make the social and economic
world go round. But these rituals also share another feature. In all these rituals the
belief in India's retro-futuristic greatness and the undeniable value of Indianness
– the very thing the elites struggle to display and often feel they lack – is delegated
to the costume. We can observe a structure of interpassivity at play here (Pfaller
2014, 2003). The situation is parallel to the functioning of the Tibetan prayer wheel,
an example given by Slavoj Žižek:

[A Tibetan prayer] wheel itself is praying for me, instead of me – or, more precisely, I myself am praying through the medium of the wheel. The beauty of it is that in my psychological interior I can think about whatever I want, I can yield to the most dirty and obscene fantasies, and it does not matter because – to use a good old Stalinist expression – whatever I am thinking, objectively I am praying.

ŽIŽEK 1989: 34

The designer garment thus both believes for Anjali at the same time as it consumes for her the commodity of national belonging and Anjali, while at the wedding stage, can think all the thoughts she wants about the sleazy uncles, dirty business, corrupt politicians and other perverts present. What really matters is that objectively she is yielding to the tradition. The garment respects the elders for her, succumbs to and reproduces the ideology for her and for others. Maybe no one really believes in her acting, and she is staging all this for an invisible naïve observer, as everyone else does. Maybe it is all an illusion without owners, staged for an idealized naïve observer who judges by appearance (Pfaller 2014). And yet, this is how objectively traditions, customs and ideologies are reproduced, structuring reality. Indeed, there is pleasure to be gained from succumbing and giving in. When inside the theatrical space, Anjali was extremely emotional throughout all the wedding ceremonies. At the same time as she despised the event and hated all the pretentions, waiting only to escape and get some vodka shots in the parking lot, she loved the event precisely in her devotion to the illusion of idealized Indianness and tradition – the great Indian wedding, when everyone becomes royalty even if only for the week of celebrations. All these rituals produce collective shared affects and affective investment in the illusion from which all impurities are sanitized – poverty does not exist, dirty business deals are covered in a veil of goodness of tradition, all illegitimate wealth is turned into a neo-feudal birthright, exploitation into aristocratic benevolence (see Chapter 4) – a paradigm for the perfect utopian Indian smart city of the future, a project of social cleansing. Beyond prestige, this is what the designers sell.

What are they buying (into)?

What the elites are buying from the designer showrooms is not something they could ever buy at the regular *bazaar*. Even if the pieces look the same, feature the same embroidery, same colour and same fabrics, still the designer *sari* is an altogether different thing. Ludwig Feuerbach's words might resonate here: 'The present age ... prefers the sign to the thing signified, the copy to the original, fancy to reality, the appearance to the essence ... in these days illusion only is sacred, truth profane ... the highest degree of illusion comes to be the highest degree of sacredness' (Feuerbach 1854: xi). The question of why the elites prefer to pay in *lakhs* to a designer for something that they could get in a regular market, equally customized, with equally good 'work', puzzled a middle-class trader in Lucknow, Preity, a woman specializing in high-quality *chikan* embroidery. She found it difficult to comprehend that the idea of handwork, as it finds its expression in the narrative of heritage skilfully connected to the nationalistic tale of the greatness of mother India, can be valorized over the actual handwork. Her sentiment might appear naïve after recounting the ritualistic tenets of elite fashion:

> I want the embroidery to speak for itself; its sheer beauty should do all the talking. People should understand the value of it just by looking at it. The delicacy of the stitches says it all. Every true connoisseur should immediately recognize that. I should be silent, only displaying it, absolutely silently. For what I am selling, no words should be needed.
>
> Interview, October 2011

Within the economy of late capitalism that has drifted away from dealing in commodities per se to trading in experiences, feelings, visions and promises of future life scenarios, this wish appears naïve and nostalgic (Roberts 2003, Böhme 2003, Joseph and Gilmore 2011, Lanham 2006). Preity once visited me and her daughter in Delhi; I suggested that we have a look at the designer boutiques in DLF Emporio luxury shopping mall. The interior of the mall is lavish, all in shades of cream and gold, a shiny marble floor with stylized chess board pattern in cream and brown, with large palm trees, sparkly fountain and glassed elevators with staff to press the button for you. Even the toilets smell like luxury, with the toilet paper's first sheet folded into a triangle, female staff that greet you, turn on the water tap for you, hand you the paper towel and then fold the toilet paper again after you leave. We visited a couple of boutiques, but Preity was largely unimpressed by the quality and even the design of the *chikan* embroidered *saris* and other garments. She felt that she herself could do much better, that her embroiderers were capable of creating more intricate pieces, but that nobody would pay her these ridiculous amounts. The designer *chikan saris* were all in a range from 1.5 *lakh* to 3 *lakhs rupees* (approx. €2,150–4,300). She kept asking me, 'what is it they have and I don't, why would people want to spend so much on something that you can buy much cheaper and then, when they come to me they argue and think I am expensive'. Preity was already frustrated when we entered Tarun Tahiliani's boutique. We were going through the hangers, when we spotted a collection of *chikan saris*. In seconds her eyes were filled with tears. I knew immediately that they were hers – the printing blocks used, the combination of *chikan* with *mukeish* and so on. Only additional pearls were stitched on to the blouse piece. All of the *saris* were in a price range between 1.5 and 2 *lakhs* (approx. €2,150–2,880). Preity sold these *saris* to a man who came by her boutique in Lucknow, claiming that he was looking for *saris* for his sister about to get married. In the end, he purchased four *saris* ranging from twenty to thirty thousand *rupees* (approx. €290–430). While this may be a common and unsurprising practice in the Indian fashion industry, the paradoxical fact remains that Tarun Tahiliani is one of the few designers known to be hard on plagiarists and is the first designer 'to get a court order on fashion designers getting intellectual copyright in India'. He is also reported to have said the following: 'you copy me at your peril, I will come after you and drag you to court' (Vasudev 2012: 14). Of course, Preity would never be acknowledged as a designer by Tarun; she has no designer persona, no fashion week shows and on top of that believes in collaborative and distributed creativity. She would never be able to challenge him, but he can easily challenge those below, who keep 'copying' his designs. Reflecting on what happened, she proclaimed: 'so it is all about the ambience? That is all very well, but you are not taking it home! Are the customers so blind that they do not see that what they are buying is the same thing that they can buy in the market? I don't understand – the thing is the same'. As JJ Valaya once said, 'when you wear a Valaya original, you are expected to naturally possess fine taste, respect for culture and a considerable amount of chutzpah' (Arora 2012). The value of the embroidered *saris* was clearly dependent on the whole configuration of objects, mythologies, and rituals within which they were placed. Only such montage could endow the individual pieces with the qualities, which were produced as its excess.

Conclusion

This chapter has identified the core rituals of the Indian luxury fashion industry that sells nothing less than lavish and proud Indianness, most obviously manifested in the crux of the business – bridal fashion that sells the utmost neo-feudal dream. Through these rituals, the neo-feudal aesthetic materialized in the fashionable attire and ornaments, becomes embodied; it becomes a lived and performed ideology. As the elite bodies move collectively through the fortified ritual spaces, clearly set apart from the everyday and from the outside heat and dirt, they participate in the highly staged and branded mythologies of Indian eliteness, of India's exceptionalism, superiority and inevitable future superpowerdom. Through these rituals, the Indian business elite have been dealing with their post-colonial trauma, with being haunted by feelings of inferiority vis-à-vis the West, and especially Britain and the US. Following the financial crisis that hit Western markets so hard, an opportunity arose for the Indian business community to re-imagine itself as a future global leader, yet one superior precisely because of its culture and traditions with their values and moralities that they imagine the West has lost. All the fashion rituals share one core ingredient, namely the celebration of Indianness as a tremendous resource, both for the present and for the future. But this Indianness, these unique roots that provide the business community with that little extra, have to be visible and shockingly opulent in order to be effective and in a peculiar way, they have to be kept at a distance. Indianness with all the traditional moralities that it is imagined to entail, is delegated by the elite to the fancy objects that symbolize their commitment for them, but at the same time a cynical distance needs to be claimed. Maybe, because identifying too much with this most precious and celebrated quality would bring the elite too close to the poor masses, those firmly localized, as we will see in the next chapter. All these rituals, these spectacles of neo-feudal excess, on the one hand reproduce the established social order, even in the logic of distantiation and delegation; while on the other hand, they contain an element of social hope. In the face of democratization, in the face of rights and opportunities being claimed and demanded by untouchables and others traditionally at the bottom of the social hierarchy, these opulent rituals serve to cultivate and maintain a small, impenetrable, tightly knit group at the top that shares attitudes, tastes and worldviews. A group of people, who through their indulgence in this neo-feudal aesthetics also, and more importantly, aim at recreating the feudal order itself, with its firm hierarchies and blatant inequalities. This is also why Indian luxury cannot be subtle, why simplicity of modernism is out of question. Indian luxury is profoundly neo-feudal not only in its aesthetics but also in the structures of its production, as we shall see more clearly in the next chapters. Indian luxury fashion is not only about crafting the aesthetics of distinction and prestige, in a uniquely Indian way, but more importantly about reproducing a firm hierarchical social order in the face of social change and pressures from the new classes of aspirants who want their share of the global wealth. But there is an element of social hope as well, namely, the hope that all of India will one day make it. It was precisely this hope that drove masses of impoverished people to vote in the new right-wing government led by Narendra Modi (2014). In this sense, the voters aligned themselves with the powerful, with the business and corporate elite and its aspirations, hoping that one day India will transform into a land of wealth for everyone.

In the following chapter, we will explore further how hierarchy, cosmopolitanism and the elite's relation to the local and the global are produced, and how materiality goes hand in hand with ideology in this production. But we will also see how social cohesion emerges as an effect of the production networks in the *chikan* embroidery cottage industry. We will trace the the movement of this embroidery, popular with India's leading designers, from the local networks of its material production by specialized and largely impoverished craftspeople (e.g. printers, embroiderers, dyers), to its immaterial production by the designers and elevation from the local to the national, and its transformation into a source of pride and Indianness staged for the imagined global Other.

2 PRODUCING COSMOPOLITANISM, HIERARCHY AND SOCIAL COHESION

In 1819, the coronation of the nawab Ghazi al-Din Haydar as the *padshah* of Awadh took place in Lucknow, the richest, most magnificent, luxurious and cosmopolitan Indian city of its times (1775–1856) (Trivedi 2010; Ramusack 1995; Llewellyn-Jones 1985). While the power of the nawabs was increasingly threatened by the English East India Company from the late-eighteenth to mid-nineteenth century, the nawabs still wanted to claim their sovereignty. While until then loyal to the Delhi Mughal court, Ghazi al-Din Haydar decided to claim his sovereignty both against the British and the Mughals. The painting of his coronation by Robert Home, a court artist at Lucknow from 1814 to 1837, captured 'the visible trappings of this unprecedented proclamation of sovereignty, which drew its authoritative symbols from Mughal and European traditions, and based its claim for legitimacy upon the Awadh dynasty's Shia ancestry' (Gude 2010: 94). Being the first coronation in the dynasty of this kind, the ceremony was carefully prepared and staged using a hybrid mixture of influences in order to display Awadh's extraordinary courtly opulence. Special regalia were prepared, coins spreading Ghazi al-Din Haydar's name and title beyond Awadh's territory were circulated; more than twenty million *rupees* were invested in the construction of the paraphernalia, a throne surmounted by a canopy, made of gold and embellished with pearls, emeralds, rubies, diamonds and other precious stones was created, covered by an umbrella made of gold and decorated with jewels.

If the throne and umbrella seemed to follow traditional Indian and Mughal patterns, the crown designed for the ceremony appears to have been of European inspiration if not pattern. . . . The crown used by Ghazi al-Din Haydar appears

to have been a dramatic innovation not only in its shape but also in its utilization
... Ghazi al-Din Haydar's introduction of a European style coronation in India
seems to have been a conscious effort to put himself into the European tradition
and context.

FISHER 1985: 260

The ceremony took place on the date of prophet Muhammad's revelation of Ali as
the first Shia imam. Ghazi al-Din Haydar 'chose this day to emphasize the
identification he sought as the true, Shi'i sovereign' (Fisher 1985: 261) against
the, according to him, illegitimate Sunni Delhi Mughal court. The emblems
associated with European kingship superficially inscribed upon the Shia-oriented
Awadhi throne manifested its sudden disloyalty both to the Mughals and to
the British. Ghazi al-Din Hayder used hybrid referents to legitimize his new
position as a king. The coronation, like contemporary elite luxury consumption,
was a hybrid montage of emblems intended for public display. Current elite
consumption might at first glance appear to us as a natural continuation of these
public displays. However, such an appearance of continuation is to a large degree
produced though commodification of the past and heritage. This appearance
is also achieved through promotion of a particular type of cosmopolitanism,
one that is the opposite of integrative and open, a cosmopolitanism that is a mark
of hierarchical distinction (Brosius 2010) and of patterns of influence (Merton
1957). The question that we are going to address here is how such a type of
cosmopolitanism comes about; how is it materially and ideologically produced
and sustained? In order to answer this question, we will delve into one particular
locality and one particular industry: namely the Lucknow's *chikan* cottage industry.
It is a remarkable case for several reasons. First, the social networks of production
of the embroidery on the one hand sustain the imaginary of Lucknow and its
cherished narrative of peaceful social cohesion by reproducing its material
conditions, while on the other hand, these same networks are kept alive precisely
through this narrative. Second, the case of *chikan* and its movement from Lucknow
to Delhi and into the global export market raises the question of the dynamic
relation between what is imagined as local, pan-Indian, cosmopolitan, and global.
This is not only a question of value, but also a question of the production of
localities, globality and glocality and their function within a system of social
inequalities. The question of the role of production of certain localities as utopian
and their inscription into heritage luxury as such, also arises (Figure 2.1). Lucknow
and the case of *chikan*, its most prestigious heritage luxury product and a physical
manifestation of successful secular nationalism, 'unity in diversity' and vernacular
cosmopolitanism, throw light onto the logic of, on the one hand the utopian
hope of social cohesion, happy cosmopolitanism and secularism, while on the
other hand, they show how the same can be used in the play of hierarchical
distinction that brings to life a peculiar neo-feudal order. The interplay between

FIGURE 2.1 Chota Imamabara in Lucknow
Image courtesy: Arash Taheri.

the lived phantasmatic mythologies of this city and their selective traditions and the relations of production of the ideological product par excellence will form the core of the following argument. And so, rather than factual history, what interests us here are the selective traditions, that is, 'that which, within the terms of an effective dominant culture, is always passed off as "the tradition", "the significant past". But always the selectivity is the point; the way in which from a whole possible area of past and present, certain meanings and practices are chosen for emphasis, certain other meanings are neglected and excluded' (Williams 1973: 9).

Dynamics of proximity and distance

In order to address these questions, let us unravel a story of the movement of a single element within the utopian montage of neo-feudal fashion. Namely, the movement of *chikan* embroidery, from the concrete networks of production to its insertion into the system of prestige objects. *Chikan* embroidery is not only unique because of its delicacy and beauty, but also because of the place it is coming from, a city known for its composite culture, vernacular cosmopolitanism and long-standing communal peace. 'Even when most parts of the country were rocked by Hindu–Muslim violence during the early 1920s and on the eve of India's partition and thereafter, Lucknow remained an island of peace and sanity. Its record, barring some isolated and sporadic incidents, has not been tarnished since Independence' (Graff et al. 2006: 11). Lucknow is the perfect example of the said happy hybrid mixture of cultures and as such particularly suitable for idealization and commodification. *Chikan* embroidery, produced in a multi-staged process that involves people from different caste, class, and religious backgrounds, and a heritage product par excellence, is turned into the very materialization of the idea of Indian composite culture, central to elitist nationalism. *Chikan* is one of the crafts increasingly patronized by Indian fashion designers. This is possibly best exemplified by Ritu Kumar (1944), one of the most famous revivalist designers, who became known for her work with craft communities as much as for designing attires for Miss India competitors. She was also awarded the prestigious Padma Shree award, the fourth highest civilian award by the Republic of India, in 2013 for her work with craft. Ritu's agenda as a designer parallels the work of the Crafts Council of India, both aiming at the revival of crafts by replicating 'the quality and finesse of the originals' of 'museum collections' (Crafts Council 2007), while adding a contemporary twist to the products. Ritu is a classic example of a designer capitalizing on her expert knowledge, craft patronage, and eloquent interpretations when selling 'idealized images of Indian culture to wealthy cosmopolitan elite' (Tarlo 1996: 315). She is first and foremost a mythmaker as her own impressive coffee table book *Costumes and Textiles of Royal India* testifies (Kumar and Muscat 2006).

Following *chikan* enables us to connect utopias, like those (re-)produced by Kumar, to their material conditions of production and unravel the dynamics of proximity and distance, that is the oscillations along the axis of locality, pan-Indianness and vernacular cosmopolitanism (Bhabha 1994); an axis of abstraction and distance that seems to work on the following principle: the further away from production, the more valuable, and paradoxically the more 'authentic'. The point is to show how the 'rural or urban or local or cosmopolitan are not temporally distinct states of being in which one evolves into another, but rather are produced in relation to each other within the same social field' (Larkin 2004: 93). 'Flows', though often appearing as disembodied in their nature, in reality 'require material conduits, and they appear because a place . . . is embedded in precise networks of social relations built over time' (Larkin 2004: 93). While some would argue that the contrasts between local and global evaporate in real-life settings (Eriksen 2003: 15), this does not mean that these dichotomies are not effective in practice – labelling things global or local has a significant social impact, constitutive of belonging as much as expulsion. Therefore these categories are worth investigating as 'categories of practice', while disposing of them as 'categories of analysis' (Brubaker and Cooper 2000).

Chikan cottage industry: structure and networks

The *chikan* craft cluster is said to be currently the largest artisanal cluster of India, even though no completely reliable estimates exist (Wilkinson-Weber 1999). In 2001, there were 250,000 embroiderers reported in Lucknow and surrounding districts (Unnao, Barabanki, Hardoi, Lakhimpur, Raibareilly, Sultanpur and Faizabad), plus roughly one million of attached labour, including cutters, tailors, printers, washermen, traders, designers, exporters, finishers, retailers, managers, contractors and so on (Arya and Sadhana 2001). I have largely worked in villages within the 35 kilometre radius and in Kakori and Barabanki. The industry has grown rapidly in the last decade, the exporters and traders I interviewed estimated doubling of the workforce, as their own businesses have grown by 20 to 50 per cent. Increased demand for *chikan* and for *chikan* of higher quality that takes considerably longer to produce, have resulted in the need for more and skilled workers. The *chikan* industry is often considered as a paradigmatic example of an unorganized sector (Varshney 1997). Yet, while the relations of production are predominantly those of an informal cottage industry, they are not so absolutely, the unorganized being clearly linked to the organized. There is a vast spectrum of putting-out relations (Basole 2012, Basole and Basu 2009), depending on a large number of factors – such as the quality of the embroidery or its purpose, such as local or international export, fast turnover, cheap, medium or elite markets, all implying different organizational models. Additionally, the variously connected and positioned workers and artisans are scattered over smaller and larger distances. Therefore, there is little centralization (Varshney 1997, Wilkinson-Weber 1999), there are few to no wage contracts, payments are mostly piece-wages, however monthly wages are becoming more common in higher end production. Nominally independent and self-employed producers tend to be locked over time into relations of financial dependency vis-à-vis the fashion designer or local trader. Since there is no social security or pensions for the workers, patron–client relations are common, patronage being both a protective policy for the clients and a despised exertion of power that locks the clients in their social position (see Chapters 4 and 5). There is a considerable difference between the role of established traders and old manufacturers who 'stress their close, paternalistic relations with producers, remarking that neither do they exact penalties over spoilt or late work like newer *mahajans*, nor do they hold back wages' (Wilkinson-Weber 1999: 38) and fashion designers, who are newcomers that often claim to be 'good benevolent patrons' and yet fail to deliver, their support being seasonal, dependent on collections and thus unpredictable and unreliable. Patron–client relations, while based on inequality, are often also long-term relationships of obligation, mutual trust and loyalty, the patron providing security in face of insecurity. And yet, it is often at the same time the patron who stands behind the insecurity – the patron offers a protection to the client from himself. Any relation of patronage 'requires the very gap which it assists the client in bridging. For surely the patron does not help his clients to change the system (or themselves) and thereby abolish the gap' (Stein 1984: 51). This is a point to be noted for our future discussions of the patronage by the designers and non-governmental organizations that successfully reproduce hierarchical relations precisely by the logic of patronage wrapped up in rhetoric of empowerment. The networks of production within the industry have the form of bridging weak ties (Granovetter 1973), that is, ties that bring together very diverse actors from across the spectrum of class, religion, gender and place them into cross-cutting networks of interdependency, some tight and some loose. These networks have expanded considerably in the last ten years. Lucknow is today plugged into trade relationships that stretch from Delhi, Calcutta, Bangalore, Mumbai, and Hyderabad to the Middle East, France, Japan, Hong Kong, Singapore and so on. This is how Preity, the *chikan* trader we met in previous chapter, herself described the changes:

> I will be able to tell you what happened in the last 30–35 years. There were a lot of people who were doing *chikan*, not too many, but a substantial number. Frankly what I see in the 20–25 past years I think we have 300–400 times more people coming into the industry and with the coming of SEWA people like Runa Banerji, the coming of the NIFT (National Institute of Fashion Technology), the designers who, I would not say patronize it, but made *chikan* a fashion statement today, it is used all over the world today. There were exporters, but on a very low scale, but now you name it and you have it. When I was a kid, *chikan* had become absolutely defunct, there was a very ordinary *kurta* which was in fashion and the quality of embroidery was bad. Now it is a big industry in Lucknow, lots of business thriving on it, and everybody is willing to understand that this is something good, they realize the value of it, and they appreciate the value, so people are taking a lot of interest in it. Initially it was something very cheap, but now it has become something very good also. *Chikan* is developing now so fast that you don't know in next 15 years what changes will come.
>
> **KULDOVA** 2009: 38, interview, February 2008

Our description of the complex relations of manufacture resonates with Marx's descriptions of the transition to modern industry. Interestingly, Marx's idea that in the domestic industries, such as in the case of home-based *chikan* embroiderers, 'exploitation is still more shameless than in modern manufacture, because the workers' power of resistance declines with their dispersal; because a whole series of plundering parasites insinuate themselves between the actual employer and the worker he employs' (Marx 1992: 591) has been appropriated in the dominant non- and governmental institutional discourse about the *chikan* industry. The middle-man, peddling between the city and villages and taking his cut from embroiderers' salaries, has been identified as the evil culprit of this system. In 1970, UNICEF published an influential study on the *chikan* industry that has firmly established the middle-man as the bad guy to be blamed for all the social evils in the industry. Even today, when the conditions and structures have changed, this is recited like a *mantra* providing a legitimization to NGOs involved with the industry. Blaming the middle-men for exploitation of the craftswomen serves as a legitimization for setting up workshops in the city (in the name of capitalist productivity) to which the far village-based craft labour should migrate – for their own good – in order to get a better and fair deal – a dubious agenda to say the least (see Chapters 4 and 5).

Networks of production

To the knowledgeable elite connoisseur in Lucknow or Delhi the *chikan* embroidery, among other things, stands for communal harmony, the core of secular Indianness. What this knowledgeable connoisseur may not know is that the economic networks of production contribute to the striking non-presence of Hindu–Muslim strife (Kuldova 2009). The production depends on collaboration of people of different religions, classes and castes. The connoisseur may also not know that the demand for luxuries by Lucknow nawabs created similar networks of interdependency and that the nawabs were, similarly to today's nationalist discourse, utilizing the rhetoric of inclusion, celebrating both *Holi* and *Muharram* and building *imambaras* that are unlike mosques open to members of all religions. Lucknow nawabs elaborated from a Shia nobility and a cultural base in Persia and have formed a specific Indo-Persian culture in Lucknow, which flourished most vigorously between the reign of Asaf-ud-Daula (1774–98), who in 1775 shifted his capital from Faizabad to Lucknow and enlivened the city with flamboyant monuments and the reign of the last of the nawabs Wajid Ali Shah (1848–56). Today's Bollywood production emphasizes often the same secular nationalist discourse of 'unity in diversity', emphasizing the same distinctly vernacular notions of cosmopolitanism (Bhabha 1994). The same goes for high fashion that remixes cultural artefacts into new creative blends (Knobel and Lankshear 2008: 22). This further stimulates the growth of industries, such as *chikan*, that are symbolically important for the ideology of composite culture and secular nationalism. But also materially speaking, the networks of production create an economic bridge between Hindus and Muslims, and thus reduce chances of communal violence (Kuldova 2009; Varshney 1997). Lucknow follows a simple rule: 'cross-cutting ties reduce the chances of violent conflict' (Eriksen 2005: 29).

Let us now zoom into the niche segment of luxury *chikan* embroidery, which constitutes only approximately 8 per cent of the *chikan* market. This segment can be divided as follows: (1) casual luxury (price range from 12,000 to 20,000 INR, the largest segment), (2) festive luxury (price range from 20,000 to 1 *lakh*, middle class wedding range/upper middle class/elite casual), and (3) the top market: high-spenders' luxury (price range from 1 *lakh* to 7 *lakhs*, mostly available only in metros and US, Middle East etc.). The multi-staged production process can be organized in many ways. All businessmen and designers have their own way of organizing the production, from utilizing managers, creative directors, branding experts, NGOs to middle-men. There is a lot of secrecy, not least due to such large external, semi-independent piece-wage labour and craft expertise. Designs are often stolen and copied, though it is often hard to establish who steals or copies from whom in the first place. Many designers complained that even before their own pieces were released on the fashion ramp, cheaper knock-offs were already available in the local market, often sold with the designer's name on it. However, as we shall see later, it is rather problematic to claim copyright infringement or design rights when the product itself is designed using printing blocks produced by local blockmakers, or old blocks owned by families of printers, the print done by a skilled printer, and embroidered by several women together, each contributing different stitches (see Chapter 4). The following is an ideotypical structure of the networks.

Designer/businessman

The businessman or designer stands at the core of the network, holding its ties together through capital, connecting producers to buyers and export networks, while taking part in the production, be it branding, design or management. The businessman or designer, or their assistant, distributes the wages to all artisans and workers involved in the production. Trust is a scarce resource in this business, therefore handling financial matters is often kept in the family or is delegated to a trusted assistant. The businessman or designer invests capital into the purchase of material needed for production (cloth, in case of *chikan* especially: muslins, tussar silk, mulls, organdies, cotton, georgettes, khadi, crepes, chiffons but recently also wool; embellishments such as crystals, Swarovski and pearls, threads for embroidery and so on). At times, some of the material is acquired through sponsorships. Artisans cannot sell their products directly, as they are typically unable to invest in the material, organization and payment of the labour in other stages of production. The business was traditionally dominated by the Hindu castes of *rastogis* and *baniyas* (Wilkinson-Weber 1999: 36). However, in the past fifteen years more Muslim and female entrepreneurs have entered the scene. The luxury segment has seen an influx of female designers and businesswomen, who often began at a hobby level, putting up fashion exhibitions around India and later being supported by their husband's capital (see Chapter 6). While the hereditary business families tend to dominate the middle and lower quality segments (yet high in turnover), self-made businessmen dominate the upper segment, pointing to a significant shift in the last decade.

Master cutters and tailors

The production begins by sending the cloth to a master cutter or tailor, either in-house or independent, who cuts the cloth into pieces according to what is going to be stitched. Master cutters and tailors are often lower class men of all religious backgrounds, even though Sunni Muslims appear to dominate this profession in Lucknow; the majority are literate. External independent tailors and master cutters receive piece-wages, while in-house tailors typically receive a monthly wage. In the luxury segment, tailors are directly employed and work in the designer's workshop. With the expansion of the industry, the city has seen a significant increase in tailoring jobs.

Blockmakers and printers

The next part of the process is printing the designs to be embroidered on the cloth using special *chikan* wooden printing blocks developed by a blockmaker (Figure 2.2) or someone already in possession of the printer. There are only about five families of blockmakers based in the old part of Lucknow, all of them Muslim and located in small lanes in the Chowk area. The workshop where several generations work next to each other consists of one room, where the blockmakers draw designs, transpose them onto wood and then carve the printing blocks. Depending on quality and size, a single block can fetch in between 40 and 300 *rupees*. Blockmakers largely supply printers, who wish to keep their designs up to date. Printers catering to the luxury segment even draw their own designs or pass on designs suggested by the designer; these then have to be adjusted by the blockmaker in order to fit the *chikan* stitches. The majority of blocks used are old, some even hundreds of years. Presently, only two blockmakers in town can replicate the quality of the very old blocks and these remain limited to the luxury segment, as only few embroiderers can embroider so intricately (Singh 2004). Printing blocks are made from Indian rosewood and most designs are drawn or copied freehand on the wood and then carved by a hammer and a chisel; after that they are given a neat finish using sand to rub off all the protrusions; then they are soaked in mustard oil for half a day (Figure 2.3). These blocks are used by printers who specialize exclusively in *chikan*, who print the motives that guide the embroiderer and that are then washed away. Traditionally, printing was a hereditary profession dominated by Muslims, Shias dominating the upper segment, and Sunnis the lower segment, but with the expansion of the industry we see newcomers and apprentices of diverse backgrounds. Several printers have turned their workshops into larger businesses, and began manufacturing, exporting and designing, thus turning into *chikan*

FIGURE 2.2 Blockmaker at work, Chowk market, Lucknow
Image courtesy: Tereza Kuldova.

traders (Figure 2.4). Printers in such workshops are largely paid a monthly wage, while most printers in the industry are paid piece-wages. Fashion designers, like Abu Jani and Sandeep Khosla, would for instance rent the whole printer's workshop for two weeks at a time, in order to ensure that the printer does not work with

FIGURE 2.3 *Chikan* printing block produced in 2009, Lucknow
Image courtesy: Tereza Kuldova.

anyone else at that time. As such, designers are both a blessing and a curse for the printers; while on the one hand bringing prestige and extra cash, on the other hand they disrupt the ordinary flow of stable work.

On a technical note, the printers use mostly a blue dye for printing, made from the gum obtained from the gum tree. Printing is done by colouring the printing block in a special tray, an innovation introduced by the father of the currently most prominent printer, and then pressing the particular block on a selected place on the cloth. Before the tray was introduced in the 1950s, the blocks used to be very small; they would fit into the palm of a hand, where the colour would be placed; due to the small size it was a very time-consuming technique. With the growth of the industry and pressures on increasing the speed of production, larger blocks and printing trays were developed. At the same time, however, quality decreased, and the blocks became harsher in design and pattern, aimed at a few simple *chikan* stitches. Today's printing is a fast process that requires a lot of skill; a good printer has the ability to imagine the finished product. With the expansion of the industry, there is a lot of competition among printers, especially in the lower segments (Wilkinson-Weber 1999). The upper segment, on the other hand, is dominated by six families of highly skilled printers with apprentices taking care of cheaper work. There are great differences in the skill and social status of the printers; some are well known for their abilities and possession of

FIGURE 2.4 Printer displaying his oldest blocks, some more than a hundred years old
Image courtesy: Arash Taheri.

exquisite blocks while others cater to the bulk market of cheap *chikan* work. The expansion of the market since the 1990s has stimulated vertical mobility especially among the hereditary printing families, where the daughters and sons often pursue higher education, some even becoming fashion designers (Wilkinson-Weber 1999).

Embroiderers and middle-men

Printed pieces are typically sampled by skilled embroiderers, who are part of the permanent staff of a designer's/trader's core workshop (Figure 2.5). Sampling is usually a back-and-forth discussion between designer/trader and embroiderer about the suitable stitches and colour combinations. Sampled pieces are distributed to the village craft centres, where most of the embroidery is done according to the sample. Distribution is done either by middle-men, in the case of the low quality segment that relies on huge quantities (employing between 30 and 200 agents, each distributing work to around 200 women), or in the case of the higher end by permanently employed shop assistants or appointed heads of the village centres, who themselves pick up the work. Depending on quality and extent, this can take anywhere from a month to half a year, in the case of exquisite pieces even a year for

FIGURE 2.5 Detail of embroidery in progress, with the blue print visible in the background
Image courtesy: Tereza Kuldova.

FIGURE 2.6 Young women embroidering *chikan* in a village near Lucknow; contrary to popular belief, all of them are literate

Image courtesy: Arash Taheri.

a group of five to seven girls. During the time of the nawabs, *chikan* was typically done by Muslim men, however, following Independence, women took over as the skill deteriorated and the craft became less profitable. Again, due to the expansion of the business, Hindu women are also increasingly practising the craft, often unmarried girls who are studying and using the embroidery as an extra source of income for the family. In the luxury segment, around 70 per cent of the women I encountered were literate; a small portion of them had even completed a BA (Figure 2.6). The proportion of literate embroiderers is higher among the Hindus; however this is most probably because they tend to be generally younger and quit after marriage. Among the Muslim women, it is more common to continue to work even at an older age; therefore the higher illiteracy of Muslim embroiderers rates than those of Hindu workers have more to do with the generational difference than with any correlation of religion to literacy.

Washermen, dyers and finishers

Embroidered pieces need to be checked for stains and mistakes, and repaired if necessary. Thereafter, they are sent for washing, dyeing and ironing. Washing has been 'a traditional, caste-based job and unlike many producers in other stages of production, *dhobis* (washermen) have been washing clothes as their hereditary occupation for many generations' (Wilkinson-Weber 1999: 48). *Dhobis* either work on the riverbanks of Gomti, or in small workshops in the old town (Figure 2.7). Higher quality embroidery however demands more careful treatment, as losses at this stage can be high. With the rise of demand for higher quality, several family businesses have reoriented themselves towards this market, turning their houses into a complete set-up where washing, dyeing and pressing take place under one roof. Washing white on white pieces is extremely difficult as the print needs to be properly removed (Figure 2.8); harsh chemicals are used and each piece undergoes up to nine stages of washing. After washing, most pieces are dyed, which requires great skill. There are various shading techniques, cold and boiling hot dyeing, and the dyer has great knowledge of different threads and fabrics, chemical and natural dyes, creating the final shades by mixing different colours in different proportions based on many years of experience (Figure 2.9). Such set-ups, in markets like Aminabad, are often family businesses owned by both Hindus and Muslims. Interestingly, one of these prominent set-ups was established twenty-five years ago by two friends, a Hindu and a Shia Muslim; they equally invested their capital in it and are still running it together with their sons. After washing, dyeing and ironing, pieces are returned to the designer/trader, checked again by finishers,

FIGURE 2.7 Washerman (*dhobi*) on the banks of the river Gomti in Lucknow
Image courtesy: Tereza Kuldova.

FIGURE 2.8 Dirty white on white *chikan* pieces at a washerman's set-up in the Aminabad market

Image courtesy: Tereza Kuldova.

flaws are repaired, pearls or crystals stitched on, sometimes *mukeish* is done, borders are stitched on, *zardozi* work, metal wire and stone embroidery is added, typically done by Shia Muslims in workshops in the old town. Then the piece is ready to be tailored, showcased, exported and so on.

Complex networks, social cohesion and locality

Throughout the brief rendering of the complex networks of production, I have remarked on the religion of the actors involved. The important thing to note here is that, similar to the experiences of Wilkinson-Weber who did her fieldwork in Lucknow a decade and half before me, 'open discussion of the communal dimension of economic relations followed my question about it, rather than arising spontaneously in conversation' (Wilkinson-Weber 1999: 58). This throws us back

FIGURE 2.9 Dyeing *chikan* embroidered *sari*
Image courtesy: Arash Taheri.

on the question of the lack of communal tension in Lucknow, as I was told 'this is how it is, this is Lucknow, these things do not matter'. While in practice tensions would arise from time to time, and indeed at times religious differences mattered, people would still subscribe to this illusion, even though nobody would really believe in it upon thorough questioning. Yet, this illusion was powerful enough to prevent violent conflicts. Rather than differences, intermingling was continually emphasized and imagined as the core strength of the locality. The *chikan* industry, where Shias, Sunnis, Hindus, and even a few Christians co-operated on a daily basis, gave the flesh and blood to the mythology of *Lakhnawi tehzeeb*. Class mattered far more than any religious distinctions, also because of the expansion of the market into the luxury segment that has brought increasing awareness of class divisions and aesthetics into the production networks and exposure to celebrity lifestyles. In the business realm, religion has become increasingly irrelevant, what matters is one's position measured in terms of capital and education. At the same time, however, the increasing amount of bridging weak ties, connected significantly different individuals (Granovetter 1983). While strong ties mostly divide society into small groups, 'integration of these groups in the society depends on people's weak ties' (Blau 1974: 632), in this case brought together through capital. These cross-cutting economic ties impact the locality and its politics; it is against the economic interest of business families, who have a say in local politics, to fuel polarizing communal sentiments and politics of divisiveness. And so while neighbouring cities have experienced waves of communal violence, riots, unrest and murders throughout their history, Lucknow has remained strikingly calm. Even following the demolition of the Babri Masjid mosque in 1992 in Ayodhya (70 kilometres from Lucknow), an act that sparked violence across North India, Lucknow, the administrative and political centre of Uttar Pradesh, remained calm. The bridging of weak ties played a considerable role in constraining the impact of the nationwide polarizing strategies of the political leaders (Varshney 1997; Kuldova 2009). Lucknow businessmen catering to the luxury segment or in the export business, supplying markets in Mumbai, Delhi and the Middle East, are closely tied to local political elites. In their own economic interest, they emphasize the language of cohesion over the language of separation. These networks have an effect of togethering as opposed to processes of othering (Ramaswami 2007). This togethering has to be continually (re)produced, not only through the material production that ties people together, but also through the work of fantasy and reproduction of ideology in everyday acts. These fantasies are rather powerfully reworked by designers and infused into their garments. In the realm of fashion narratives, 'the Lucknow spirit' is a powerful fragment in the montage of elitist nationalism and prestige. In the process, the garment undergoes a series of abstractions, qualifications and requalifications, as it moves from the local to the national, global and cosmopolitan. Products, as Robert Foster rightly points out, are mutable, never quite finished, 'contingent outcome of negotiations – even conflict' around their qualifications (Foster 2007: 713). These successive requalifications happen as the object travels across the networks from one locality to another, and enables certain consumers 'to move fluently between the local and the global, as well as between the concrete and the abstract' (Mazzarella 2006: 18).

Phantasmatic Lucknow

Lucknow is a city overflowing with phantasmatic myths of itself; myths that provide relief from the pains of everyday life to its population. Even its dirt disappears as the imagination spins images of the luxurious, extravagant and opulent culture of the times of the nawabs, their refinement in poetry, beautiful courtesans, delicate cuisine, seductive fashion, elaborate etiquette, marvellous architecture, *imambaras* and mosques, celebrations and festivals, and all the pastimes: *kathak* performances, kite-flying, cockfighting or just time to sleep and relaxing. This is the Lucknow that lives on in imagination (Mitchell 2000; Appadurai 2000, 1995, 1996) and it is fuelled to new phantasmatic heights through the branding mythologies of the designers and Bollywood cinema, from movies like *Chaudvin ka Chand* (Sadiq 1960), via *Pakeezah* (Amrohi 1971) to the two versions of *Umrao Jaan* (Ali 1981; Dutta 2006), or heritage tourism. Phantasmatic Lucknow comes alive on fashion ramps, dance, music and theatre performances organized by the local cultural patrons, such as the fashion designer and film-maker Muzaffar Ali or organizations like Sanatkada, a local NGO and crafts store devoted to reviving the nawabi culture, magazines such as *Uppercrust* or *Márg: A Magazine of the Arts*, with special issues and regular coverage on Lucknow but also tales told by the locals to their children. The local upper classes and elites indulge in private nawabi theme dress-up parties, where *mujras* and *ghazals* are performed and haute Lakhnawi cuisine is devoured. The past as a symbol of present and future greatness is in vogue. Also, the fact that Lucknow, as compared with for example Rajasthan, has not yet become 'vulgarized' by the influx of Western tourists, which, as one of the designers working with *chikan* pointed out, makes it desirable for the discerning elite tastes. The only Westerners in Lucknow are either those who pass by en route to their next destination, students of Urdu at the American Institute of Indian Studies, businessmen or academics. Even though it is known for its laid-back attitude to life, Lucknow paradoxically attracts the frantic businessmen and academics, who significantly contribute to its phantasmatic (re)production, together with local literati comprising of professors, writers, poets, artists, performers, lawyers, descendants of the nawabs, IAS officers, luxury fashion producers, elite businessmen, heads of non-governmental organizations, politicians, ex-army officers and members of the Handicrafts Board. All these people frequent Ram Advani's bookstore that stocks most books ever published on Lucknow, the local Golf Club and the elite MB Club (Mahomed Bagh Club Ltd) that was originally open only to Defence Services Officers, but since 1947 has opened up to civil services officers, *taluqdars*, and prominent citizens as well. MB Club was originally 'Brit' men's club, but following Independence traditional *sherwanis* and Nehru jackets were allowed – a sign of times changing. Today it is a perfect glocal combination of the Lakhnawi and the British. Entry to the club is only possible together with a member; at the moment there is a fifty-year waiting list for membership, which can be circumvented only by several *lakhs* in extra donations to the membership fee of five *lakhs*. Events such as celebrations of Deepawali, Lohri or rock concerts, *ghazals* performances, fashion shows, or Bollywood nights take place there, in addition to regular nights out. Artists like Shreya Ghoshal, Asha Bhosle, Jagjit Singh, Diler Menhdi, and Sonu Nigam have all performed at the MB Club. Many initiatives aiming at the revival of local culture, often led by wives of the members of the MB Club, began to take shape in early 1980s, a period when Lucknow was also rediscovered in academia. Between the 1930s and 1970s there was no book published on Lucknow. It was first in the 1980s when historians were captured by the compelling narrative of the Siege of Lucknow – a prolonged defence of the Lucknow Residency during the unsuccessful Indian rebellion of 1857. Since the 1990s, books about Lucknow proliferated, focusing largely on the nawabi era, thus selectively stabilizing the oral narratives, memories and fantasies of the Lakhnawites and reinserting them into the contemporary and future Lucknow. This bookish knowledge has been appropriated by advertisers and designers, who own and use the visually powerful coffee table books about Lucknow to stitch their own myths. Even virtual Facebook communities of Lucknow lovers have popped up, further fuelling the positive myths of the city. When talking of the city, local elites use expressions such as, 'Lucknow has a distinctive aura', or 'Lucknow is what dreams are made of'. Even visitors are said to appropriate the city as their own and succumb to the transformative and overpowering atmosphere of the city, much like the elite customer buying into the affective atmosphere of the designer studio. The same rhetoric is found in popular academic books such as *India's Fabled City: The Art of Courtly Lucknow* (Markel and Gude 2010). Lucknow as a place is produced through iterative processes, iconographies and materialities of consumption (Goodman et al. 2010) through performative re-enactments such as the said dress-up parties, where the fantasies of the city are transformed into lived myths supported by cherished academic coffee-table books. The value of research cannot be emphasized enough when it comes to elite distinction and connoisseurship (see Chapter 3). This is another reason why *chikan* embroidery lends itself as a trophy of elite distinction, with its elaborate lengthy production, phantasmatic worlds that it evokes and research that it demands in order to be understood. And yet, *chikan*'s meaning and role is significantly different in Lucknow and Delhi. Among the Lucknow elites, it is firmly connected to a sense of proud local identity. Among the Delhi elites, Lucknow is turned into one among many symbols of the Indian composite culture, incorporated into the notion of pan-

Indianness. Delhi elite tends to view India as if from the top through a possessive gaze that wishes to both own the local others and to transgress the locality, which is itself a local enough obsession. The elements that Delhi connoisseurs emphasize differ too; important to them is the evocation of shared pre-colonial courtly history of Northern India that speaks to the memories of unpartitioned homeland of the people of *al-Hind* (Kesavan 1994), reflecting the pan-Indian spirit of an eclectic mixture, and interconnectedness, so ferociously reproduced in both fashion and Bollywood. Maybe this is a way for the Punjabi-dominated Delhi to distance itself from the stereotypes of Punjabi vulgarity, bling, violence, honour culture and local identity, and an act of creation of alternative narratives that would position them as rulers of a composite territory, both Indian and by extension of the logic also global. Let us now delve into the world of nostalgia, vogue of the past and the branding of cities for their consumption elsewhere.

Vogue of heritage

Environments we live in are 'pregnant with past' (Ingold 2000: 189), they are like an echo-chamber of voices of ancient alien Others in which and from which we emerge (Anton 2011, 2001). Representations of past structure our present (Mead 1929). Today, this is increasingly happening through commodified images of the past that feed off our sentimental nostalgias, longings for better days that were, or our search for authenticity that we project into the imagined past. Micro-local distinctiveness, tradition and nostalgia are powerful marketing tools (Demossier 2011) in a fast-changing world, where traditional hierarchies and moralities dissolve. Commodified nostalgias projected into the future serve the reproduction of the idealized traditional order, possibly even with more determination than in the imagined era of tradition. Heritization is fuelled globally by organizations such as UNESCO and local NGOs that emulate them and by appropriation of protective laws such as the Geographical Indications of Goods (GI) Act that indicates the origin of a product and guarantees its quality and distinctiveness, defined by geographical locality, region or country. As a member of the World Trade Organization (WTO), India enacted the GI Act in 1999 and it came into force in 2003. So far it is the only protective measure for crafts such as Lucknow *chikan*. Yet, there are barely any companies registered under the GI Act. Nonetheless, GI is important on the ideological level, granting localities a special sense of self that lends itself to commodification. This imagined self is often translated in branding into an essence, something that is imagined as permeating the product and emanating from it. While local essence imagined as emanating from a certain product has been a staple of luxury consumption throughout ages, in recent years we have witnessed an acceleration of the business of branding localities and cities (Conley 2008). References to origin are always a significant feature of luxury brands, their brand mythologies and logos, functioning as vehicles of desire (Maxwell 2012). History, heritage, and provenance have become next to beauty and uniqueness the core of contemporary luxury myths (Puddick and Menon 2012). This vogue of the past, as Gilles Lipovetsky points out, can be seen in

> the success of old objects, of antique hunting, of everything that mimics the past, everything 'vintage', all the products stamped 'authentic' that arouse nostalgia. More and more businesses are referring to their history, making the most of their heritage, communicating with their past, launching products that encapsulate memories and make the old times come alive again. . . . everything old, and our nostalgia for it, have become sales techniques and marketing tools. . . . There was use-value and exchange-value: in addition we now have the emotional-memorial value associated with feelings of nostalgia.
>
> **LIPOVETSKY** 2005: 59–60

Luxury market business experts in India, advising companies on how to enter the market, sum it up in the following manner: 'The next few decades will be about recreating the class differences by upgrading people to lifestyles that mark out their exclusivity. . . . Local and traditional motifs will play an increasingly larger role in expanding the idea of luxury. India wants its luxury products and services to conform to the international class, albeit in an Indian way' (Sinha 2012: 10–13). Places turning into brands not only endow objects with a particular essence, but like other brands also become 'part of the mundane context of action within which we become subjects' (Arvidsson 2006: 5). Buying exquisite *chikan* equals buying an experience of a royal lifestyle. Immaterial and phantasmatic value dominates this capitalism that relies on 'autonomously produced externalities as a source of surplus value and profits' (Arvidsson 2006: 7). Turning places into brands and mediatized images means subsuming them under the logic of capital. As Adam Arvidsson pointed out, 'the mediatisation of life-world is nothing but a consequence of the process that Marx theorized as the "real subsumption" of life under capital; the process in which capital enters the social fabric "vertically" to penetrate its every fibre, to become part of the very basic, bio-political condition of life itself' (Arvidsson 2006: 13), a process of colonization of everyday life by corporate power (Klein 2002). Branded past, as Appadurai points out, is 'not a land to return to in a simple politics of memory. It has become a synchronic warehouse of cultural scenarios, a kind of temporal central casting, to which recourse can be had as appropriate, depending on the movie to be made, the scene to be enacted' (Appadurai 1990: 4). Along similar lines, Lipovetsky has argued that:

> tradition no longer calls for the faithful repetition and revival of the way things were always done: it has become a nostalgic product to be consumed, a piece of folklore, a wink and a nod at the past, an *object of fashion*. In its institutional

guise it used to regulate the collective whole: its value now is merely aesthetic, emotional and playful.

LIPOVETSKY 2005: 60–61, emphasis in original

While we could argue that its value is aesthetic and emotional, in the Indian context, hierarchical value takes precedence. Past is not necessarily something democratically shared. Selectively appropriated elements used in branding of localities and objects from these localities, tend to be distinctly elitist, aimed directly at reproduction of hierarchical difference. 'The mythical past is thus established both as specifically "Indian" and as a locus of languorous expertise and opulent pleasure' (Mazzarella 2006: 139) that is beyond the reach of the majority of the population, but still forming a shared imaginary space, being central for the local as much as pan-Indian 'communities of sentiment' (Appadurai 1995). Movie makers, advertisers and branding experts all draw on popular stereotypes and myths, thus stabilizing them as authoritative narratives and (re)producing them as normative. It is instructive to consider the way cities and their cinematic inhabitants are portrayed in popular Bollywood movies. Let us look, as an example, at the movie *Ladies vs. Ricky Bahl* (Sharma 2011); it captures nicely the imaginary dynamics between Lucknow, Delhi and Mumbai. Ricky (Ranveer Singh) is a conman, specializing in conning rich women, daughters of wealthy families and professional women with access to capital, be it their own or of a corporate group. A Mumbai-based PR businesswoman, Raina (Dipannita Sharma), whom Ricky conned and persuaded to buy a fake painting by M.F. Husain for 60 *lakhs*, makes a statement on the television promising to find the man who conned her. Two other girls, also conned by Ricky, see this, including Dimple (Parineeti Chopra), a daughter of a self-made man and creator of Chaddha Industries and a young Lucknow widow Saira (Aditi Sharma), a daughter of a local *chikan* manufacturer and trader. The three women join forces and try to con Ricky into giving them their money back; they hire Ishika (Anushka Sharma), a smart saleswoman at Home Town, who tries to con Ricky back. But then he finds out that he is being conned and cons the ladies again, however this time falling in love with Ishika and in the end returning the money and proposing to her. The representation of the three women, and the three cities of Lucknow, Delhi and Mumbai is more interesting for us than the plot. When Saira appears for the first time, we see her on the rooftop of an old building dressed in *chikan* suit with a *dupatta*, shyly speaking in the typically Lakhnawi dialect with the panorama of the old city behind her, an embodiment of the phantasmatic Lucknow. Virtually all Lucknow shots take in the old city, around *Bara* and *Chota Imambara* and the *galis* of the Chowk market, where her father's store is located. Architectural monuments built during the nawabi era dominate the screen, while Hindustani classical music plays in the background. Hazratganj, the centre of Lucknow, which was built by the British and beautified, or rather facelifted during Mayawati's rule, an act of sanitization and heritization, was mentioned, but never shown. Lucknow was intentionally portrayed as stuck in the nawabi era, while the post-1856 era was effectively erased. The Lucknow of shopping malls, luxury hotels, coffee shops and multi-brand stores, fancy cars, motorbikes and gated communities, night clubs and posh restaurants, fashion events and parties, or lavish weddings is non-existent, and so is the political Lucknow, whose architectonical landscape was transformed by the former chief minister Mayawati's construction projects that included statues and memorial parks to herself and to Bhimrao Ambedkar, the father of the Indian constitution and Dalit activist. The Lucknow that aspires to become a metro and refuses to be provincial, while claiming its historically grounded cosmopolitanism, is just not part of the script. Cosmopolitanism as an important qualification of Lucknow tends to be overlooked in its stereotypical portrayals, and yet it is an accepted knowledge among the literati and glitterati; it is something that qualifies the embroidery, but only for a selected few. Back to Ricky and his cons. Ricky always dresses up appropriately for his cons – when he cons Dimple, the Delhi girl, he chooses cool, branded clothes, showing his attitude on the dance floor; conning Raina, he dresses up as an artsy gallery owner, with a scarf and glasses and messed up hair; conning Saira, Ricky pretends to be a small town boy from Bareilly, dressed up in a black embroidered *kurta*, styled with moustache and sleek hair. Gaining her trust, he is introduced to her father and shows him a piece of exquisite *zardozi* embroidery, claiming that it was done by his *karigaars* in Bareilly, and that he can sell it for 500Rs a metre. Saira's father gives him 10 *lakhs* in advance and Ricky promises to come back in two weeks, which he of course never does. Throughout the movie, the provincial, traditional, and cultured Lucknow is juxtaposed with hectic corporate Mumbai and the metropolitan Delhi of booming nightlife, fancy cars, self-made millionaires, designer clothes, and style. In the case of Delhi, its representation is equally selective; *bazaars* of Old Delhi and North Delhi are pushed into non-existence. South Delhi is selected as representative of the whole of Delhi, in the same way as selected elements of contemporary Lucknow that remind of its past are exaggerated into representing the whole of Lucknow. Even the characters are designed to match the cities: Saira is always shy and modest, Dimple is girlish and spoiled, and Raina determined and tough. Lucknow is selectively purified of its modernity, Delhi, on the contrary, of its past; the first becoming a heritage location, the other a hypermodern metropolis. They need each other, at least in imagination as they define themselves against and through each other. Similarly, as was clear even in the movie, despite the Hindu majority population, Lucknow is still imagined as a centre of Muslim culture, a reason why Ricky turned into Iqbal Khan during his Lucknow con. Yet, if we recall the coronation of Ghazi al-Din Haydar, we know that the city was a mixture of unique international influences, as much as it is today. Precisely its vernacular cosmopolitanism is an important and valuable qualification of *chikan* for the Delhi-based revivalist designers, who capitalize on it when educating the current cosmopolitan elite or engaging in one of the rituals of celebrating Indianness. While the Delhi elite insists on being first Indian and then global citizens, the Lucknow elite insists on being first Lakhnawi, then Indian and then global. The Delhi elite thus systematically tries to dissociate from any notion of the local, imagining itself rather as (trans)national. The nawabi Lucknow fascinates the contemporary Delhi elite because of its tastes that allow for an imagined continuity of privilege and eliteness. As Llewellyn-Jones recounts,

> In the golden days of the nawabs, Lucknow attracted people and goods like a magnet, drawing them in from other parts of the country, from West Asia, from Africa, from Europe and Britain. River traffic seemed almost a one-way phenomenon as luxuries sailed up to the fabulously rich court. Anything and everything has sailed along the now deserted Gomti, rhinoceros from Assam for the nawabs' zoos, shire-horses from England, barrel-organs from the best organ-makers in Europe, huge looking-glasses from France, musical clocks and trinkets from Switzerland, crockery and silver from England, and room-sized chandeliers from Bohemia. To supply the nawabs' mania for building, the best teak came from Burma, and bamboos, needed for the scaffolding, from all over Awadh. Crushed sea-shells for chunam, the delicate marble-like plaster, came from Madras. The goods that went down the river seemed pedestrian by contrast – indigo, tobacco, saltpetre, and piece-goods, bound for the British and European markets.
>
> **LLEWELLYN-JONES** 2003: 25–28

Architectural obsession was as prominent among the former elite then as it is now; recall the smart cities or gated farmhouses and Punjabi baroque villas. Persian and Mughal influences were mixed with interpretations of buildings from England and Western Europe (Llewellyn-Jones 2003), much like in today's elitist gated abodes. The nawabi cosmopolitan mastering time and space through luxury manifested also in their favourite *aina khanas* or glass houses, where they presented their gifts, luxury objects from faraway places, collections of European and local artworks and rarities (Gude 2010).

If we now return to the production networks, we must again emphasize that they at the same time materially sustain the ideology and are ideologically sustained by the Lucknow Ganga-Jamuni *tehzeeb* dating back to the nawabs; an ideology that informs even today's notions of cosmopolitanism and signifies the friendship between Muslims and Hindus in the city that is considered as exceptional. Ganga and Jamuna refer to the meeting of the two holy rivers and their smooth blending into each other. As the *chikan* trader Preity put it,

> You will find Ganga-Jamuni *tehzeeb* in so many other cities too, like Varanasi, but in Lucknow there is a different aura about this. I have been brought up in an

area with *imambaras*; it has a very good effect on your mind, sort of tells you that this is our heritage... there is a difference, we have a lot of Muslim–Hindu mix, which you do not find in so many other cities, so I like that.

Interview, March 2008

The nawabs are often remembered for taking part in all celebrations, no matter their religious association. Wajid Ali Shah (1822–87), the tenth and last nawab of Awadh, incorporated the Hindu pantheon into his own poetry, turning it into a statement of communal cohesion. As the popular sentiment goes, 'faiths were bridged when the king, Wajid Ali Shah, wrote and danced as Lord Krishna or a lovelorn yogi' (Ali 2007: 61). Even in discussions about Partition it is claimed that 'there were no riots in Lucknow ... due to the efforts made from time of Wajid Ali Shah who created an atmosphere of friendship between Hindus and Muslims' (Aziz 2007: 49). The nawabi history of Lucknow has contributed to the largely positive image of the Muslims, especially Shia Muslims, in Lucknow, who are associated with culture and refinement, rather than with poverty and illiteracy as elsewhere (Frøystad 2005). The utopia of Lucknow as an oasis of peace, an ideal and idealized place, is proudly reproduced by journalists:

> Keeping the spirit of 'Ganga-Jamuna *tehzeeb*' of Awadh alive, the descendants of the nawabs in Lucknow continued to organize *Holi* festivities and celebrate the festival of colours with their Hindu brethren. The royal families residing around the city station area in Lucknow have been organising *Holi* functions to share the joy and mirth associated with the festival, strengthening the bonds of brotherhood nurtured since the times of nawab Wajid Ali Shah. ... By celebrating the festival together, an atmosphere of trust and confidence has been created in Awadh and these festivals reinforce it time and again, the descendants of law minister of the first ruler, Shah Ali Khan Bahadur, Prof Nawab Sayed Ali Hamid said.

Express 2009

Ganga-Jamuni *tehzeeb* is also reproduced in the cultural field intended for local and international consumption, from the Delhi-based International Melody Foundation promoting the idea of Awadhi communal harmony through music, to *kathak* dancers Manjari Chaturvedi, who created what she calls Sufi *Kathak*. As she says,

> Here [in Lucknow], we are not only taught to respect every faith and community, we do it in every aspect of our lives. I think perhaps Awadh is the only truly secular place in all of India. There has never been a line of demarcation between the two cultures.... Not just in my dances, the amalgamation is so apparent in other aspects too, like my dress for Sufi *Kathak*. If you notice, I do not wear the

traditional *Kathak* dress of an *anarkali* with a *churidar pajama*. Instead, I wear a long *anarkali kurta* with looser pyjamas, which is reminiscent of Awadh's Peshwa link. In fact, the inspiration for my dress comes from the Peshwa miniature paintings from Awadh. This is how I have chosen to represent my culture and anyone who has some idea of Lucknow's history immediately connects with it.

CHANDRA 2012

Relating Ganga-Jamuni *tehzeeb* to her Lucknow *zabaan*, she speaks of the language as follows, the 'sweetness is very tough to discard. *Waise toh Hindi har jagah boli jaati hai* (Hindi is spoken everywhere), but the Hindi spoken in Lucknow is unique because it is so mellifluous' (Chandra 2012). Ganga-Jamuni *tehzeeb* is closely related to the eloquence and luxurious refinement of the local way of speaking, its *nafaasat* (finesse) and *nazaakat* (delicacy). These words are also applied to luxury embroidery, poetry, demeanour, architecture and even cooking. Lucknow is imagined as the ultimate city of luxury, since all universal basic human needs – sustenance, shelter, clothing and leisure – are refined (Berry 1994), perfected and elevated to an art form and all inhabitants, elite or low class, are imagined to partake equally in this local culture of refinement and of languorous grace. Embroiderers were said to create poetry in their hands, the eloquence of language materialized in the delicacy of the embroidery known as royal work. Lucknow cuisine, too, had to match the beauty of the poetic language. 'Sensuality ruled and food became a very powerful statement of class and social position. Cooking turned into art, the site for a grand mingling of the material sciences with sensibilities and heritages both indigenous and European, especially French' (Mangalik 2003: 43). Today's haute cuisine turned into an art-form comes to mind. And so, at least in fantasy, 'this refinement, delicacy of sensibility, elaboration, and versatility are all part and parcel of that distinctive quality people call *Lakhnawiyat*, or "Lucknow-ness"' (Petievich 2010: 107). The role of the distinctive refined language known for its Persian loanwords, prominent in Urdu *ghazals*, cannot be overemphasized here. It was the language that distinguished social classes and it was the language that had to be carefully matched with the finesse of attire and bodily demeanour. The cultural elite indulging in the seductions of the *zabaan* gave meaning to the delicate embroideries and created their place within the larger myths of the day. Is it not exactly the same thing that we valorize in contemporary economy that privileges the intellectual over the manual? Is it not why fashion designers are celebrated and why they are sought after as *gurus* who possess the aesthetic and the language of power?

The origins of *chikan* are till today covered in mystery (Singh 2004, Wilkinson-Weber 1999) that ignites the imagination of local producers, academics as much as the fashion designers. One legend recounts how a courtesan of the nawab's harem embroidered a prayer cap for her master. It was so fine, that he, impressed, ordered that a workshop be started in his court where this style of embroidery would be developed and patronized. From then on, the craft flourished – many craftsmen came to the courts and articles of great beauty were prepared. Since the nawabs were the settlers of fashion and the humbler nobles and *zamindars* would imitate them in every way, *chikankari* received much impetus and it was at its peak during the central part of 19th century.

RAI 1992: 6, emphasis mine

These prayer caps still feature strongly in the imagination of *Lakhnawiyat*. Private *chikan* collections often feature at least several of these, often with very fine embroidery. Even though small in size, these caps have an immense evocative power. Other legends place the origins of *chikan* in Persia, believing that it was brought to India 'as a part of the cultural baggage of the Persian nobles' (Tyabji 2007: 33), whereas others claim it came from Bengal, brought in by male artisans who came to work under the patronage of the Nawabs in Lucknow (Irwin 1973, Wilkinson-Weber 1999). Embroiderers, more romantically, tend to trace its origins back to Noor Jahan, the beautiful wife of the Mughal emperor Jahangir, a story that points to a past of extensive mutual influences and secularism of which the embroidery has become a material manifestation. Embroidery was an imperial pastime that Noor Jahan herself indulged in, much like the women in *zenana*, who were after the male artisans the most skilled in the craft. As an inspiration, the seventeenth century Mughal artists used extensively floral sketches from the botanical albums and florilegia of sixteenth and seventeenth century Europe. As we know, the flowers on the Taj Mahal did not ever grow anywhere near the Mughal Empire. Noor Jahan and her stepson Shah Jahan patronized the flower motifs that were so dear to Jahangir, and that were heavily influenced by the import of luxury embroideries from England (Findley 1996: 9–10). 'The reciprocal trade in embroidery between England and India began initially with gifts to the Mughal court' (Findley 1996: 13) and by the end of the seventeenth century embroidery patterns and even finished embroideries were being sent out to India to be copied, but they already displayed signs of cross-cultural influences (Crill 1999). It is apparent that the cross-fertilization of designs was more than Indian style elements in England and English in India. Not only were the styles themselves already a mixture par excellence of influences, places and people, but the cross-fertilization was itself a 'product of conscious effort, noted here on the Indian side, to copy designs as accurately as possible the minute they were available and then to incorporate them within the larger schemata of artistic work' (Findley 1996: 14–15). Imitation, appropriation and cross-fertilization of designs and styles have always been part of the industry and as is by now obvious also a significant part of the elite's desire to master time and space and of its passion for powerful symbols of sovereignty.

Producing cosmopolitanism and social cohesion

So far we have followed the journey of *chikan* from its material production to its imaginative production and back, to a place where the phantasmatic is transformed into a quality imagined as inherent to the object itself. And we have seen not only how authoritative narratives of the past are reproduced and localities constructed in the process, but also how the past itself becomes a projection of contemporary desire and nostalgia for imagined tradition or even invented tradition (Hobsbawm and Ranger 2003). Depending on the perspective, the embroidery can stand for the local and a particular identity such as *Lakhnawiyat*, while from another angle it can easily be incorporated into the idea of pan-Indianness or of cosmopolitanism, one that encompasses a 'translation of symbols, a translation of sites ... which confuses what is general and what is the specific, what is part and what is the whole' (Pinney 2002: 14). Commodification and heritization of royal pasts, their branding and mediatization and their dominant use in elitist fashions, are conductive in the reproduction of authoritative narratives about certain places, narratives that select desirable elements, while discarding others. Such narratives sanitize the past and favour phantasmatic perfection bordering on utopia, one that can be projected into the future. It is not only that myths, as Roland Barthes correctly pointed out, serve the ideological function of naturalization, thus making values, beliefs and attitudes seem objective, natural and self-evident (Barthes 1977: 45–46). But when it comes to mythical narratives, narratives that have power to affect us and push us in certain directions, we have to always ask, in what direction is this myth pushing us? The utopian Lucknow of the past, projected into the future, is deeply ambivalent in this respect. Frederik Jameson's remark comes to mind, when he talks of anxiety and hope being the two faces of the same collective consciousness. Mass culture, and within this scenario also fashion, function as 'the legitimation of existing order – or some worse one – cannot do their job without deflecting in the latter's service the deepest and most fundamental hopes and fantasies of the collectivity' (Jameson 1979: 144). Or as Ernest Bloch has argued, there is always a subversive element of hope in the utopian production of popular culture, advertising, fashion and so on, no matter how much it reproduces the status quo at the same time (Bloch 2000). In the phantasmatic utopia of Lucknow, we see two simultaneous tendencies. First, a tendency towards the reproduction of hierarchical distinction with all its emphasis on mastering of time and space; a cosmopolitan desire of possessing and selectively appropriating the world, with its language of superior refinement. Second, a tendency towards a hopeful utopia present within the idea of cosmopolitanism that addresses the persistent anxiety and fear of Otherness and of potential communal violence and replaces it with a successful secular society that fetishizes its own narratives of harmony and peace and of unity in diversity. Fetishes seem to be much more successful sources of social cohesion than, for instance, patriotism alone. We have pointed out the remarkable role of the national fetish of the economic rate of growth, and of Indianness grounded in mythological narratives like the one of Lucknow, where luxurious lifestyles of the royals become fetishes in their own right. We have also seen that it is distance and distantiation that increases market value as much as prestige of an object. And we have seen that it is often by way of eloquent language that such distantiation is most effectively produced, a distantiation from the material tenets of actual production and materiality itself.

Conclusion

In this chapter we have dug deeper into what the neo-feudal aesthetic introduced in the first chapter entails in terms of its material production. We have seen that even a fragment of the opulence takes enormous labour distributed across complex networks of production that cut across the formal and informal economies. This clearly shows that the formal always goes hand in hand with the informal rather than existing independently of each other. These networks of production also cut across divisions of caste, class, gender, locality and religion, creating economic interdependencies across the social spectrum and forcing people with different skills into economic alliances and relations. This economic interdependence has as its unintended consequence a larger degree of social cohesion in Lucknow and low levels of communal strife. This fact both lends itself to idealization of the city as a paradise of communal harmony and is further fuelled by already existing historical myths about the exceptionalism of Lucknow in terms of the collaboration and peaceful cohabitation of diverse communities. These myths, supported by the actual networks of production and economic relations on the ground, in turn feed into the desires for displays of Indianness and in particular for a commodified idealized past, for commodified locality that offers itself to the elite as a fragment of a montage of its prestige, one locality of many they can possess and show. This fetishization of heritage locations and with it of their locals paradoxically increases the distance between the elites and the rest, those who remain 'local' and thus also 'stuck in the past', as the elites say with derision. In order to be turned into luxury, the familiar needs to be 'encoded in the glamorous language of the outside' (Pinney 2002: 12) and of distance – social and spatial. In the next chapter, we investigate more closely this dynamic of distantiation by looking at the tense relation between design and craft and the strategies of legitimization used by designers; strategies that not only distance them from the artisans but also turn them into cheap local manual labour. In what follows, we will see how designers' narratives about creativity, innovation and artistic genius systematically push craftspeople into invisibility, inferiority and passivity, and deny their creativity, individuality and agency. It is here that we begin to see more clearly how the neo-feudal aesthetics not only illustrate the ambitions of the elites, but is also complicit in the (re) production of a feudal-like social order marked by clear inequality and rigid hierarchy. Only the strategies used to achieve this have changed. And so in what follows, we will see how the designers' authoritative discourses and acts sanitize heritage luxury from the polluting bodies of the craftspeople, at once celebrated as emblems of national traditions and despised for their poverty and low classness. Only in their sanitized form can these luxurious garments be consumed by the elite and the hierarchies effectively reproduced.

3 DESIGN GENIUS AND HIS GHOST OTHERS

Rohit Khosla died of cancer in 1994 at the age of thirty-five, but he turned out to be one of those 'dead who govern the living', as August Comte would put it (Comte 1973: 381). Steeped in myth and nostalgia, Rohit is the Indian fashion fraternity's founding father, who set the trend and defined the terms of the game. Rohit is credited with introducing the concept of a fashion designer to India, but more importantly, he legitimized the profession as a form of modern art and created an authoritative narrative that distinguished fashion design from craft, tailoring and to costume design in the film industry (Wilkinson-Weber 2013). The tale of his journey and creative struggle still shapes the industry, be it through memory or curriculum at design institutes across the country. Two years after Rohit's death, Rohini Khosla, his sister and partner in business, wrote a book about her brother, *Vanguard* (Khosla and Johnston 1996). The introductory words to *Vanguard*, written by Nikhil Khanna, a journalist, read as follows:

> Rohit Khosla embodied a unique creative spirit. . . . His designs always bore an unmistakable Indian sensibility. He believed that clothes were a complement to one's inner being. The harmonious exploration in Rohit's work offered the contemporary Indian woman, evolving out of her traditional mould, new options for expressing herself. . . . Many professionals involved in the applied arts affiliated to it, regard Rohit as the pioneer who brought together and galvanized the start of the Indian fashion movement. At a time when there was no awareness of fashion as a creative expression, Rohit struggled to realize what he believed in. Fashion is finally a lucrative and recognized business in India, supporting a cast of thousands from models to age-old crafts.
>
> **KHOSLA AND JOHNSTON** 1996: cover

Rohit's tale is one of a uniquely creative individual determined to pursue his personal desires, of a man who broke with his family and ran away at the age of seventeen only to pursue his dream of Western fashion. When he proclaimed in 1975 that he wanted to be a fashion designer, he was met with laughter: '"*Bade hokar darzi banna hai kya*?" / Do you want to be a tailor when you grow up?/' (Khosla and Johnston 1996: 21). At that time, there was no designer label and the idea invited mockery; but even today it resonates as not all parents have accepted fashion design as a legitimate career path. This fact increases the pressure on legitimizing one's profession, a pressure on distantiation from the manual and association with the more highly valued abstract. In the previous chapter, we emphasized what it takes to produce a single piece of embroidery, a single element in the montage of elite prestige, a single element in the construction of Indianness. The extent to which designers are dependent on these networks and on the hundreds of artisans who work for them has to be continually dismissed as insignificant and pushed into invisibility. And that too no matter how much artisans in their abstracted, purified, and idealized form are celebrated and cherished as the very core of Indianness in the designer's production. These interdependent worlds have to be kept separate; bifurcation into the parallel worlds of fashion weeks and urban poverty is not only essential for value creation, but also for reproduction of firm hierarchy. This requires a great amount of discursive, aesthetic and manual labour. Rohit Khosla was not only instrumental in legitimizing the profession and its power in India, but also in adapting the fashion industry's framework imported from London to Indian conditions and in creating a designer persona for others to emulate. After several years of studying in London, he went to Bombay and in 1987 started his own label together with his sister, co-founding in the same year also Ensemble, together with Tarun Tahiliani, Sailaja Tahiliani, Neil Bieff, Amaya and Abu Jani and Sandeep Khosla, India's first haute couture store, which continues to house top designer labels under one roof. Ensemble created a platform for the new and at that time marginal specimen of fashion designers, a platform where they could showcase their collections. But there are also other designers such as Rohit Bal, 'India's master of fabric and fantasy', as *Time* magazine once called him. Bal opened his store in the mid-1980s, at the same time as when NIFT was established. And even though Ritu Kumar's fashion boutique was opened already in 1966, it was not really until the mid-1980s that the concept of a fashion designer began to take hold and larger infrastructure, from media to colleges, celebrity networks, and fashion advertising began to take shape. Rohit Khosla set the trend by using the well-tried strategy of turning fashion design into an art-form, utilized already by pioneering legends such as Charles Worth, in order to carve out a niche and legitimize his position. As his sister recounts, 'styling gained new recognition as an art form in its own right.... He wanted to seriously show clothes in the right context as an applied art form, and not as cabaret' (Khosla and Johnston 1996: 37). Rohit himself was clear on this point, remarking that:

> In terms of designing as creative art, yes, it is. It is not a purely commercial endeavour for me and for the ones that it is, they are not designers, they are

tailors with good taste. For a true creative designer designing clothes is a way of life. I have always said that first, I am a fashion creator and then I am Rohit Khosla. For me bolts of silk and crêpes are my personal canvases. And what I create is art for me.... I became a truly liberated free spirit to whom nothing matters as long as you are creatively happy and creatively rampant and wild.... I am interested in the past as a road to the future. I don't want to be nostalgic; I want to design for my time. I love India's history, but I also love the music, art and movies of today, and I want my clothes to express these influences on me. To this day I believe that to be a happy faced fashion designer in India you have to be a happy schizophrenic.

KHOSLA AND JOHNSTON 1996: 11

JJ Valaya, who trained in his early days under Rohit Khosla, has pointed out that the fact that the word designer means something in contemporary India and to its consumers, was 'one of the major battles' they 'needed to win'. He said:

We had to establish ourselves as relevant sources of ideas and inspiration.... Besides addressing the needs and requirements of the affluent, fashion today is making our craft tradition relevant to new consumers, a new youth who are just taking their first steps into the upper class consumer segment. What we are managing to do, and do quite effectively, is creating a path to make our heritage in textile, our heritage and history relevant and desirable for a whole new generation.

VALAYA 2009: ix

Fashion designers often function as cultural brokers, both (re)producing the heritage discourse and partaking in the material production of its content, at the same time as they have to continually distance themselves from tradition. This uneasy middle position means that they have to continually legitimize their own status within the hierarchy as superior to all other producers. Their in-betweenness in the production of luxury, their proximity to the material and to the low class bodies marked by impurity and pollution means that devising strategies of distantiation becomes a dominant preoccupation of the designers. These strategies and techniques of power are not always necessarily conscious; rather, they have emerged as such during the analysis of the collected data, therefore there is no 'reductionism of the symbolic in terms of the utilitarian ... implied here', neither is there any cynical purely utilitarian and instrumental 'assumption here that the manipulation of the symbolic process is done consciously and rationally' (Cohen 1981: 219). These strategies of distantiation, elevation of value and legitimization can be grouped as follows, by appeals to (1) creative genius and art, (2) innovation and development, (3) expert knowledge and research, (4) intellectual property right protection, by (5) purification and sanitization, and finally by (6) patronage and benevolence. Let us address the first five strategies here and devote next chapter to the last, as it grows from the first five and is by far one with the largest impact on the lives of artisans.

Creative genius and artification

'The Boys' are the best. There is a rare eloquence in all that they create, which is rare and unique. I use the word 'eloquence' and not 'elegance'. Several designers in India create elegant garments. But only Abu-Sandeep manage to make their garments speak! Mind you, it really is the garments that do the talking ... the wearer is merely the vehicle. When you are an Abu-Sandeep loyalist, you don't have to say a thing! You merely float into the room for conversation to stop and the clothes to take over the rest of the communication! That's how it has always been for this talented duo. ... Their aesthetic is distinctly their own. And one only has to recognize their immense talent for what it really is – a divine gift. 'The Boys' are blessed. Their art remains as ethereal and undiminished as it was when they began their fascinating voyage into the unknown, eccentric, egotistical world of fashion 25 years ago.

Dé 2012

This is how Shobhaa Dé, a famous and immensely popular Mumbai-based columnist and novelist, sums up her experience with Abu Jani and Sandeep Khosla, a designer duo. In 1986, they started their boutique and couture house Mata Hari, after working with Xerxes Bhathena, the 'high priest' of Bollywood costume design. They are also known, among other things, for dressing up Judi Dench in a *chikan* outfit in 2002. Dé's insistence on eloquence reminds us of the importance of refined language, an insistence on transcendence of the material, an insistence on refinement of basic needs, such as clothing, to the point of luxury and desire. A few lines later we read of their 'divine gift' and 'ethereal art'. It is fair to say that the battle identified by JJ Valaya, has been won. It is not only people like Shobhaa Dé who have appropriated this designers' artspeak, but most clients, journalists, bloggers, teachers and lecturers, regularly employ it when talking of contemporary Indian fashion design. Divine creation becomes one with the eloquent language of design as art, where words like 'revelation', 'inspiration', 'creation ex-nihilo', 'trance', 'meditation', 'calling' etc. are chanted like *mantras*. Even the Hindi alphabet, called *Devanagari*, which literally translates as the abode of the Gods (Tambiah 1968), hints at the power of language and its power to create. Designspeak, the language of fashion, has become over the last twenty-five years in India, since Rohit Khosla's days, not only an adjunct to power (Simmel 1957; Wilson 2007), but also an authoritative discourse that effectively separates designers from artisans and expels those unwanted from the boundaries of the elite club, turning them into invisible ghost Others. This also sheds light on why Raghav, whom we met earlier, presents himself as and is called by others a *guru*. When it comes to power mystique, authoritative interpretations are as important as their dramaturgy (Cohen 1981). Let us now investigate these interpretations further, before proceeding to their dramaturgy.

Raghavendra, a revivalist designer based in Delhi, working among other things with *chikan*, much like Abu and Sandeep, has made both the problem and its solution clear in one of our interviews:

> R: According to the Indian tradition, arts and crafts were one, the craftsman is the artist, there is no distinction between designer, artist and craftsman, we all do the same thing, fundamentally, we all are artists.
>
> T: What is it that differentiates you from the craftsman?
>
> R: I guide the craftsmen; their creativity is of different nature, they repeat, they cannot innovate. That is where I step in. I create original pieces, they make my vision happen. And obviously, craft is great inspiration.
>
> Interview, September 2010

Raghavendra refers to the concept of *kala*, in which craftsman and artist are one, similarly to the Western concepts of *ars* and *tekhne* which 'meant much the same thing, namely skill of the kind associated with craftsmanship' (Ingold 2001: 17). As Troy Organ pointed out, there is no word for art in Sanskrit; the closest we can get is the concept of *shilpa*, which is a 'word meaning "diverse" or "variegated". This term was used originally to mean "ornamentation", but later on was extended to denote skills in the broadest sense: painting, horsemanship, archery, cooking etc.' (Organ 1975: 11). Ananda K. Coomarswamy, the pioneering philosopher of Indian art, who promoted the idea of the Indian craftsman as a metaphor of the Hindu order and tradition, once noted that the idea of an artist struggling to express himself and his passion while suffering a lack of patronage is ridiculous to Indian thought, since Indian art always responded to the market demand (Coomarswamy 1966). For Raghavendra, like most other designers, artisans (if they ever can be compared with artists), can be artists only in the traditional sense of the word. This means that they are positioned as a collectivity imagined as frozen in a remote past. So while designers imagine themselves as future-oriented individuals, taking recourse to the past only in order to shape the future, the artisans are labelled by these designers as a collectivity stuck in the past, unable to comprehend the present, not to mention relate to the future. Only such a split can legitimize the price tags and position of the designers (Figure 3.1). The first move is to insist on the separation of the intellectual and creative from the manual and repetitive, to insist on a purification of everything associated with matter and body while projecting it towards the bottom of the hierarchy. The second move is the insistence on a divine gift, or on unprecedented passion, a staple of designspeak, a

FIGURE 3.1 Designer Samant Chauhan posing with models after the inaugural fashion show of the *Fashion India: Spectacular Capitalism* exhibition at the Historical Museum in Oslo

Image courtesy: Adnan Icagic.

passion that as they say ignites a fire of creativity and aligns them with largely Western notions of high art. The designers' magical formula is: 'I imagine, they execute'. Soumhya Venkatesan has, in her work on the Pattamadai mat weavers, argued along similar lines, showing how the discursive production of categories like craft community and traditional Indian craft serves to deny the agency of the craftsmen (Venkatesan 2009, 2006). I argue that the artisans are being denied individuality and personhood in the process. This is how boundaries are (re) produced and maintained, and this is how artisans are pushed into invisibility. This strategy of artification, turning non-art into art, has become a popular strategy of adding value to one's product in the fashion world globally (Radford 1998; Geczy and Karaminas 2012; Muller 2000). Artification is about drawing distinctions (Korolainen 2012) and about value creation. This process has culminated in the rise of the fashion exhibition in art museums worldwide during the last two decades (Melchior and Svensson 2014; Steele 2008); these exhibitions far too often represent the designers as artists and are often co-curated by designers and even funded by famous fashion houses, thus turning into authoritative spaces that transform brand messages into worthy knowledge (for a critique of this see Kuldova 2015). This can be viewed as another step in the long historical process of fine art's outstripping of craft's cultural capital and value, as we have seen in the

West over the last century (Lees-Maffei and Sandino 2004). And so while designspeak, following the example of artspeak, plays on notions such as artistic vision, individuality, inspiration, creativity, progress, innovation, change, future and so on, craft is associated with nationhood, tradition, collectivity, stasis, repetition, rigidity, and past. This split, the dependence on the artisans and the need to claim superiority through the aforementioned strategies, is clearly visible in the following press release for Tarun Tahiliani's bridal collection *Artisanal: Bringing the Craft to the Fore*, a press release that shows remarkably well how something can be simultaneously 'brought to the fore' and pushed into invisibility:

> Real beauty, luxury and elegance require no tricks to seduce us. It is, rather, the timeless appeal of fine workmanship that truly pleases the style connoisseur. In India, the caress of luxury is the result of millions of artisan hands that pour their energy to define the ancient artisanal skill, exquisite taste and patience. Only a fusion of soul and expert technique will produce fine craft. Intricate workmanship, along with the return to organic textile celebrates and feeds Indian Couture, reinventing our historical traditions in the form of the Modern Mughal.
>
> **TAHILIANI** 2011

Rohit Khosla, too, 'was interested in the evolution of traditional arts and crafts, not just the reproduction of ancient techniques' (Khosla and Johnston 1996: 113, Maya Anavaratham on Rohit Khosla). The rhetoric used is one and the same. While it would be reasonable to argue at this point that it is indeed the education and class background of the designers, no less their ability to speak English, that actually sets them apart and to claim that many designers, such as Abu Jani and Sandeep Khosla, do come from privileged business family backgrounds, this would be too simple an explanation. Indeed, it is clear that the educated elites, plugged into the global expert knowledge society, have the power to decide who is to be traditional and who is to be modern (DeNicola 2004), no matter how much the reality defies this separation. Yet, the question here is also how class privilege and hierarchy is reproduced and created in a democratizing society and within an industry that has seen an influx of newcomers and self-made men even from underprivileged rural backgrounds. These self-made designers, even though a minority, have learned to effectively employ these strategies, and use the same designspeak in order to differentiate themselves from the masses of artisans on whom their businesses depend. No matter the background, all designers legitimize their current position through a rhetoric of creativity, a rhetoric that is nothing else than a vehicle of the ideology of meritocracy. As one designer, preferring to remain anonymous, told me: 'we must accept a few of low class origin among us, but not too many, otherwise what would be the credibility of our creative passion'. The 'charismatic ideology of creation', as Pierre Bourdieu called it in his *Rules of Art*, not only systematically draws our attention towards the individual creator and away from the question of who created this creator with all his magic power of transubstantiation (Bourdieu 1996), but possibly more importantly, it hides away and denies all the creativity, imagination and skill of hundreds of others without whom there would be only fancy words. At the same time, this charismatic ideology effectively devalues the artisans in the process, and in our cases reproduces their poverty, while feeding them the meritocratic narrative that says: if you have passion and creativity enough, you too can succeed. As Soumhya Venkatesan has observed, a 'successful trader transcends the relatively powerless role of object producer, becoming instead a producer of images' (Venkatesan 2009: 140). The designer supersedes the trader by realizing the power of narratives attached to these affective images. As William Mazzarella points out in his ethnography of advertising, any 'play with images remains incomplete if the affect that it generates cannot be captured and formalized within a discursive set of product narratives' (Mazzarella 2003: 46). As pointed out earlier, any successful mobilization of affects resulting in a capture of the individual's power to act requires narratives in order to push these affects in the desired direction, that is, into alignment with the master-desire. This is why the narrative of the self-made creative genius becomes so powerful; it not only induces admiration, but also identification, all the while legitimizing the social position of the designer. To the elite, the designers rather than their clothes, become the embellishment, together with their narratives of creativity, passion and signature. What is bought is no less the power of the designers over the vast networks of artisans that they command (Figure 3.2). Through the designers or rather by possessing the designers' signature garments, the elites master the Indian space and time. Designers are often treated as if they are owned by the elite women and men often demand certain things to be done for them according to their wish. They treat the designer as a tailor who can be commanded and should obey. The insistence on unique creativity and value is therefore as much driven by the designers' cries for independence and their attempts at resisting the elites, and at dictating what the elites should wear. It is still a struggle for the designers to be respected as educators, *gurus*, or sources of expertise and knowledge, even if it is precisely these qualities that are in demand by the same elites. It is said that for this reason Rohit Bal, the *enfant terrible* of Indian fashion who likes to portray himself as an artist, refuses to meet most customers in one-on-one sessions; he refuses to be dictated and told what to design. We are reminded of the legendary Charles Worth and his struggles with and against his customers while establishing himself as a designer.

It is telling to consider the fairly accurate observation of Hindol Sengupta that Rohit Bal's 'brand is defined by Rohit Bal the man. It is almost as if the brand is merely an extension of the edgy (or at least perceived to be edgy) life of the man' (Sengupta 2009: 150). As one of my interlocutors among the elite buyers said, buying Bal is 'an investment, it is like buying art, it has value which only increases in time'. But possessing Bal is also about including his creativity and the networks he himself possesses, the value lies as much in the amount of work that is put into the production

FIGURE 3.2 Model posing in Samant Chauhan's design

Image courtesy: Adnan Icagic.

itself, the amount of hands that fall under the power of the creative head, that is Bal. Collaborations between artists and designers are also increasingly popular (see Chapter 7) and seem 'to serve the purpose of endowing the garment with new meaning, and to elevate it to an art form' (Taylor 2005: 454). This is how simultaneous valuation and celebration of craftspeople and their devaluation takes place. Here we return to the power of language with which we began; the designer garment, like art, opens up 'the possibility and the necessity of interpreting the work, of offering a theory as to what it is about, what its subject is' (Markowitz 1994: 60). It is the meaning that is imagined as transcending the material that is significant, in other words, the level of connotation, symbolization and mythmaking (Barthes 1983). It is through the power of such myths and affectively charged narratives of superiority that the artisans are turned into relics of the past that need to be protected, educated and helped and whose crafts need to be continually revived for them. The modern orthodoxy separates conception from execution and thus legitimizes the hierarchy of creativity and knowledge. These authoritative narratives underpin the local notions of us and them, sustain neat hierarchies and (re)produce social boundaries (Barth 1969). The master of international art English is the Lucknow designer, socialite and mythmaker Muzaffar Ali, who hails from the royal family of Kotwara and runs the label Kotwara together with his wife Meera. Muzaffar Ali is also known as a film-maker, especially for his movie *Umrao Jaan* (1986), and a poet actively participating in Lucknow's cultural life, and promoting Sufi music and other cultural performances. While he often represents himself as a patron of the arts and crafts, following his royal legacy, among the artisans he is largely known for delayed payments and unreliability. Muzaffar Ali is extremely skilled in creating affective narratives about himself and his art, while distantiating himself from the manual:

Clothes for me are the epitome of inner grace.... They can transform a human figure, add an ethereal dimension to realism, they are visionary and timeless. They are a spiritual relationship with an ambiance. They are the essence of nostalgia, the fragrance of the present, and the dream of the future. When I sketch clothes, I design a trance made of moments of the past and present, and project them as valuables that people would cherish. To me clothes are sacred as they enclose the temple of the human form.... They change lives, heal the body, enrich the soul.... Clothes to me are like long lost friends, they come to me through those who wear them and the aura, which they live with ... a revelation, a high, a dance meditation. They go beyond comfort to becoming one with the body. They are in essence simple, self-effacing, yet radiating. They are futuristic because they will speak to you a decade from now.

ALI 2009

Such affective language is a language of seduction and power, a language that glamours clients. To glamour is to have power over those glamored, exactly the way vampires are said to operate, when they charm humans 'in a way that more or less forces the glamored person to do anything the vampire wants' (Irwin et al. 2010: 14). The power to glamour reveals the way in which fashion is always an adjunct to power (Simmel 1957; Wilson 2007). Valued as an abstraction and devalued as real living individuals, the artisans find themselves both celebrated and despised; the credit for their work is captured by a staged image of a creative individual legitimized by an ideology that sees creativity as separate from body and matter. And yet, there is something dirty and low about them that seems to attract, something earthly, a connection to the roots and the dirt of the national soil; this is a quality that seems to be in demand no matter how much purification and sanitization they are subjected to. Is it so that they have to be turned into dirty and low precisely in order to be desirable for the elite? Before we address this question, let us look at the second tactic of distantiation.

Development and innovation

Innovation, it is said, is what counts in the creation of new commodities in the competitive neo-liberal market (Liep 2001), innovation fuelled by creativity that 'has come to be seen as a major driver of economic prosperity and social well-being' (Hallam and Ingold 2007). In classical economic theories innovation is often considered as the sole autonomous cause of economic development (Schumpeter 1934). The celebration of innovation can be traced back to the split between art and craft and the nineteenth and twentieth century modernist belief in progress and innovation as inherently good. As Maruška Svašek points out,

> Forms of cultural production that did not aim for novelty were ridiculed for being outdated 'stuck in the past'. In the arts, 'creativity' was equalized with 'originality' and 'innovation'. In this view, traditions were either 'authentic, unchanging practices' or 'boring repetitions', and copying had to be regarded as ultimate form of non-creative conventionality.
>
> **SVAŠEK** 2009: 64

Prior to the beginning of the nineteenth century innovation was considered dangerous and suspicious, denoting a 'perverse and deranged mind' (Girard 1990: 9). After the turn of the century, as René Girard pointed out, 'innovation became the god that we are still worshipping today.... The new cult meant that a new scourge had descended upon the world – "stagnation". Before the 18th century, "stagnation" was unknown; suddenly it spread its gloom far and wide' (Girard 1990: 10). Stagnation was discovered by the colonial administrators everywhere in India, stasis becoming 'akin to mortal sin' (Pollock 2001: 5). Craft, considered static, repetitive and imitative became the example par excellence of the inability to progress, innovate and develop. The European 'opposition of body and mind, savagery and civilization' (Howes 2003: 5) lurks in the arguments of the majority of designers, who claim that design intervention and innovation of contemporary craft is necessary. As the educator and industrial designer Singanapalli Balaram (Balaram 2011) writes, 'one of the most pressing needs is helping people with design. This requires educating students to give design training to people who are illiterate. . . . It also means leaping from past traditions to future aspirations; connecting traditional materials, forms, techniques, and wisdom to the world's future materials, techniques, and needs' (Balaram 2005: 20–21). Similar attitudes were to be found among lecturers at the National Institute of Fashion Technology in Delhi, who claimed that the designers need to guide the craftsmen, who cannot orient themselves in the market. This is a typical rhetoric of the developmental discourse, in which the craftsman is perceived as 'skilled but not knowledgeable' (Venkatesan 2009: 38), a discourse that has been part of the education and socialization of the new generations of fashion designers. The same rhetoric is present in the UNESCO's advice on design intervention for the Indian crafts sector (UNESCO et al. 2005), a standard reference in the training of the designers. The designer is turned into an instrument of development, an 'instrument of good'. Time and again, the artisan is positioned as someone who needs help and external expertise; the gap is widened even further through these authoritative developmental narratives, so widely appropriated by the designers that most of them run or claim to run an NGO in addition to their business. Those NGOs typically claim to provide ethical working conditions, fair wages and further development of skills. Paradoxically, in reality it is the designers who learn from artisans, often things that are never thought at the design institutes and yet are essential in order to survive in the market that demands opulent ornament. Not to mention that artisans are continually developing new designs, as for instance in the case of *chikan* printers, who continually offer new designs. Women doing *chikan* sampling keep trying out different colour and stitch combinations, continually striving to present something new to the trader or designer, showing off their skill and imagination. This has been the case for other crafts as well, as Smritikumar Sarkar shows in his case study of the Kansari's craft in Bengal:

> the conventional notions of the unchanging or stagnant and backward Indian craft technology are much too simplistic. The reasons for the frequent repetitions of such interpretations are primarily two: absence of in-depth studies of Indian artisanal industries and the Eurocentric notion of technological change, which prejudice such studies. The case of *Kansari's* industry clearly suggests that technology in Indian artisanal industries did change in response to market demand. If such changes appear rather timid and slow, it was because a radical transformation of the technique of production was never a pressing and unavoidable need in India.
>
> **SARKAR** 1998: 140

Any polarization should be viewed with suspicion, not least because as René Girard remarks, 'our world has always believed that "to be innovative" and "to be imitative" are two incompatible attitudes. This was already true when innovation was feared; now that it is desired, it is more true than ever' (Girard 1990: 11). The denial of the fact that every innovation is firmly grounded in numerous acts of imitation is an ideological denial that has little to do with the nature of skill and creativity, but has all to do with power and (re)production of inequality. The show must go on! Innovation is a matter of survival; it is no wonder that designers and marketers worship it.

Expert knowledge and artistic research

Ritu Kumar, with her almost encyclopaedic coffee-table book on Indian royal fashion (Kumar and Muscat 2006), set the precedent for the valorization of expert knowledge among the Indian designers. We have encountered this already as part of the rituals of celebrating Indianness in the designer studios. Let us now consider it as a strategy of legitimization, distantiation and value creation. We can consider the case of Aisha, a fashion designer now in her forties, who has been in the industry for past twenty years, encouraged by Rohit Khosla. Since then she prides herself on her 'research based' and 'innovative' collections. Indeed, to her too, Indianness is the USP; but again, the talk is of an Indianness translated into contemporary times and looking towards the future, in her case a sexy and spiced-up version of India, where women are liberated by skimpy and tight-fitting clothes. Her research consists of 'hanging around the artisans' and 'digging out and digging deeper' into the Indian history of textiles and crafts and recreate the greatest things, as she says. Instead of indulging in what anthropologists term participant observation, Aisha engages in something more akin to spectator observation, thus keeping the artisans at a distance by means of her vision and exclusive interest in the pragmatic mapping of the techniques and design possibilities of their work. She is also an avid collector of books on textile and fashion, displaying them proudly to her visitors. Combining this research or expert approach with 'spicing up' tradition and making it sexy, is the self-proclaimed staple of her design. However, while her insistence on tradition and expert knowledge is very much in line with currently dominant trends, her insistence on empowerment and liberation through sexiness thrown into this mixture, is not – or we should rather say, not any more. A strong and visibly sexually liberated woman, with tradition only as an ornament, has been Aisha's signature, even when she was selling her garments to housewives, who only dreamt of independence and sexual self-determination; Aisha's garments acted 'interpassively' (Pfaller 2003), they were liberated and modern for these women rather than liberating these women. But increasingly, the customers who used to swear by her in the 1990s, have been shifting to other designers, claiming that 'her garments have become unwearable'; even though equally daring garments were perfectly wearable earlier. Aisha's idea of the modern Indian woman has become dated and trickled down to the middle class woman, and so her garments too became dated, at least in the eyes of the elite class she aims to cater for. Distinction and prestige is today heavily embellished and women proudly cover themselves in tradition. Maybe they have just become too modern and need the garments to be traditional for them. Also, the perception of the Indian designer as the expert on Indian fashion, bridal wear and opulent bling, has been established. As one customer remarked, 'if you want skimpy clothes, then go to Zara, why go to an Indian designer'. The USP of Indianness has taken over the local fashion industry, turning the designers paradoxically into experts on tradition rather than on modernity. Even if they are thoroughly 'modern' experts, while so-called traditional artisans conceived as pre-moderns cannot ever be experts even when they actually are experts and when it is their expertise that is sought after by the designers (Figure 3.3). Aisha on the other hand believed that instead of creating heavily embroidered royal-like attires, Indian fashion designers should better follow the footsteps of their Western colleagues and stick to only superficial embellishment in craft on distinctly Western silhouettes. But even she has recently given in to the market pressure and turned to Indian silhouettes. Sometimes she felt that the fact that she has been successful in the West, sold in

FIGURE 3.3 Backstage before the inaugural fashion show at the Historical Museum in Oslo

Image courtesy: Adnan Icagic.

New York, London and Italy, and designed for people like Naomi Campbell, goes against her in the local market that amounts to the majority of her income. Even her idea that Indian fashion should be about modernity in the Western sense and about 'catching up with the rest of the world' is dated and appears to provoke some of her former customers who claim that they have already arrived and conquering the world is only a matter of time. Aisha on the other hand feels that having to produce more traditional and Indianized fashion in order to satisfy her clientele is a sign of the Indian elite customer turning regressive instead of progressive in the modernist sense. As she says, the 'Indian elite women were more liberated in the early 2000s than now'. But the battle is not one of liberation, it is one of power and distinction, where symbols that have trickled down to the middle classes are being rejected, and as the inequality between rich and poor deepens, the more the elite likes to imagine itself as neo-royalty of incontestable birthright to power. Yet, all these contradictions and tensions visible both in Aisha's struggle to stay in business (even though her lavish villa with armed guards and dogs is not exactly an image of struggle) and in the power struggles over creativity and expertise, are contradictions inherent to modernity, where life itself is a maelstrom of frenetic change, ambiguity and desperate holding onto selected traditions and utopian visions (Berman 1983). The ideological regime of confidence and pride in India not only demands certain aesthetics but also punishes the disobedient designers, at least in New Delhi, the seat of power. Mumbai, as she depicted it, was different, fast-paced like New York, more cosmopolitan, less moralistic and full of working women, unlike the rich housewives of Delhi concerned 'merely with showing off' their wealth. Designers like JJ Valaya, who are more in sync with the current ideological zest, talk of connoisseurship, eternal style, and tradition, while emphasizing their expert knowledge. The modernity becomes both legitimization and property of the expert designer, while no longer being a visible property of the ornamentalist garment. In Valaya's own words:

I therefore consider myself to be supremely fortunate to have been born in India – a country that never ceases to surprise and enrich with its resources. . . . It gives me untold freedom to experiment – to bring alive a language of elegance and grandeur. . . . I feel Indians need to get more confident about making and believing in indigenous statements about their own sense of researched style rather than constantly looking towards the West for acceptance. . . . It is a labour of love and like most things special, it commands a higher value which connoisseurs of fine craft and those looking for spectacular clothing relate to, affluence of course does help a lot. . . . In spirit I like everything to have a sense of history, culture and antiquity but then I tremendously enjoy the freedom that fashion allows me when I contradict these very beliefs with something modern and new.

VALAYA 2012

Intellectual property rights and markets

Tarun Tahiliani, the famous Sindhi designer born in Mumbai, has fought a relentless legal battle for an exemption on his income tax from overseas earnings, by claiming to be an artist, under the section 80RR of the Indian Income Tax Act. In November 2010, the Bombay High Court held that designers are artists and hence entitled to exemption. Tahiliani reasoned at the court hearings that designers are indeed artists due to the fact that their work is all about individual creativity and conceptualization. In his struggle, he was supported by the Fashion Design Council of India (FDCI) and the fashion community at large; such ruling would be beneficial to everyone recognized as a designer. This ruling effectively and legally separated the designer from the craftsman. The artist has a signature or a label with an appropriate logo that can be protected under the copyright law and intellectual property rights. Originally, IPRs 'used to be considered as "grants of privilege" that were explicitly recognized as exceptions to the rules against monopolies. To consider them as privileges underscores their temporary and unstable nature. Shifting to the term "rights" suggests that it is the sovereign's duty to uphold them' (Sell 2014: 5). In practice, these rights and protection they offer are available only to those already privileged, at the same time as they legally reinforce their privilege. Complaints about copyright infringements are widespread among designers, court cases are being filed, even though with the speed of Indian courts they are rarely resolved. While designers freely appropriate what is deemed as traditional designs, out there to be taken, revived, innovated, developed and so on, none of this is of course considered a copyright infringement. Reversed, the artisans are regularly accused of copying designers on commission by traders and businessmen. But the question is: can you really steal from yourself? Legally speaking, the artisans can. Crafts are under the copyright law protected by the Geographical Indications of Goods Act from 1999, which has a clause that deals with the protection of traditional knowledge of localized communities. This also means that whereas copyright laws protect to a degree designer labels, craft is out there for the grabs. Its copyright belongs to the nation. The craftsman is perceived as a part of a collective national heritage, and consequently being imagined in terms of a collectivity himself, rather than as an individual with intellectual property rights over his production. In practice this also means that if you produce *chikan* outside of Lucknow, it is not considered a traditional product anymore. The law itself associates craft with repetition, tradition and immobility, while rather conveniently drawing a line between traditional knowledge of a collectivity and individual expert knowledge. Individual creativity is denied even to the most excellent and innovative artisans, and with it also an individual existence. Originality and individuality is thus a matter of class, the legal framework enforcing this status quo. In practice, only a member of the Anglophone bourgeoisie (Elias 2011) has the rights and privileges of individual intellectual property. Designer discourse is perfectly aligned with the legal discourse of the state and the global discourse of IPR. The logic of these boundaries is reinforced in everyday encounters. Consider this: when designers decide where to place the *chikan* blocks that they select on a piece of *sari* cloth, instructing the printer to do their bidding, it is called design, but when the printer makes the exact same design decisions he is 'merely placing the blocks on the cloth', as one designer put it. This logic turns the same act into a mechanical manual procedure devoid of conceptual thought. Abstraction is produced as a scarce resource; scarce resources equal power, leverage and desire. In practice, however, it is copying and abstraction that are inherent to the industry as to any other creative endeavour. The negative concept of copying, closely tied to the rise of the individual and to the ideology of meritocracy (Jodhka and Newman 2007), functions to legitimize claims to originality and value, while intellectual property rights protect the markets and create value in the face of competition. In reality, it is hard to find anyone who would really subscribe to the idea of unique creation *ex nihilo*. Yet, even as an illusion without owners, it structures the hierarchical universe, translates into capital and reproduction of privilege. All my interlocutors have upon my questioning admitted that creativity in fashion translates into an omnipresent and endless hybridization of designs fuelled precisely by copying. Fashion can only exist in a regime of open appropriation. Copying is essential both to the creativity of the industry and to its functioning. Furthermore, copying is rarely 'very harmful to originators. Indeed, copying may actually promote innovation and benefit originators' (Raustiala and Sprigman 2006: 1691). However, in the context of profound inequality, where open appropriation translates into exploitation of artisanal creativity, the effect of the illusions sanctioned by law becomes deeply problematic. Fake, copy, and original become themselves positions within a hierarchy. Recognition is simply not distributed equally and the current legal framework makes sure that this does not change. At the same time, designers capitalize on the fact that 'copying is a way of life in India' (Roy and Liebl 2004: 60) and everyone freely appropriates designs no matter where they come from. Another still relevant fact plays into designers' cards, namely that 'traditional Indian artists (and this includes musicians, dancers, vocalists, sculptors, painters, potters, metalworkers, poets, and many others) do not hold sacrosanct the notion of individual creativity. Rather, the most important task of the artist is seen to be the interpretation of a classic theme, rather than the creation of a new one ... design ownership is seldom organized or respected at any point in the crafts industry' (Roy and Liebl 2004: 61). In such a world, the fact that artisans keep developing designs is nicely covered up by a modernist ideological smokescreen that opens up the possibility of pushing artisans into invisibility and turning them into ghost-like creatures. And yet, the agency of these invisibles is often feared by the designers and so they grow secretive, trying to establish larger workshops and contain the new designs within them, while demanding loyalty and silence. Still, most embroideries are outsourced to external craft workshops that work on commission for designers as much as traders, which also means that sometimes designer 'copies' get into the stores even before the designer manages to put them on the ramp. However, in this blurry landscape of appropriation, the object of desire for many clients is very often the designer's signature, the label, the logo, that which is protected by the law, the proof of the original, rather than the original itself. This is especially true of the aspiring clients, who cannot really afford the signature. A case of two girls of upper middle class background testifies to this. Prior to the wedding of one of them, they visited JJ Valaya's showroom in the high-end DLF Emporio mall, where they tried on several dresses. While in the dressing room, they clicked pictures of these dresses and the detailing and to top it all, they clipped the JJ Valaya label from the garments and walked out as if nothing happened.

> We were so tensed until we left the mall, it felt like stealing the garments. It was totally crazy. Next day we went on a hunt for the fabrics and then had the embroidery done, which took some time and then had it stitched, and finally we stitched on the label, at home, by ourselves. It was too exciting and my God, so cheap too, like it cost us close to nothing; I still tremble when I look at the dresses.
>
> Interview, November 2011

Clients are a vital fuel for the copy market, while often contributing their own vision and personal taste. Most clothes are after all custom-made; even ready-mades bought at a shopping mall are adjusted, altered, embroidered, and so on, to match personal desires. Elite clients, too, often demand to be listened to, and so designers constantly struggle to subject such clients to their vision that they present as superior and knowledgeable. These strategies of legitimization thus work not only against the artisans but also against the clients, who too need to be subjected and forced into uncritical admiration of a designer who claims to know better what suits them than they themselves do. As one trader in Delhi told me:

> People in India are used to getting their clothes done on measure, to fit exactly both their bodies and their minds. Customers often come to me with a clear idea of what they want, they would be carrying a design, now recently a photograph, clicked with the phone, of something they have seen here or there and that is too expensive. Then they want me to make a copy and have it adjusted to their personal preference and body shape. Some might condemn this behavior, but it drives the industry, it speeds up the innovation and demand for new designs, at the same time as we learn in the process, we develop our creativity and our minds, we learn by copying and then add our very own impetus and aesthetics to that.
>
> Interview, November 2011

Purification and sanitization

The logic of abstraction mirrors the logic of purification and sanitization. And so while the artisans are essential to the production of Indianness, traces of their real living and breathing bodies have to be sanitized from the fabric; they must be separated from the materiality so that they can be re-made in the imagination. Only the designer has the privilege of being celebrated as a living and breathing human being; quite paradoxically it appears that only a disembodied mind can have a body that is equally recognized as valuable. The real bodies of artisans have to be melted into thin air, so that the abstracted artisan can be celebrated as a symbol of the nation. Artisans' real bodies are considered a social nuisance, a problem to be perpetuated in the name of solving it (see Chapter 4). Effective commodification of heritage demands sanitization; in its 'raw' and 'unprocessed' form, directly from the hands of the artisans, heritage luxury appears to the Indian elite and even middle class buyer as unhygienic and polluting, both in a moral and physical sense. *Chikan* embroidery is a case in point. The complex production process during which *chikan* passes through many 'low class hands', appears to the elite consumer but even to many designers as 'disgusting' and 'appalling'. *Chikan* has to be thoroughly washed, purified and sanitized. It is worth paying attention to the most widespread tales told by designers and traders about *chikan* production, also observed by Wilkinson-Weber in her study of *chikan* from 1999 (Wilkinson-Weber 1999). These tales all incorporate an imagery of the threatening stained and dirty embroidery. While dirt is unavoidable considering the time and conditions under which the embroidery is produced, what is striking is that most stains are imagined as bodily fluids, as sweat, slime, blood, mucus blended with dust and dirt. Most dangerous are the blood stains often believed to be menstrual blood. Even a tiny blood stain renders a piece of embroidery instantly worthless, and triggers a designer's violent reaction of anger and disgust. Such a piece goes straight to the garbage bin. Only sometimes is the blood stain covered by a dark colour dye, but still the piece sells for much less. The designers try to prevent their favourite customers from buying it, so that the inauspiciousness of the piece is not transmitted onto them; instead they try to sell it to a newcomer. As research into the nature of disgust has shown, primary triggers of disgust are bodily fluids, corpses, urine and other things that tend to remind us of our animality and thus also mortality (Rozin et al. 1986; Rozin and Fallon 1987). The disgust that the unwashed and unfinished pieces of embroidery triggered in the middle, upper and elite classes, is thus directly related to the idea of class pollution, corresponding to the logic or law of contagion, and thus to the principles of sympathetic magic (Frazer 2009). The fear of class pollution has in my view replaced, or extended, the fears of coming in direct touch with those considered untouchable. The reminders of our animality that trigger disgust are projected outwards and downwards in social hierarchy, onto groups of people that are constructed as less than human, inferior or worthless, or directly as shit – according to Alan Dundes the crucial factor in making sense of untouchability (Dundes 1997). As society becomes increasingly anonymous, and as inequality increases, material signs of poverty, rather than caste belonging, fuel fears of pollution. The logic of untouchability is now transposed onto the low class without further qualification. Martha Nussbaum has famously argued that the very content of emotions such as disgust includes 'evaluative judgements, and it would seem, as well, that one cannot consistently have such evaluative judgements without having the corresponding emotion' (Nussbaum 2004: 9). Philosophers and psychologists tend to agree that emotions such as disgust provide us with a kind of basic moral sense (such as in cases of disgust aroused when witnessing torture), yet at the same time, disgust is a kind of response conditioned by appropriated social norms and values, which means that it is changeable. As such these emotional responses are revelatory about prejudices and moral fabrics of the given society at a given moment in time, as much as about the ambiguity of the low classes that are for the elites both an object of disgust but also an object of desire (see Chapters 6 and 7). The rigorous washing of the embroidery has to be understood in terms of sanitization of low classness from the very matter, so that it can be turned into an item of heritage luxury wearable on an elite body. The physical sanitization by use of harsh chemicals that eat into the flesh of the hands of the washermen is thus a clear precondition for the imaginative sanitization, that is, abstraction and association of the matter with concepts larger than life – such as a nation – and a parallel disassociation from the materiality of the low class bodies. The process of sanitization and purification of the 'raw' and dirty embroidery, can thus be likened to the process of cooking, that is, to the process of 'civilizing' and endowing of the matter with abstract and ideological forms of value, which trigger desire, pleasure and positive emotion in the elite customers (Lévi-Strauss 1983). Indeed, to be consumable by the elite, the artisans need to be boiled, turned into vapour preferably. The 'raw', the repulsive and full of germs, needs to be also pushed into invisibility. The visible and invisible here is parallel to the split between the formal and the informal economy, that is, the pure and the impure economy, white and black economy. Again, we see the bifurcation of the social world into parallel universes at play. And yet, time and again it seems that it is precisely the low-classness that attracts the elite clients; the imaginary dirt still inherent to the garment is an object of desire (see Chapter 6). This purification and sanitization dominating the heritage luxury industry out of fear of class pollution is mirrored in increasing numbers of purification and beautification projects of the urban landscape and in the rise of gated communities (Brosius 2009; Waldrop 2004). Even the main street of Lucknow, built by the British, Hazratganj, was given such a facelift (2009–11) in a 400 *crore* project. All the *paan* stains were removed, pavements reconstructed, new benches appeared, all shop signs were remade in a unified black and white style, and several buildings were reconstructed. Two months after the facelift, newspaper articles mourned that

Hazratganj is back to dirty, portraying the misbehaved Lakhnawites as incapable of protecting, preserving and playing along the heritage protection logic of conservation. Even some designers, like Raghavendra Rathore, are consciously aiming to expand their fashion brands to include city beautification projects in the future. All these incentives aim to sanitize middle class and elite neighbourhoods from signs of poverty and from the working class bodies. Leela Fernandes calls this 'politics of forgetting', arguing that it should be viewed as 'an active political process that involves processes of exclusion and purification' (Fernandes 2004: 2428). It should be viewed as a political project of forgetting subordinated social groups, of turning them invisible or even denying their existence altogether. Statements such as 'there are no poor people in India' can be regularly heard among elites in Delhi and Lucknow.

Conclusion

Following up on the discussion in the previous chapter on the role of distantiation in the creation of value, we have now zoomed onto the tensed relations between the design and craft. We have seen that as fashion designers sought to establish themselves as legitimate experts on fashion, something that four decades ago any tailor, artisan or housewife could claim to be, they had to both differentiate themselves from these 'traditional' experts and establish their own value vis-à-vis the wealthy elites, their patrons. Trained in Western fashion centres and inspired by the Parisian fashion industry, they sought to use the division between material and immaterial labour, and in particular the value attached to Western high art, in order to legitimize their fashion endeavours and their own value within India. We have also seen how their authoritative narratives about creativity, innovation and unique artistic genius, now ingrained in the fashion education system, function as instruments of power capable of monopolizing individuality, while delegating the artisans into the realm of collectivity, tradition, past, inferiority, passivity and so on. In effect, the designers' authoritative discourses and acts sanitize heritage luxury from the polluting bodies of the craftspeople, at once celebrated as emblems of national traditions and despised for their poverty and low classness. Only in their sanitized form can these luxurious garments be consumed by the elite and the hierarchies of the social order desired by the neo-feudal elites, effectively (re) produced. This sanitization of heritage luxury from the materiality and physicality of the low class bodies of its producers needs to be read also within the aforementioned context of the momentary ideological confidence of India related to its economic boom and the rise of its millionaires. However, at the same time, as we will explore in the next chapter, the 'polluted' low class bodies lend themselves as perfect 'objects' of patronage and benevolence, and other power techniques that (re)produce distance and inequality. The designers' strategies have to be read in the context of the rise of philanthrocapitalism in India, and globally. The next chapter thus further develops the theme of the power relations between design and craft, and between the rich and the poor. Many designers working with craftspeople also run non-governmental organizations to 'empower' these workers, while cultivating the rhetoric of ethical business and philanthropy, and offering their customers in addition to luxurious clothing also good conscience. As we place such initiatives within the larger trends of corporate social responsibility, philanthrocapitalism and ethical business, we will see how these manifest goals translate into effective covert power strategies that reproduce the existing power relations rather than unsettling them.

4 CHARITABLE NON-LOVE AND PHILANTHROCAPITALISM

Back in Raghav's studio, another ritual takes place. Geeta, an older customer of Raghav, a marketing manager and wife of a CEO of a company dealing in Chinese green energy technologies, looks for the perfect attire for her speech about India's sustainable future; she has an image of powerful womanhood in mind, a combination of Sonia Gandhi and Madhuri Dixit, the heroines of politics and cinema respectively. Geeta's husband had explicitly instructed her to do her best to project an image of trust and confidence, since an important merger was at stake. Superstitious as she was, Geeta believed that only Raghav could do the magic and give her the right dress that she would bless in a temple the day before her talk. Geeta wanted Raghav to draw for her, always mesmerized by his lines, but he refused, and suggested instead a *sari* in white and gold silk *khadi* with subtle white *chikan* and gold *zardozi* border, matched by a long-sleeved blouse in deep green with some more gold. After a great deal of convincing, she agreed to the idea, but when Raghav mentioned the price tag of seventy thousand *rupees* (€900), Geeta began protesting: 'for a regular *sari*, you have gone mad!' Raghav coldly insisted that price is non-negotiable, 'this is not a *bazaar*'. She did not stop. And so Raghav decided in favour of his second favourite tactic, second to invocation of national pride, namely emotional blackmail. He dragged her to his workshop at the back of the building. The perfect juxtaposition to the designer space – shabby, badly lit, *paan* stains on the wall, where some of his *zardozi* workers were embroidering. Raghav instructed her: 'look at them, look carefully'. She peeped in briefly and said annoyed, 'I have seen places like that before, what is your point?' Raghav softened up a little, 'darling, how can you be so heartless? You ask me why I want that money, it is because of them, I have a responsibility to take care of them'. Standing in the door, not willing to step inside, she turned even more annoyed, 'please, don't try this "I am helping the poor kinda attitude", it won't work'. Raghav did not give up that easily, 'well, you can try to bargain with me, but you should not bargain with them'. For a while they continued, but then Raghav decided to pull out his best card and took her back into his seductive studio together with a small kid, Raju. Raghav was determined to make this 'heartless woman' connect with his 'workers', show her that he was a benevolent designer taking the cause of uplift from poverty seriously. To prove the point, he switched to Hindi and began interviewing Raju, a well-rehearsed act that he has successfully pulled off in front of many other customers before. Raju told a moving story of how his father died, leaving his mother alone with him and his two younger brothers. When his mother turned for help to her brother, he kicked her out. She was miserable for months until she accidently knocked on Raghav's doors. Raghav took over Raju's story here and shifted to English, 'looking into the mother's eyes, and the kids around her, I could not throw them out'; he decided to give her work, enrol Raju in a local school and give him training in *zardozi*. Geeta began to melt. Then Raghav turned back to Raju and asked him to confirm his benevolent deeds. In a *filmi* style, Raju proclaimed, '*Raghav saheb hamare liye bhagvaan jaise hai* (Raghav Sir is like a God to us)'. Suddenly the Ravi Shankar's sitar raga playing in the background gained a whole new meaning; everything was intensified. Geeta hugged the little boy with a tear in her eye, just what Raghav wanted. The staged presence of Raju, dressed in worn-out clothes, flip-flops fixed with a plastic tape, munching on his biscuit, sitting on an antique sofa and calling Raghav his god inside the lavish museum-like studio, created a unique affective atmosphere. In this extraordinary staged moment, class and pollution boundaries were transgressed. Geeta apologized to Raghav, agreeing to pay for what appeared as redemption from her privilege. Raghav won the game. Indeed, 'with the help of games, it is possible to compel people to feel guilty' (Pfaller 2014: 246–247) and to present oneself as the remedy for this guilt, capitalizing on it in the process. One of the reasons being that these games appear to be, in Robert Pfaller's words, far 'more fascinating than even life's positive aspects because', they unite 'both positive and negative aspirations, adding them together … precisely because the game is "nonsense" in their eyes, a mere game, and because they therefore disdain and hate the game (while simultaneously loving it, whether for the suspended illusion that is presented in it or for the repeal of such), they fall under its spell' (Pfaller 2014: 103–104). Raghav's ritual is more of a coerced game that enacts the ideology of ethical business, invokes capitalism with a human face, and provides the customer the great pleasure of guilt and its redemption, not to mention their transformative effect. Geeta claimed that following the encounter, which she perceived as completely authentic, she re-emerged as 'a new person', she felt 'reborn'. But still, she would be the first to claim that charity was about nothing else but business, self-interest, and public image. In the act of intense play, even Raghav got partly seduced by his own act, and so in order to keep his distance, once Geeta was gone, he gave Raju a tight slap, instructing him to make up for the lost time.

In real life, Geeta did not even know the names of her servant's children, they did not impress her, but she kept remembering Raju, who belonged in the play-sphere. She even decided to use his example in the talk she was giving a few weeks later on corporate social responsibility in front of the elite business community, another play-sphere where imagined economy with its philanthrocapitalist heroes is enacted, an illusion no one really believed in, but one that warms their hearts, fills their pockets and gives them a sense of power over impoverished labour power. As an effect of the affective play, Raju became a treasure of memory (Huizinga 1955). This is how ideology quite literally plays out in practice and materializes, or just simply exists in the material. Even the boundary between the designer studio and the workshop is strategically exaggerated, a feature shared by all designer studios with attached workshops that I have visited. One studio even had a large glass sliding door that separated the spaces, where the designer could at all times observe what the artisans are up to without sharing the same air with them and where his customers could get a staged view of the production. The artisans were displayed like in a living museum; they were, too, instructed not to meet the eye of the customers. It is not that the designers do not have resources enough to fix up the walls, light, and clean up the space, no, the space must look as shabby as possible. We are reminded of Oscar Wilde's words on the utter non-love of charity: 'They try to solve the problem of poverty, for instance, by keeping the poor alive; or, in case of a very advanced school, by amusing the poor' (Wilde 2004: 1). The dramatic visual contrast of these spaces of material and 'immaterial' production is strategically exaggerated to provide the necessary legitimacy to the claims of the separation of craft and fashion, and of the need for ethical business and to sustain and reproduce this false opposition between material and immaterial labour in the first place. The designed aesthetic boundary between these spaces is a boundary between knowledge, art, power, luxury and dirt, oppression and poverty. The space itself is constructed such as to perpetuate and legitimize the distinction between the designer and the artisan, as much as the logic of the 'perpetual need to uplift' – what would such claim be with the space being clean and neat? Another designer, gazing at his artisans behind the glass, once said to his customers: 'you have to realize that by buying this you are also doing good, making sure our five thousand year old civilization goes on'. What is at stake is nothing less that reproduction of hierarchical structures and inequality. Even vision and gaze is complicit in reproduction of these social boundaries. The artisans are instructed not to meet the eyes of the customers; the customers gaze down at them; the customers engage in the *darshan* of the designer, gazing deep into the designer's eyes. In his study on the role of eye and gaze in the Veda, J. Gonda argued that seeing in India is also a way 'of participating in the essence and nature of the person or object looked at' (Gonda 1969: 4). Everyday reproduction of hierarchy is in the gaze. With this in mind, let us now turn back to the encounter between Raghav and Geeta and attempt to understand first the socio-economic context of his insistence on his benevolence and then on the role of the NGO that his sister runs on the side for him.

Philanthrocapitalism and the new national heroes

'Greed is good, in fact, it is a virtue, only the super rich can save the world!', thus spoke Ravan, a Delhi-based businessman and self-proclaimed philanthropist. Within the echo-chamber of the transnational business and corporate elite circles, this peculiar belief is reiterated, reinforced and amplified, spreading like a virus through global markets in an attempt to exterminate or co-opt competing views. In 2008, when I was in India for the first time, newspapers regularly reported on the terribly greedy and selfish billionaires interested only in accumulation of capital. In 2011 the rhetoric in the same newspaper was turned on its head, now greed was good and billionaires were the saviours, the real hope for real progress and development and transformation of India into a high-tech nation. Since 2009, magazines like *Forbes India*, that established for instance its annual Philanthropy Awards, began pushing the idea of business as a 'force of good'. The recent victory of BJP in the 2014 national elections, with the PM Narendra Modi backed by India's and the global corporate elite, was not only a victory of the muscular unscrupulous Right over the 'effeminate' intellectual Left, and of Hindu nationalism over secularism, but also of the philanthropist billionaires over the state. These millionaires and billionaires are increasingly celebrated as national heroes, noble selfless saviours, celebrities and iconic role models for the aspiring classes, as much as for our designers and their clients. This democratically sanctioned corporate coup d'état and victory of philanthrocapitalism (Bishop and Green 2008), has practical lived consequences, such as de-politicization, reproduction and intensification of inequality and further multiplication of systemic edges, that is, internal borders within current configurations, that when crossed, lead to 'expulsion' of those considered undesirable and undeserving (Sassen 2014). These expulsions go uncannily hand in hand with impositions of notions of 'need' and 'good life' onto the 'poor', as with our designers who run NGOs as part of their business and who like to see themselves as benevolent patrons and selfless philanthropists.

We have already touched upon the importance of the imagined economy for India's national self-definition (Deshpande 1993), and the role of the factish, a combination of fact and fetish, of the rate of growth (Latour 2010). Economy as a source of national pride creates an opening for the intermingling of global and national symbolism and, as we shall see, also for a smooth merger of the ideologies of *Hindutva* and neo-liberalism, especially in the currently rising form of philanthrocapitalism. As we saw during the elections, the magical rate of growth equated with 'development' became the ultimate emblem of Brand India's future glory (Crane 1999), with Narendra Modi as both its CEO and brand ambassador, who sells the illusion of a confident, buzzing, hypermodern, developed and highly sophisticated India to the world. The rate of growth has become over the last several decades an unexamined virtue, with the growth of consumption no longer perceived as luxury, but instead as a national imperative. The poor artisans, portrayed as they are, as we have seen, as pre-modern tradition bound collectivities, become within this discourse an obstacle to growth, development and progress. While once this used to be the business of the state, today the state is proclaimed by corporate lobby, popular economists and other ideologues as incompetent, corrupt, inefficient, overtly bureaucratic, unprofessional; they say it is creating a dependency culture through welfare policies. Right-wing populists are only too happy to jump on this and argue for the need of private–public partnerships or direct outsourcing of its jobs to corporations. In this context, we see a rise of philanthrocapitalists attempting to hijack the state. The current pro-business BJP government is geared towards strengthening the role of both philanthropy and CSR. Philanthropic trusts and foundations are strategically portrayed as both committed to nation building and as the future solution to all collective social problems; the exact same logic as the one utilized by the designers. This relation between poverty and philanthropy of the wealthy feels like a return into England of the Victorian era, 'rich industrialists are being given the authority to determine the availability of public assistance and character of recipients', where the aim of the philanthropic societies was 'not to provide genuine solutions to poverty, but rather to affirm the providence of the market and the importance of self-help, while also assuaging the guilt of well-heeled do-gooders' (Polsky 2015). They thus promise to relieve the inefficient state of its responsibility (Nickel and Eikenberry 2009) and begin taking on roles previously reserved for government, thus skilfully inserting themselves into governance and depoliticizing it in the process by pushing the market into invisibility together with its negative impacts that create the 'need' for philanthropy in the first place (Nickel and Eikenberry 2010). Where the goal should be the abolition of this need, the result is its perpetuation, and creation. Philanthrocapitalism, an idea programmatically promoted by books such as *Philanthrocapitalism: How the Rich Can Save the World and Why We Should Let Them* (Bishop and Green 2008), has resurrected the old eighteenth century idea of the moral value of capitalism, and Adam Smith's notion that free markets if left to their own devices will naturally promote public good, cooperation between nations and bring welfare to all (Smith 2000). What we are witnessing is a new revamped version of Adam Smith's invisible hand, where social conscience and market reunites for mutual benefit (Žižek 2006).

In India, philanthrocapitalism has its well-established heroic families and heroes, such as Ratan Tata, Jamnalal Bajaj and GD Birla, who have been essential during the freedom struggle, supporting Gandhi's movement and popularization of *khadi* and village industries. Gandhi motivated women to engage in philanthropy, and has defined the realm of trusts, foundations and NGOs as a legitimate sphere for women's public engagement. This legacy goes on; today, predominantly female family members of businesses, industrialists, designers and CEOs run philanthropic and charitable foundations on behalf of their family's wealth (see Chapter 6). Even Narendra Modi has recently declared that women are best suited for charitable work. During the building of modern India, the euphoria of independence, the business community invested its wealth in setting up cultural institutions, commercial and technical colleges, hospitals, museums, public parks and so on (Sundar 2013). Still, philanthropy was typically viewed with suspicion, as the wealthy could control others through their capital, implement policies and enforce moralities – not unlike the situation today. In her study of the Sanatana Dharma Sabha movements between 1915 and 1940, Malavika Kasturi has shown how socio-religious gifting, or *dana*, became a crucial cultural and political terrain where the elites articulated their power, reinforced hierarchies and reworked relations of patronage and authority, in an attempt to regulate 'the people' and demarcate the deserving from the undeserving poor. In the process, they aimed to create a Hindu public crucial to crafting modern civil society, nationalism and citizenship while reproducing the status quo of the wealthy (Kasturi 2010). However, immediately after Independence high taxes replaced donations and philanthropy was discredited by accusations of shady business, misuse of trusts, money laundering and reproduction of the status quo, combined with interference in the lives of the beneficiaries. But then again, towards the end of the 1960s, the rhetoric of the state's inefficiency began to take hold and arguments about 'dependent' masses created by social welfare policies came to propagate the idea of charity as an alternative solution. The 1970s saw the enforcement of laws providing tax exemptions for donations and thus also a massive rise of NGOs that suddenly took over the developmental work. Under the post-1990s neo-liberal regime, NGOs became increasingly swallowed into the governmental and corporate body politic and in the process prevented or directly prohibited any critical opposition. They have become executioners on behalf of the state; a state that by co-opting NGOs successfully curbed any civil society opposition. Commenting on the emerging dominance of NGOs in social and developmental policies, Rajni Kothari has already in 1986 argued that control, repression and exploitation under this new regime that marked a shift in capitalist thinking on the role of the state, took 'extremely sophisticated forms' and 'a human face' that 'successfully neutralize both existing and potential sources of protest and dissent' (Kothari 1986: 2177). As we will see, the NGOs run by designers are a perfect example of this. They serve the goal of co-option of the workforce in the effective capitalist mode of production that benefits the designer but has little to do with welfare of the artisans, all in the name of so-called development and empowerment, notions dictated by the middle classes and the elites. The rise of the fashion industry and especially its emphasis on revival of crafts of the last decade coincides with the time when the superiority of the market over the state as a means of rapid modernization was established, together with the superiority of the private firm, and the subjugation of the state to the new transnational corporate ruling class (Kothari 1986). Over the last two decades, the processes described by Kothari have only intensified as the talk of the need of CSR with its managerial professionalism and celebration of the philanthropic heroes are considered an unquestioned good. During the eighteenth and nineteenth centuries industrialists used philanthropy in order to establish their authority as political and social actors; in the twentieth and twenty-first centuries CSR works to authenticate and extend their authority and power, while re-embedding morality into the market (Banerjee 2008) and turning consumerism into the main form of (pseudo)political action and markets into a showcase of humanitarian ethics. This effectively destroys any potential for non-market politics and solutions, while feeding the world with the fairy-tale story that 'one can celebrate a culture of global capitalism while sympathizing with its victims' (Nickel and Eikenberry 2009: 279).

Globally, wealthy philanthropists have become unquestioned celebrities, whose success in wealth accumulation turns them into worshipped leaders. In India, the iconic example is the Tata family, the role model of philanthropic and business success, spanning across India's economic history. The story begins with Jamsetji Tata (1839–1904), who began building India's largest iron and steel works in the face of British resistance in 1907 and was later labelled by Jawaharlal Nehru as one of the great founders of modern India; the story continues with the iconic Ratan Tata (1937–), who turned Tata Sons Limited into the world's sixth largest corporation and a powerful international player venturing into diverse businesses such as steel, luxury hotels, tea, salt, motors, chemicals, digital services and so on. Ratan Tata is not only every Indian entrepreneur's idealized hero but also one of the most celebrated philanthropists; a devoted promoter of capitalism with a human face. Guided by the spiritual wisdom of *Bhagavad-Gita* (trans. Prabhavananda and Isherwood 2002), Ratan Tata has established Tata Trust as one of the world's most generous corporate trusts. Indeed, it is less known that Tata Trust has poured more cash into Harvard Business School than into any educational institution within India, not to mention that protests against land grabs by the company across India and Africa are notoriously silenced. Within the realm of imagined economy, corruption, illegal practices and notorious exploitation do not exist. Tata Sons regularly rank highest among the most trusted Indian companies, while Indian spiritualism merged with business pragmatism produces the very leverage and imagined superiority of India against the West. Being Indian at the core, the very quality the designers are so keen to deliver to their elite clients is central to doing business the specifically Indian ethical way. Moreover, it adds to their heroic spirit. In the non-fiction bestseller *India Unbound*, Gurcharan Das (Das 2000) portrays the entrepreneurs as heroes, 'these entrepreneurs are as mad as our medieval Rajputs who went to battle ... when they knew in their hearts defeat was their only prize' (Das 2000: 294). Philanthrocapitalists embody national greatness, princely and/or spiritual.

Resonances between Hindutva and neo-liberalism

Hindutva, the ideology that insists on the dominance of a Hindu way of life, has often been invoked by my business interlocutors, designers as much as by India's philanthropists. Recently, we have seen a resurgence of the rhetoric of Hindu superiority, as history books are being rewritten by Y. Sudershan Rao, the appointed head of the Indian Council of Historical Research, who claims that the holy scriptures suggest that 5,000 years ago Indians were flying aeroplanes, engaging in stem cell research, used cosmic weapons and as Narendra Modi himself claimed, were experts in plastic surgery – how else could the elephant head of Ganesha been stitched onto human body, he asked? The Hindutva activist organization led by Dinanath Batra, *Shiksha Bachao Andolan Samiti* (Committee for Struggle to Save Education), known for censoring textbooks for content that is deemed anti-national and anti-Hindu, fought a battle against Wendy Doniger's book *The Hindus* (Doniger 2010) for her supposed distortion of Hindu culture and her obsession with sex. Penguin consequently withdrew the book from the Indian market. Many Hindu elite businessmen and even several designers, subscribed to the claims of racial superiority made by these Hindu ideologues. Most Western and Indian academics, particularly those labelled 'Marxists brainwashed by Christian missionaries', are today accused of being anti-Hindu propagandists. The important point for us here is that it is the ideology of Hindutva that provides Indian neo-liberalism with moral order. Shankar Gopalakrishnan has in his article from 2006 (Gopalakrishnan 2006) pointed towards important resonances between Hindutva and neo-liberalism, resonances that are even more prominent today. First, both ideologies reduce social processes to individual choices or individual moralities, thus doing away with any conception of social structures and power relations. Second, both ideologies divide societies into 'internal' and 'external' realms, where 'the actual existence of social divisions is then explained by identifying certain division as *the boundaries* of "society" itself. Outside those boundaries lie "external" entities, which produce "disharmony" within society ... those "outside" must be "educated" into the "understanding" necessary for social functioning, or, if this is impossible, destroyed' (Gopalakrishnan 2006: 2805, emphasis in original). Following this logic, in the India Shining campaign, where neo-liberalism most clearly overlapped with right-wing nationalism, 'those without "shining" lives were simply not Indian' (Gopalakrishnan 2006: 2808). Third, what Hindutva and neo-liberalism have in common is the rhetoric of transformation through the main ideological principle at hand – either market or *dharma* (Gopalakrishnan 2006). In the case of philanthrocapitalists, ethical businesses and CSR in India, we see these two increasingly teaming up for highest impact. *Dharma* provides the moral high ground to neo-liberal capitalism, while promising to transform India into a global power capable of nothing less than saving the whole world from civilizational crisis. And who could do this better, they say, than those self-made rich? After all, those who themselves come or claim to come from impoverished backgrounds, are said to be more likely to 'give back to society'. In the design world, as we have seen, the individual is carefully crafted in opposition to the masses of undifferentiated others; it is therefore no wonder that the ideology of meritocracy works well in synergy with *dharma* and the promise of transformation through the free market. Meritocracy belongs to the most popular and persistent of the mythologies of 'spectacular capitalism' (Gilman-Opalsky 2011) that incorporate ideas such as that anybody can make it only if they work hard enough or that with time capitalism will eradicate inequalities. The realities on the ground more often than not resist these myths. From privileged or underprivileged backgrounds, most designers like to claim their achieved status (Linton 1965), the former systematically pushing into invisibility their ascribed status of hereditary wealth. The paradigmatic example of a designer who climbed the social ladder from middle class to an elite position is Kolkata's Sabyasachi Mukherjee, who, like Rohit Khosla, went against his family to pursue fashion design at NIFT. After his graduation in 1999, prominent awards rushed his way, topped up by Femina British Council's award for most outstanding young designer in 2001. He has shown everyone that all that matters is talent and determination; now he sells in London, UAE, Singapore, Kuala Lumpur, New York, Dubai and Milan. He likes to portray himself as relentless in his pursuit of money, sacrificing personal relations, because, as he says, he loves accumulating money, money that he rarely spends. The accumulated money is a symbol of his self-made status and a measure of his worth in the capitalist marketplace. Recently, he was invited onto a popular TV show sponsored by Teacher's whisky, *Achiever's Club* at Star World channel, moderated by the actor Boman Irani. This show features interviews with India's prominent self-made men and systematically reproduces the myth that all that matters is dedication and vision. As Sabyasachi proclaimed on the show, 'today in India, if you really believe in who you are, the world will come to you'. Sabyasachi has focused his career on the idea of the necessity of return to Indianness and the urgency of putting an end to 'aping the West', as he says; he believes that dressing 'Indian' brings forth the confidence in Indian people and confidence in turn brings success; his clothes become a vehicle of such success. The meritocratic ideal also allows a tricky move and that is never to argue that the artisans find themselves where they are because of any possible structural conditions, no, the only reason they are where they are is because they lack individual skill, creativity and drive to self-development (Figure 4.1). The title of

FIGURE 4.1 A group of village women embroidering a *chikan* sari, a popular target group of diverse empowerment organizations

Image courtesy: Arash Taheri.

the Indian bestseller, featuring entrepreneurial stories of twenty-five MBAs from the Indian Institute of Management in Ahmedabad, *Stay Hungry, Stay Foolish* (Bansal 2008), says it all – poverty is a matter of individual idiocy. Pratap B. Mehta has quite correctly observed that in contemporary India, 'meritocracy has become part of the self-justification of elites ... being thought of as part of meritocracy is elevating; it is also part of our identity' and that 'what we are seeing on display is not just greed; it is a society struggling to find measure of worth' (Mehta 2011: 7–11). The problem with meritocracy is that it systematically legitimizes social inequality by arguing that success depends on the individual's abilities and talents, while ignoring altogether the structural conditions of opportunity in the first place (Jodhka and Newman 2007) and creating an illusion of open society, precisely through cultivating few examples like Sabyasachi. We have seen how philanthrocapitalism works with meritocracy and the ideology of Hindutva; now let us turn back to the charitable designers and look at how this works in practice in the case of *chikan* embroidery production.

'Empowerment', co-option and expulsion

So what are the benefits of making ethical claims or running NGOs for the designer-firm? While most 'ethical' designers and philanthropists like to claim to be selfless givers, invoking the scriptural notion of *daan*, a disinterested gift without an expectation of return, a liberatory mechanism (Bornstein 2009) or even of the *gupta-daan*, that is a gift given secretly to prevent 'the increase in donor's public status' (Laidlaw 1995: 297), in practice even the secret gift (that somehow eventually everyone gets to know about) is never really disinterested. Nietzsche knew quite well that there is often rarely anything less disinterested than such claims to disinterest: '"And the praise for the self-sacrificer?" – But whoever has already offered sacrifice knows that he obtained and wanted something for it – perhaps something from himself for something from himself; that he relinquished here in order to have more there, perhaps in general to be more, or to feel himself "more"' (Nietzsche 2008: 104). Beyond that, there are many other benefits, from lower tax rates, customer loyalty, enhanced brand image, and positive public opinion. But most importantly for us here, are three crucial functions: (1) the reproduction of labour power; this labour power must precisely be reproduced as 'skilled but not knowledgeable' (Venkatesan 2009: 38), to use again Venkatesan's observation (2) the co-option of the so-called 'weak', often of those at least partially independent, into the capitalist system, precisely in the name of their 'empowerment' and 'development' (3) formalization of labour (without that necessarily translating into formal contracts). The NGO working on behalf of the capitalist functions as an ideological state apparatus that runs primarily on ideology and only secondarily on repression (Althusser 1971). While typically the two aforementioned functions would be achieved by the capitalist educational system, here it is the NGO working on behalf of the designer that secures most effectively the reproduction of the relationships of production. Yet, we must not forget that institutions such as NIFT that educate India's fashion designers, encourage their students as several NIFT lecturers explained, to become patrons of crafts and 'do some good', help elevate the craftspeople and provide them with 'design assistance', or even to take on board a particular craft and 'devote themselves to the cause of its revival'. The educational system thus fuels the agendas of the NGOs that many designers set up after they graduate. Even designers focusing on the middle and upper middle class youth market, creating artsy and edgy fashion statements of rebellion and subversion, such as Jagdish, share the enthusiasm for craft revival after having studied at NIFT:

Craft is the backbone of Indian fashion. It is the second largest employer in the country, so you can imagine how big this industry is. . . . India is starting lots of brands, which is so much like a capitalistic point of you, whereas a crafts sector is still, I think, rather than a sector a revolution that you undertake against mass production, against something which is not of that quality, so in that sense the craft sector of India will always be special. But in certain segments where it has not been explored lot of crafts have perished in India. I have my NGO after graduating from NIFT. I have run it for three years now. I was staying with the tribals documenting their crafts in the northern part of India, in the Himalayas. That is where I realized that although if you go to Rajasthan, Gujarat, Lucknow, Orissa or some other states, you find primarily crafts from these states visible in the market, or designers are working with them. But as such there are lots of other crafts, in fact, there is a storehouse of them which has still not been discovered, the quality has not happened, lot of craftsmen have left their professions because of not having a market or not having a knowhow or awareness as far as the trends are concerned, the colours and the quality or the kind of products that one would require in today's market. So there are designers who are working with these clusters where you go and produce a certain collection. So it is a long process, probably next two or three decades, that more and more designers will penetrate this industry and you will see exquisite craft, which will relegate to the fashion and come into the market.

Video interview, April 2012

Arturo Escobar famously argued that development is a historically and culturally specific project that 'created a space in which only certain things could be said and even imagined' (Escobar 2011: 39) and a discourse in which only certain things are visibly problematic: 'women', 'illiteracy', 'backwardness' and 'stagnation'. Typically, the modernist development discourse is blind to other possible shapes of the good life beyond the strictures of bourgeois ideals and it is thus hardly a coincidence that it serves the interests of capital owners and that 'the solution to failed philanthropy is more of it; the failure of philanthropy is its success' (McGoey 2012: 196); the failure of philanthropy is precisely its success in securing the reproduction of the relationships of production.

The stated goal of the designers or their family members running NGOs is to empower the artisans and give them dignity and self-respect, educate them and provide a fair wage, document the craft for them, conserve the living heritage (sic!), popularize it and create or expand the market for it, innovate and develop it and increase its quality. But how do all these claims fair in practice? The obvious contradictions of these goals notwithstanding, let us look at what the insistence on these goals attempts to do and does in practice in terms of the reproduction of 'skilled but not knowledgeable' labour power.

Let me now consider the cases of three designers and Preity, who we met earlier, running their NGOs and/or ethical businesses, all of whom work in particular with *chikan* embroiderers. These designers are all urban based, in Delhi or Lucknow, and all fully dependent for their livelihood on their business, the only source of their income. All of them run workshops both in the city and centres in the villages, each having between 150 and 400 women working for them in total. This puts them into a tricky position, which often goes unacknowledged and undercommunicated – namely their complete dependency on the craft workforce. After all, they have built their careers on high-quality embroidery and they need to reproduce this image. We already know that the production of *chikan* is complex and extremely time consuming, in particular the crucial embroidery stage. While there are female embroiderers in the old city of Lucknow, most of the embroidery is produced in the villages surrounding Lucknow. Most designers have a few workshops in the city, but still most of their production is located in the villages, periodically inspected by themselves and/or by their managers. Some embroiderers work for informal monthly wages while others are on piece-wages. It is crucial to understand at this point, that there is a great difference between the organization of the labour in the city and the village. The whole production is marked by great insecurity for the designer, from untimely deliveries, via women opting out of the work, pieces spoiled by stains, to fights, arguments and women passing work amongst each other, often to the less skilled, resulting in inadequate quality. The designers, in their race to deliver orders and collections on time, have to devise strategies of making the production more effective, controlled. In a word, strategies that would enforce a strict and effective labour regime and control over the notoriously disobedient workforce. Here the differences between the embroiderers in the city and those in the village become most obvious. The city workshops are marked by strict technologies of control; they are often run by a male manager (in few cases also female), typically of a slightly higher social standing than the embroiderers, who has full control over the comings and goings of the fifteen to thirty women employed in the workshop. These women are expected to work six days a week, nine to twelve hours a day; Sundays are free. The manager keeps strict records and the women are paid according to how many days they have worked in a month. But the calculation of the wage does not depend solely on the amount of hours spent embroidering under strict observation and in complete silence (except for the lunch breaks when they are allowed to chat). Calculating the wage can be a trickier matter. We have earlier encountered the woman who samples the pieces and her special role in co-creating the design to be embroidered. Such a woman is typically extremely skilled and creative and she has done high-quality embroidery for more than three or four years; typically she is also unusually fast. When sampling the piece, the time she spends on embroidering one printing block, discernible to the skilled eye, is measured. This time per block is then used as a standard, in Marx's words the 'socially necessary labour time' (Marx 1992), a standard all other embroiderers are expected to live up to, both in quality and speed. In practice, this means that those who are less experienced and have only worked on high-quality pieces for a couple of months or even a year, lacking the precision in speed, may have worked for nine hours in a day, but will be paid for three or four. Women often also embroider the same piece, especially in the case of time-consuming *saris*, together, often in groups of four to seven. In this case, each woman is minding two or three different stitches she is especially skilled in, some women doing the difficult stitches, such as different types of *jali*, others doing the easier stitches. At the end of each day, the manager carefully counts how much each girl or woman has done and records it in his notebooks. The final monthly salary is counted by the designers' assistants or in case of Preity by herself. The monthly salaries of the women in the city workshops thus vary considerably, from 800 to the maximum of about 3,500 rupees. For comparison, one *sari*, depending on the amount of embroidery, is sold for between 25 and 200,000 rupees. The discrepancy in the salaries is considered an incentive to 'encourage the women to learn and develop the skill in order to become empowered'. One of the designers thus pays the best woman in the workshop to give free lessons to other women and newcomers from the villages or the city, in quality embroidery. These workshops go on daily typically for two to three weeks, and women learn while embroidering simpler pieces for free, in the name of learning and qualifying for a future job, after which they may get the entry level salary of 600 rupees a month.

The rural women have for decades worked from their own households, their work being delivered to them by the middle-men. Typically they were embroidering in their free time, in between other household chores and care for their agriculture. In the studies of the industry, it is paradoxically this form of labour that has been criticized most heavily for being exploitative (Wilkinson-Weber 1999, Arya and Sadhana 2001, Jafri 2011). In particular, feminists have strongly argued against such 'exploitation', demanding better work conditions and higher pay. While it is true that the middle-men have often taken a great share in the process, this would be just attacking another small guy, who turned out to be nothing more than a scapegoat for enforcing developmental agendas. Today, the landscape has somewhat changed and traders and designers alike have made a great effort to organize village centres, with appointed leaders recruited largely from the more resourceful women in the village (also often Hindu), who have bigger houses connected to electricity, where five to fifteen women meet on a daily basis to embroider, watched over by the more privileged one of them, who has the responsibility for all pieces in her centre and for all deliveries. Even so, women take along their children, chat, drink tea, have breaks when they want, pass on the work to someone else, often someone more in need of cash than them, and they come and go largely as they want (Figure 4.2). Each time I visited the village with one designer or another, only one or two women would be working, sometimes none, and they were all called in at short notice. Sometimes a kid would spot our car approaching, notify everyone and they would gather and nicely stage their dedication to work. They delivered in the end, often with delays, and on their own terms, mocking the discourse of effectivity. Time was not the same in the village, and this is not to idealize the rural life that has its own difficulties. The crucial point here is, unlike the urban based embroiderers, these women were not dependent on the income for their survival. They had fields, brothers, husbands, fathers, father-in-laws, who all combined their incomes from diverse activities. But most importantly, these women had land and often also cows and they understood

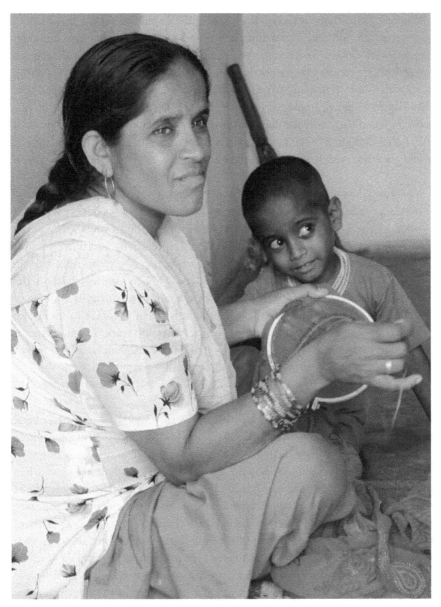

FIGURE 4.2 *Chikan* embroiderer with her son
Image courtesy: Tereza Kuldova.

their value. While the designers would try to convince them that the skill in embroidering is their greatest asset, they would laugh and say it is a pastime, then they would take me to their land and their cows and say, 'this is our wealth'. Some women would engage in the embroidery only as a pastime, a hobby, as in the case of younger girls, others would ask the trader or designer to give them printed cloth and cut it off from their pay, and they would embroider trousseaus for their daughters or clothes for themselves. Some were more interested in having an opportunity to escape to the workshop from their homes and engage in delightful chats with other women and so on. They were not scared to demand services from the designer either, or to leave if he or she did not live up to their expectation of a reliable patron. To others, the designers were a 'hassle' that destroyed their 'peace of mind' (see Chapter 5). One of the designers in business since the 1990s summed up the 'problem' with rural embroiderers as follows:

> In the old days, when I began with a small studio, it was a hassle, I used to travel to the craftsmen, wherever they were and tried to get things done, everything took so much time and energy, late deliveries, unreliability, you know yourself how these people are, they have no sense of responsibility and time. But now things have changed, now the craftsmen are at our doorsteps, right here in Delhi, most of the things you need can be done over here, one travels only to fix special things, but even for that I have people now. But *chikan* is still one of those things I have to go fix myself, especially when it comes to important orders, you cannot trust it to anybody if you want good work. The problem is it is done by women, so it is harder to make them migrate to a city, maybe Lucknow, some do that, but Delhi is still impossible.
>
> Interview, November 2010

The rural women were the great 'problem' for the capitalists and neo-liberal moralists insisting on their version of the good life. The fact that many of these women would opt to leave the work altogether in the case of dissatisfaction with the work provider was perceived by the designers, NGOs and middle class urban intelligentsia as a 'great loss', a 'sad fact', a 'problem', something that needed to be remedied. They were labelled the enemies of progress, the enemies of the state, with all their poverty and illiteracy. Even though this illiteracy claim is a persistent trope, in actual fact most embroiderers below thirty-five are literate, some were even village school teachers while others held long-distance bachelor degrees. Only certain older women would be truly illiterate. In this context, it does not come as a surprise that the designers and increasingly traders like Preity, exploit the discourse of ethical trade and strategies of NGOs, their aim being to enforce standards and control either at the village level by establishing centres, or even better, by convincing the women to shift to the city. However, the women have little interest in their labour being formalized. Even though many have understood the commercial potential of the embroidery, very few are really interested in transforming this home-based spare time activity into a serious career option, a similar case to what Edwards observed among the textile workers in Gujarat (Edwards 2010). For others, another concern is the observation of *purdah* that prevents them from leaving the village. Interestingly, *purdah* was often invoked in cases when the man was already working in the city, either commuting on a daily basis or staying over during the week. In such cases, *purdah* prevented women from seeking jobs in the city, and instead pushed them to take care of the land. One husband of an embroiderer commented on this, claiming that 'people from the city come and plant ideas in the women, they dream, but they don't understand it is lies'. He was referring here to the interactions between designers/traders and the rural women, interactions that typically emphasized the logic of female empowerment through waged work and increased skill, an idea that in the future they may progress and achieve something. The designers would typically provide examples of women who have received national awards for their embroidery from the Crafts Council and the Ministry of Textiles, yet these awards mean very little beyond a paper of recognition (see Chapter 5). Talking of dreams of the future, it is important to think of plays with temporality here. Designers, traders, managers, or their middle class NGO employees come to the village to preach to these women, typically emphasizing the importance of their work in terms of heritage, the necessity of upgrading and perfecting the skill and quality (which they equate with 'education'), while reinstating the promise of a better future 'only if they work hard enough now'. Hidden in their discourse is the promise of agency, the Faustian dream of self-development and self-transformation, the promise that everything depends only on their hard work and dedication. They are indoctrinated in the mythology of meritocracy and given examples of people like Sabyasachi or of successful women they can see on the TV. The promise goes like this: 'if only you do as I say, work hard, dedicate yourself to work, you too can be like them. Indeed, it you fail, it is because you have not worked hard enough. The trade-off is this: yes, if you shift to the city, for a short period you might be in an even more precarious position than you are in now, but eventually, you will learn and be better off and able to send money back to the village, provide for education of your children, save up and realize your dreams.' This systematic and repetitive preaching to the women during the visits to the village, and to the craft centres, visits intended to either establish functional craft centres or to relocate the women to the city, utilizes classical advertising strategies. Typically, first the women are reminded of their value for the nation, their role in preserving heritage, in being heritage, they are reminded that *chikan* pieces are in the museums, private collections, worn by celebrities. Then they are reminded of their lives in poverty, in dirt, lacking basic amenities, not owning enough clothes, electronic devices, and so on. They are told that they are uneducated, unwilling to learn, progress, develop, even dream and that this is the true reason for their failure. The fact that they prefer to stay at home, work from home on an occasional basis (for wage), is turned into patriarchal repression, 'your men hold you back'. The husbands are demonized as lazy alcoholics, or *bhang* addicts, or wife-beaters and so on, one story is enough. The problem and the potential for change are established. And now comes the time when the designer, trader, or their NGO worker proposes himself or herself as the very remedy to this problem. And the remedy as we know is – getting training, increasing quality, working at least eight hours a day, joining the village centre or directly moving to or commuting daily to the city, after all they deserve 'good working conditions', especially 'better light' not to ruin their eyes and of course those toilets.

In a recent ethnographic account of the Tirupurr garment cluster in Tamil Nadu, Geert De Neve has observed similar dynamics at play (De Neve 2012). In his case, parallel systems of employment exist in the local garment industry – one of the Fordist assembly line and the other of smaller flexible workshops. Even though the scale and level of formalization is different, the arguments are the same. The capital owners argue for the necessity of supervised workshops that promise higher wages, a clean environment, fixed time, predictability, security as opposed to unpredictability and insecurity of the flexible workshops. Ethical business in practice means exactly this: fulfilling the criteria of a good/healthy environment, standard working hours and a 'fair wage'. As De Neve points out, this produces 'a form of governance that seeks to maintain strict control over production regimes and workers' movements' (De Neve 2012: 7). The same can be observed in both Delhi and Lucknow in the case of the male-run *zardozi* workshops that can be divided into two types (1) family run (2) and those run by manufacturers and designers, with appointed managers. Whereas the first tend to be lively spaces, where men chat, listen to radio, watch TV while working, or have breaks when they please and so on, the second type is again marked by silence and by focus on effectivity, while the workers become easily disposable and replaceable if they refuse to obey. It is here that the secondary feature of the ideological apparatus steps in, namely its operation by repression that manifest in what Burawoy called the despotic organization of work under capitalism (Burawoy 1979). The exact same repressive mechanisms can be observed in the city workshops, all in the name of empowerment and better working conditions. Workers in Tirupurr, much like the rural embroiderers, as we shall explore in the next chapter, mocked the urban settings of production and the designer's 'mindset', thus seeking to avoid being co-opted into the neo-liberal labour regimes. De Neve's ethnography shows how the workers critiqued the neo-liberal labour regimes, precisely because of the discrepancy between what they are assumed to or should be valuing according to the capitalist and what they actually value. In both cases 'workers value those work environments that allow them to retain control over their working lives' and 'seek to evade regimes of time discipline and spatial control that reduce their freedom at work. The avoidance of particular work regimes effectively amounts to the avoidance of the "production gaze" that seeks to rob them of basic freedoms and dignity at work' (De Neve 2012: 9), the very same dignity that the designers and their NGOs promise to deliver. And again in both cases, the workers dwelled 'at length on the differences in temporal routines and supervisory regimes' (De Neve

2012: 12). The labour regimes that the designers and traders-cum-designers, as much as NGOs attempt to put into place using the rhetoric of empowerment are often 'divorced from the actual needs and aspirations of the workers on which they are imposed . . .; these largely Western projects of imposition do not go unchallenged when viewed from a worker's perspective' (De Neve 2012: 21).

Before we proceed to the next chapter, where we will look more closely at the actual interactions between these designers, NGO representatives, Preity and the embroiderers who they employ, let me include and conclude with an observation made by Irfan, a famous printer in Lucknow, who has worked for many well-known designers and who himself supplies work to around 350 women both in Lucknow, though home-based, and in the surrounding villages. Irfan has worked over the last three decades for designers like Abu Jani and Sandeep Khosla, Rina Dhaka, Ritu Beri, and others. These designers, for whom *chikan* was only temporarily on the agenda, or who patronized other crafts, often used Irfan to mediate the work for them instead of going to the villages on their own, because, as Irfan claimed, 'they could not take it'. When I inquired more into this, he was convinced that the reason was of a 'psychological' nature. Of course it was practically much easier to outsource the work to Irfan, who would take care of the whole process, acting as a printer-cum-designer, while having none of the glamour of the designer attached to him, thus remaining safely within the bounds of his 'place'. Since Irfan finds himself in between many famous designers and urban as well as rural embroiderers, he turned out to be a particularly interesting discussion partner. For Irfan, dragging the women from the village and establishing centres in the city, was related to the idea of village as a threatening leisurely space, in other words a space that resists the capitalist logic. Once the women were in the bounds of the urban workshop they would be under control, under a regime of work which did not allow leisure. It is not a coincidence that the villagers enjoy *bhang* on a daily basis, while the designers are self-proclaimed *coffee* addicts – the first being a drug of anti-capitalist slow time, the second being a drug of capitalistic effectivity, high speed, and stress – the same reason why marihuana was prohibited by the British. One day we discussed with Irfan SEWA Lucknow, the most famous organization working for the empowerment of *chikan* craftswomen run by the feminist Runa Banerji and established on the impetus of a study of *chikan* workers conducted by UNICEF in 1979. I had a chance to visit their set-up in Lucknow on a couple of occasions. The main building in which the whole production of *chikan* is concentrated resembles a factory – there is a room for printing, several rooms where the embroiderers sit on the floor and work, there is a room for washing and a room with finishers and finally Runa's office on the top floor. The work that is traditionally done by men, printing and washing, is here done by women, in accordance with the logic of female empowerment, which here meant a complete elimination of men from the production process. Men were demonized as eating up from the salaries of the embroiderers, while women were presented as victims of patriarchy and they had to show they could outdo the men. In the whole building there is marked silence, every woman is minding her own business, nobody talks or laughs, and all my attempts to talk to the embroiderers were repeatedly discouraged. Only two girls were picked out to reproduce in front of me the authoritative narrative of the positive benefits of the organization. Indeed, the organization managed to revitalize the craft, expand the market, improve the quality, and revive forgotten stitches and the organization has been effectively marketing their products on the basis of their ethicality since they started, showing their work in Paris, Milan and New York. At the same time, however, Irfan opposed the way this 'empowerment business' was organized. While he may hold a personal grudge, his points are still relevant:

> They are the only one who does their own printing. You know where the blocks come from. They copied my blocks and had them done. They still keep coming and try to copy this or that. This Runa thinks *chikan* belongs to her. Then she teaches these girls how to do printing. Printing has been always done by us men. She puts all of *chikan* manufacture in one house. That is not the right way.... She puts all these women in one house, there they sit whole day, from morning to evening. Most of them come from village. I know since some of them are now working for me. They left that place and went back. They did it for money but they had no life. When they are in village they can decide when to work, how much. Nobody controls them, nobody tells them now you have to sit for twelve hours, now you eat.... Now you see what they do, they tell you it is all about empowerment of women, but you see what is happening in reality. The only one who profits is SEWA, they have all under control, then they have their store and people buy because it is for a good thing, they make exhibitions all over India, they even travel to Italy and Paris, sell at international exhibitions and who is getting the money? They behave the same as the designers. I mean they are good in many ways, they promote the craft and we all profit, they made the market bigger. That is good for everyone, but they do not really care for people. They do not understand *chikan*, even if you try to explain it to them. *Chikan* takes time, it should be done *aaraam se* (at leisure), otherwise it does not have that quality in it.... You know these designers keep coming to me and talking about empowerment and recognition, it often makes me laugh, who gives me recognition? In the end, I do most of the designing.
>
> Interview, November 2010

Conclusion

Building on the previous chapters, where we discussed the tensed relation between design and craft and the persistent creation of distance – special, aesthetic, economic and social – this chapter has turned to an investigation of the social and economic power that comes with claims to charitable benevolence. Through rituals staged in designer studios, and on fashion ramps, rituals that are put up in the name of the empowerment of impoverished artisans, buyers can not only be compelled to feel guilty (and shop as a relief), but structures of inequality can be more or less visibly (re)produced. Designer studios are set into aesthetic opposition to craft workshops that remain intentionally dirty. But there is more to this. Throughout this chapter we tried to grasp the peculiar convergence between neo-liberalism, especially the emerging philanthrocapitalism, and Hindu nationalism with its return to traditional moralities. Working in tandem, the philanthrocapitalists and ethical designers are trying to convince us that capitalism can be a force for good, that greed is good for everyone and that even people like the impoverished artisans benefit. The famous Indian philanthrocapitalists have become the national heroes, the saviours. Yet, in practice we have seen that NGOs, trusts and other initiatives are first and foremost aimed at turning the 'loose' workforce, casual labour, and so on, into organized labour (even if without actual contracts). The aim is co-option in the neo-liberal system, all in the name of dignity and self-respect that the designers promise as a reward for following their orders and delivering on time. Building further on this knowledge, the next chapter turns back to the villages surrounding Lucknow and to the female embroiderers, revealing how these women resist the attempts of the designers at patronizing them in the name of their own good. These women, as we shall see, often use irony and laughter when confronted with the charitable discourses that position them as vulnerable, poor and in constant need of rescue and they defend their way of life, their values and even their anti-work ethic.

5 INSUBORDINATIONS OF THE LAUGHING CRAFTSWOMAN

Once, a *chikan sari* was commissioned for the museum ethnographic collections. Following a discussion with Preity, the *sari* was printed by Irfan and embroidered collectively by six embroiderers in the village and three in the city, who did the sampling, advanced stitches and finishing. During one of our visits to the village to check on progress, the following conversation took place between Preity and 'her girls', as she calls them. Preity, as she always does, preaches to them work ethics and national pride:

> This *sari* will be exhibited at a faraway museum. People over there will know about our craft. You should be proud of yourself; they will see India, our nation, through your work. You should be very proud, you represent Indian heritage and people from far away appreciate it. They give you dignity and self-respect.

> (The 'girls' are giggling, listening with a dose of scepticism), then Zehra says: It is only words – nation and tradition – what does it mean, it means nothing (laughs). What difference does it make to us?

> (Other girls start nodding.) Jameela says: We are sitting here and ruining our eyes for nothing. What nation, what kind of tradition? You get your work done, you get your money, and what do we get?

> Zahra continues: You people only talk, it is only words. All you do is take credit for our work, I have TV; I see the designers. We do the work and they just talk, as if they knew anything, they just live of us, like you do.

> Mubinah steps in: I don't care for any of that, the work is just useless, I do it while waiting to get married, to pass time; there is nothing else to do over here.

When I get married I will live *aaraam se*. What kind of pride? Everyone does it here. I don't want to learn new stitches. I just want to *relax*.

(On the way to Lucknow, Preity reflects on the events of the day while driving.) These girls just want to live *aaraam se*, they don't want to learn. Then they envy us, they know what kind of people buy their work and they envy me. They think how much she has and we do all the work. But they don't realize what it takes to manage everything and the risk involved. No one can anticipate sales; these are expensive pieces only few can afford. The investments are high, there are so many people involved whom I have to pay. And you have to keep checking them all the time, you can't entrust the work to anyone, you cannot rely on any of them, they can't see all that.

Interviews, May 2011

Another Lucknow-based niche designer, who supplies several well-known designers in Delhi, also experienced being regularly mocked by the village-based craftswomen. Even though she publicly displayed confidence in the discourse of empowerment, fair wage, education and so on, being a self-proclaimed feminist, academic and activist, in addition to playing on 'ethical business' notions, in private she displays a dose of scepticism. After our interview on camera, she shared some of her experienced tensions off camera. On camera, she talked about the history of *chikan*, the patronage of the *nawabs*, the exquisite pieces of the past. She talked of SEWA Lucknow, praising the organization for giving workers a proper, clean environment, better wages, standardized working hours, and training. Like most other designers, she believed that the only solution for the *chikan* workers is their inclusion in the organized sector, and she even managed to organize most of the labour in her house, convincing women to come out of what she perceived as notoriously oppressive conditions of the rural household. But the dependence on the family is merely replaced with a new dependence, namely on wages. However, this new dependence is framed in terms of self-reliance, self-development, and independence. Capitalist relations of subordination are skilfully erased from the discourse, while dependency is notoriously individualized and turned into individual laziness, unwillingness to learn and progress. When it comes to the failures of the artisans, all of a sudden they are turned into individuals! As Kathi Weeks rightly points out, 'as an individualizing discourse, the work ethic serves the time honoured ideological function of rationalizing exploitation and legitimating inequality' (Weeks 2011: 53). While for some women, for instance the urban landless poor, or widows, and so on, finding work is a matter of necessity, and therefore this might truly be a way of surviving even if on a mediocre wage, what is our concern here is the insistence on bringing the rural women into the organized sector of the city and breaking their unwillingness to work and employing strategies that would turn them into 'willing slaves of capital' (Lordon

2014). This repetitive bias clearly tells us that what is at stake especially in the 'developmental agendas' is the self-interest of the designers and their need for expanding the workforce and exercising more effective control over it, making it faster, more productive, skilled and no less willing:

> The *chikan* workforce is really large and fragmented. But for them it is a matter of survival. Let's face it. They cannot decide. . . . *Chikankaar* should move from the unorganized sector into the organized sector. I don't know when and if that is possible. But only then can the *chikankaar* be paid proper wages. And if that happens, the quality of *chikan* will definitely improve. . . . See, these are unskilled workers, when I say unskilled, they are unlettered, illiterate. Their work is not market driven, if it were market driven they could be really paid very well, unfortunately it does not happen that way. So they are economically dependent on other people. . . . They have to become part of the organized sector, get better working environment, better wages.
>
> Interview, April 2012

As we know by now, the insistence on the illiteracy of the *chikan* embroiderers is purely ideological, or mythological, in the sense of having a narrative structure that has (affective) traction in social life, shaping the way we collectively imagine social reality (Citton 2010). The narrative of illiteracy is recited like a *mantra* in the ethical fashion discourse, and as with any ideology, knowing better is not capable of unsettling this myth (Figure 5.1). Even if in reality, illiteracy among *chikan* workers is largely limited to women over fifty, an estimated 5 to 8 per cent of the workforce, the myth persists. It becomes unimaginable, and unbelievable that in reality there are village school teachers and women studying long-distance bachelor degrees, among the workers. The discourse of empowerment cannot function without this insistence on dependency for survival, on victimization, the inability to act, to understand and even to read, and if it is not really there, it needs to produce it, else it would lose its cause. And not to forget, it needs to proclaim middle class life as the ultimate social good. Off camera, she expressed her unease when trying to convince these women who resist such impositions:

> They do not understand what is good for them. They laugh at me. They tell me, 'why would I need all that?' But I feel they too deserve that, they should have that. They should have a better life. Then I think, maybe they are happy the way they are, but then that must be wrong. Once I came to the village and tried to educate them about *chikan*. They don't even know the value of their own craft. Then one of them stood up and said, pretending to be very serious: 'Now sisters, understand that what she is saying is right, we are doing all of this for our nation, for our Great India, it is a question of our honour, we are tradition, those that live far away respect us a lot, even Aishwariya (famous Bollywood actress)

FIGURE 5.1 Women laughing while embroidering high-quality *chikan* pieces and listening to Bollywood songs

Image courtesy: Arash Taheri.

is wearing our work, understand that!' (translated from Hindi). But then all of them began laughing, I did not understand. Then one of the others said, 'what nonsense, what rubbish'. Then I understood that they were making fun of me. I still don't know what to make out of it, you can't help those who do not want to be helped. I told them they should not talk like that. But I still cannot forget the incident. I don't go to that village anymore.

Another day, in a village near Lucknow, I was chatting with the girls about designers while they were embroidering and watching a soap opera, then one of them said:

No matter what you see in the TV and what those designers claim to be, we all know that it is us who make the clothes, without us there would be no designers, they would be lost, we may be poor and dependent on them to get our money, but they would not even exist without us. We are the real heroines of *chikan*.

Interview, August 2010

All of us began laughing, indeed, without them there would be no designers; they were the dependent ones. This point was made clearly in another encounter between a different group of rural embroiderers and a Delhi-based designer who went in person to check on some of his special orders for a couple of *saris* for a wedding trousseau of one of the Delhi millionaire daughters about to tie the knot. He was unhappy with the quality of the embroidery, expecting something more delicate and he became instantly frustrated and stressed, thinking of the problems ahead with the delivery. He began to shout at the women, blaming them for being irresponsible and lazy, for lacking a work ethic. Then he threatened them with cutting their wages or giving the work to someone else. The women sat still, staring at him, and then one of the older women began laughing, threw the *sari* at him and shouted:

> Take it! We don't care for your money, we don't need people like you here shouting, get lost, and remember, we don't need to do this work, we do it because there is nothing else to do in the day; you come here and give us work and what do you think you are? You designers come and go; one piece here, one piece there and think you are saving us. You are the irresponsible people here, not us. We don't care for your work, take it! You come here and you want embroidery, we don't run after your work. You are the one who is dependent on us. Without us you are nobody, you can't do anything. Now stop shouting and making a fool of yourself and either get lost or let us continue working.
>
> June 2011

The other girls nodded, supported her and laughed at him. He was angry and frustrated, complaining that these women are so hard to deal with. Even he plays the ethical card and has established several centres in three different villages in order to increase his workforce, all around twenty-five kilometres from Lucknow and he tried to provide them with training from older embroiderers, but even when these women were actually very skilled, they were not particularly interested in working beyond their chosen workload. And so he too alluded to the distinction between the workshops in the city and the village:

> Those who are in the city are much easier to handle, they do what you say and keep their mouth shut, they are dependent on the work you give them, and that makes them thankful and obedient, these women here think so much of themselves. They make my life hell. . . . The moment you step in the village, you are stepping on their territory, no matter how poor they are, they let you know that you don't belong there, when the same girls are in the city, you can make them do anything, they know who is the boss.

Even when all these designers, traders and NGOs systematically try to swallow and co-opt the potential female labour force in these villages into the logic of money, profit and conspicuous consumption through the discourses of empowerment, education, a fair wage and so on, the village strikes back with its ironic voice of denouncement and resistance. For the women, the city is often imagined as a space of neo-liberal pollution, of misery and filth. Their men often travel to the city to do different petty jobs and there is nothing the women envy about that. The unease that designers often feel when they come to commission work in the villages is often caused precisely by their systematically repressed realization that these women do have some power over them, that the dependency can be easily reversed. On one rare occasion a female designer once admitted to me in the comfort of her luxury farmhouse close to Chattarpur, in Delhi, that sometimes when she meets the craftspeople she feels guilty:

> Everybody praises me for my work, I take all the credit. But to be honest, I would be nothing without the craftspeople. I studied fashion design at NIFT, but what did we learn? Western cuts, stitches, marketing, we only got to know little about different crafts. But then if you are into fashion in India, you have to do embroidery, else you won't survive a day in the elite market. So I had to go to the craftsmen and learn from them. I learned from them more than from NIFT. Sometimes I feel without them I would be nothing. I mean, what do I really do? … They know I am more dependent on them than they are on me. These people will always manage one way or the other, but me, without them I cannot do anything. But you cannot say you learned from craftsmen.

Work ethic versus anti-work ethic

The designers are often haunted by these ironies of production and the discrepancies between the dominant ideology of the work ethic to which they subscribe (Weber 2005), and its realities of the reversals of dependency, that manifest themselves in the problems of securing reliable, willing and obedient workers. This is precisely why statements like the above are rarely heard beyond the safe private space, the boundary between the speakable and the unspeakable needs to be reproduced through everyday acts and the voices of resistance to this narrative need to be silenced.

Following Michael Herzfeld, these ironic, mocking acts that trigger the sense of a reversal of dependency, capable even of provoking guilt and unease among the designers, can be understood as acts of insubordination. As Herzfeld points out, insubordination 'is not always resistance: it can lock one into the structures of power more firmly than ever – a considerable price for the momentary satisfaction of symbolically inverting the prevailing order. Those who mock the educated and powerful, for example, may nonetheless play the game of clientilism because it is pragmatically stupid not to do so' (Herzfeld 2001: 71). Herzfeld also points out, and I believe rightly so, that taking irony seriously as an analytical perspective also translates into 'a recognition of one's informants capability of theoretical reflection of their own predicament' (Herzfeld 2001: 65) – the very ability that is systematically denied to them by the designers. Being ironic necessarily implies an awareness of one's circumstances and the ability to reflect on these circumstances. The reflections that these women present us with bring forth their insistence on the designers' notions of the 'good life', of the value of work, of 'development', of 'empowerment' and so on, as contingent, and not necessarily universally shared and sought after. The women, through their ironic insubordinations, invoke an alternative anti-work ethic that valorizes for example children, relations, community engagement, leisure, chatter, and so on, over a clean working environment, eight-hour working day and 'empowerment' through petty bonuses on wages. However, while alternative work ethics, as Kathi Weeks imagines (Weeks 2011), siding with the autonomist Marxists, can function as a tool of insubordination, as a form of resistance to the normative discourse of work ethics employed by the designers, NGOs and so on, at the same time a dose of scepticism is necessary when considering its liberatory potential per se. What it however achieves in our case, is to protect the world of these embroiderers, with their anti-work ethic that valorizes laziness, leisure, and protects the community from what Baudrillard called the romanticism of productivity (Baudrillard 1975), where the 'virtuous productive' is juxtaposed with the 'immoral unproductive' (Tseëlon 2011). The craftswomen engage here in a powerful critique of the ideology of productivism that considers a dedicated work ethic an ultimate moral virtue. This critique also enables these women to maintain their lifeworld with its values and notions of well-being, and notions of what life is worth living for, at a distance from the designer's hectic schedules. Most importantly, the fact that they repetitively insist on claiming that it is the designer/capitalist who is dependent and not them, the way the capitalist likes to paint the relation, enables them to claim their freedom from oppression by strict labour regimes and what they often perceive as 'the curse of money', money that destroys lives and breaks families.

This interpretation is grounded in observations of diverse and often bold ironic interpretations of the position of the artisan, which take on the form of mocking, ridicule and laughing at the designers and joking about them, their beliefs and lifeworld, as we have seen in the examples above. We have seen that the women call into question concepts such as nation, tradition and heritage, the central 'mythical attractors' (Citton 2010) of the discourse of the benevolent designers. These women, unlike the designers and their clients obsessed with staging their Indianness, were very little concerned with these 'big words'; nation appeared not only as an altogether laughable matter but also as an instrumental concept that 'politicians use to get their votes', as one woman proclaimed. Moreover, these women were well aware that elites invest a lot of time and energy in preserving crafts, which meant forcing the artisans to remain where they were. These women also clearly recognize, especially in their mocking and ironic subversions and reversals of the logic of dependency that is imposed upon them, that without them there would be no nation, that the elites are fundamentally dependent on their material production and even on their bodies that as we have seen, sanitized and abstracted, translate into the 'essence' of Indianness, which can then be flaunted by those far removed from the spaces and bodies of their producers. In order words, they clearly recognize that their craft products are necessary in order to Indianize modernity (Hancock 2002), both for the middle classes and elites, while they are being turned in the process into an abstraction that pushes their real bodies either into invisibility or expels them (Sassen 2014) beyond the internal boundaries of the nation – they are neither good consumers, nor dedicated producers. The fact that Indianness emerges only at a social and imaginary distance from those who are among its most pronounced abstracted symbols lends itself easily to irony. Being treated as an idealization tends to be rather offensive to real people. The craftswomen who are turned into ghost-like creatures, existing only as a fantasy, a dream, a non-present present, then reveal in their irony the hollow character of contemporary ideals of neo-liberalism, progress and capital accumulation (Nietzsche et al. 2001). Their irony, which represents a clear conflict of perspectives, the very antagonism of the worker against the capitalist, works to discredit and critique the ideal of productivism, work ethics and capital accumulation. These women also mock the very idea of craft as the spiritual–humanistic ideal of unalienated labour. They call into question all those nostalgic theories inspired, among others, by the young Marx – theories that romanticize handicraft production as a source of fulfilment (Fromm 2013).

Without knowing it, these women stand for an autonomist Marxist position in which 'workers are to be conceived not primarily as capital's victims but as its antagonists. By this estimation, neither capital nor labour power is the primary creative element; rather, working-class insubordination is the dynamic force in history' (Weeks 2011: 94). In this rendering, influenced by the 1960s and 1970s Italian social movements, it is the working class' insubordination to and struggle against capital that defines it (Tronti 1966). These perspectives emphasize the role of 'the imposition and organization of work' (Weeks 2011: 97) over the role of private property in understanding the dynamics of capitalism. It is precisely this organization and imposition of work that the rural women systematically resist. In this sense, what the craftswomen force upon us here, through their ironic statements that mock the designers and question their obsession with the work ethic, is a perspectival shift: from labour theory of value, in which we have engaged so far, to value theory of labour, where 'the point is not to grasp the process by which value is constituted by labour, but rather to fathom how labouring practices are organized, shaped, and directed by capitalist pursuit of value' (Weeks 2011: 97). Yet, the two have to go hand in hand.

Value of leisure and virtue of laziness

The craftswomen push us here towards a rethinking of the value of work, and of the work ethic that dominates contemporary capitalism. Like Paul Lafargue, they provoke us by their statements about the value of laziness (Lafargue 1883); they want to live *aaraam se*, as they say, without bother, without hassle, without control, without cutting up of their day by strict work routines. Indeed, the 'virtue of laziness' is powerfully embedded in the well-known mythology of Lucknow as a city of leisure and indulgence, where even street vendors behave like the *nawabs*, lying throughout the day on their beds, smoking or playing games. Even the women kept saying that their favourite activity is to roam around, visit relatives, chat with neighbours, walk through the fields and so on, without any specific purpose or agenda beyond leisure and enjoyment. This anti-work attitude drove the designers, traders and NGO workers mad, as one designer pointed out, it was the main obstacle for her dealing with her 'workers':

> they always have enough time, they are never in hurry, in fact they have no concept of time, they just want to lie around; they don't understand one cannot live life like that. It is so hard to come by anyone hardworking, they all just want to relax, that is the Lucknow *tehzeeb*.
>
> See Chapter 2

Like all the other designers, she juxtaposed her hectic working tempo, with no space left for relaxing, with the slow-paced leisurely life of the craftswomen. As she said:

> They don't understand that I have to run around whole day, manage all orders, manage designers in Delhi and Mumbai, distribute work, design my own pieces, sample pieces for abroad, you have to market it, you have to network and all. They don't understand that I have to do all that in order to be even able to pay them.
>
> Interview, September 2010

In the view of the craftswomen, the designers are always stressed, always running after something, always giving orders, always hectic, as they say '*yeh log aaraam aur shaanti kabhi nahi milte hain*' (these people never relax and get peace). This position recalls the traditionalist perspective that Weber invokes, a perspective that resisted the Protestant ethics and preferred to work less, to work in order to live, and not to live in order to work. The women's 'traditionalist' or 'anti-work' perspective is clearly visible when they are confronted with the designers' attempts at turning them into good and proud workers with 'dignity', 'self-respect' and 'self-worth':

> I keep telling them, learn this new stitch, it is not an easy one but you will get paid more, but they don't care, they won't learn. And I can't force them. So the exquisite parts of the embroidery have to be done in the city, those city girls are

under control, they do what you tell them, but with these village girls it is always a hassle, they do as they please.

Interview, December 2010

All the women had to say to this, was the following:

Why should I learn? What difference would that make for me, the only one who takes advantage from this is the designer. And should I do it for extra money, how much, hundred *rupees* in a month, why would I care for that? I am not the one who is crazy for money, it is the designers, the businessmen; they are slaves of money (*paise ke ghulaam*). They always come here looking so miserable.... We laugh at them, they have everything but still they are miserable. They think that we are poor, that we don't have anything. But we have everything we need (*zaroorat*). Look at the village, everything is here, air, water, fields, food, and look at the city, it is just dirt and people miserable and fighting, and they come to teach us how to live?

Interview, August 2011

The designers clearly miss the point, neither the women's dignity nor their self-respect is grounded in the idea of work ethics and they have a hard time convincing them that it should be the case (Figure 5.2). They also fail to understand something that Weber already recognized, namely that material need alone is not necessarily a stimulus enough to work. Designers, interpellated by contemporary capitalist ideology with its obsession with productivity and creativity as a source of individual fulfilment, joy, and status and prestige to be demonstrated through consumption, who pride themselves on being as good consumers as producers, typically fail to understand that this is not the only way a life worth living can be imagined. Through the same estrangement – by way of confronting us with the 'traditionalist perspective' – Weber could tell us something about the development and contingency of the work ethic and our irrational commitment to work that poses as the most rational thing to do (Weber 2005). These women clearly stand for the:

refusal of the ideology of work as highest calling and moral duty, a refusal of work as a necessary centre of social life and means of access to the rights and claims of citizenship, and a refusal of the necessity of capitalist control of production. It is a refusal, finally, of the asceticism of those ... who privilege work over all other pursuits.

WEEKS 2011: 99

Paul Lafargue provocatively blamed the workers and their passion for work for all the misery in the world rather than blaming the capitalist, 'all individual and society misery takes its origin in the passion of the proletariat for work' (Lafargue 1883: 8).

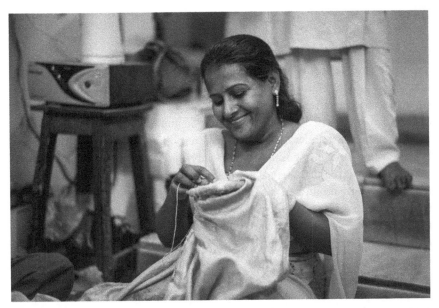

FIGURE 5.2 Woman embroidering and laughing during our interview about 'empowerment'

Image courtesy: Arash Taheri.

This idea powerfully resonates with the women's experiences with the 'miserable designers', and with experiences of those craftswomen who went from the village to the city, and who fell for the preaching of the capitalists about empowerment and a brighter future, as they said – those 'seduced by things'. While some embroiderers imagined that with more money they would have more time for leisure, of course the opposite turned out to be the case. Experiences like this only add to the reasons for the ironic subversive attitudes – they know quite well that they are not those meant to succeed even if they embrace the ideals. Observing the stressed designers, these women often relate this to their own stories of the effects of money. These stories are marked by an ambiguity of, on the one hand, the necessity to have some money and, on the other hand, of having too much, which can quickly flip into a bad thing marked by a sense of loss of life itself. Irfan, working for a series of wealthy designers, once acquired enough capital to start up a construction company and he closed down his printing workshop. This lasted only for about two years, he got into difficulties and some projects did not work out as planned, and he decided to go back to printing and re-opened the workshop. Irfan remembers the time when he had the most money as the worst years of his life, years filled with troubles and worries, sleepless nights; he even believes that he was meant to eventually go almost bankrupt and return to printing, since that was the only way to regain his 'peace of mind'. Such stories were a persistent trope, especially among the village craftswomen.

The curse of money

One of the embroiderers, after a lot of encouragement from a Delhi designer, decided to work really intensely; she stayed up to master new stitches and worked nine instead of four hours, as she used to. She chose to believe that with money she could buy independence, and she could move from the village or improve her life, as the designer promised. The other girls were laughing at her sitting up late, telling her in their fatalist manner that it won't make any difference. And indeed, once she began earning more, her husband who clearly has not embraced the ideology of self-making, realized that there is no need for him to work and so he left his jobs and began to laze around. In the end, she even took a loan from the designer to reconstruct the simple house they were living in; and so in the name of a better life she enslaved herself for at least fifteen years to the designer, whom she in addition calls a great patron; to her he is good and benevolent. She took on all the responsibility, pays her children's school fees and so on. What she achieved was the reversal of the traditional roles of the wife and husband, and she turned into a dedicated and indebted wage slave. Embracing the designer's discourse was the only way for her to cope with the situation, while trying to convince her husband to work. Other women, who came originally from villages but whose husbands began working in the city and who themselves moved into the city, mourned the times when they were in the village. Now they had to work six or even seven days a week from morning to evening, the only thing they felt they were good for was earning money that was barely enough to reproduce their bare life. 'Money snatched away my life from me', as one of them said. They only wanted to go back to life in the village, but now the situation changed, their relatives were keen on the money from the city and their living expenses were also much higher and so they felt trapped in the city. Men recounted similar stories. One of them used to be a *zardoz* in Lucknow but managed to take up driving and shifted with his wife and kids to Delhi and over the course of several years drove a taxi; his income increased considerably. And yet he cursed this money at every occasion. He knew that he was nothing if he did not have money in the city, so he kept taking up more shifts, working long nights, lacking sleep; also, he blamed money for all his troubles with his wife:

> The moment she saw I can earn, she became obsessed with it, she would argue about anything I wanted to send to my parents, she wanted it all for herself, now she stopped working too and only keeps roaming in the markets. First three years of our marriage were great, we did not have much money, and we had a simple home, but we had each other. When the money came it destroyed everything. I am ruined because of having money! I used to laugh at the designers and business people who used to come to my home to give me work, I saw how they were worried all the time. Now I am helpless too, I work night

and day and when I get home we fight about money. Now I am slave of money, without it I am nothing. When I used to be a *zardoz* I was poor, but life was easier, I would work at home, my kids were around and my wife too and we had good time. There were quarrels and local fights in village, but still we lived *aaraam se*.

Ironic attitudes derive as much from experiences of 'neo-liberal pollution', of which the dirt of the city and its notoriously stressed designers, are the most visible manifestation to the village women. The curse of money seems to be related to the positional treadmill thesis (Frank 2001): 'One has to walk faster (consume more conspicuous goods) to keep up with the treadmill (significant others in the community who consume conspicuous goods). This eventually leads to lower levels of subjective well-being, due to the inflation in costs.... The positional treadmill ... acts as a vicious circle' (Linssen et al. 2011: 69–70). Running after money and wealth was, according to the village women, symptomatic of the city and its people and was incompatible with life lived *aaraam se*. Money equated to tension, hurry, problems, jealousy and so on. They instead preferred leisure and 'freedom that can't fill the stomach' (Basole 2012), to borrow an expression from Basole's work on Indian informal economy and the Banarasi weavers. Their 'craft pride' came eventually more from the ironic knowledge of dependency of the designers on the women than from pride in their actual skill or national heritage.

Irony and unwilling slaves of capital

So, did some of the designers succeed in their efforts in the face of all this mocking, laughter and notorious disobedience? Did they manage to produce willing slaves of capital (Lordon 2014), did they manage to manufacture consent (Burawoy 1979)? Their efforts at co-optation and subtle coercion turned out to be effective in several cases, they managed to force some of the women to embrace the fundamentals of capitalism, even against their ironic language or maybe precisely because of it. While the designers are effectively interpellated by the discourse of self-realization, self-fulfilment, and personal growth that dominates the designer's world and try to impose this ideological vision onto the women, they realize that this does not really work in the village. In the workshops they have already come up with an effective strategy: divide and rule. The obsessive measuring of the productivity and quality of each woman is there for a reason – to produce an incentive to compete, an incentive capable of producing jealousy and rivalry among the women, thus diverting their attention from the designer, whose words become true – 'if you work harder, you will be rewarded'. The women are thus presented with an illusion of choice within the highly restrictive environment of the workshop (Burawoy 1979) and are made to believe, in line with the training in meritocracy that they receive, that their destiny is in their hands – even if they try to resist and mock this thinking, it nonetheless becomes effective in practice.

Even in the villages, the designers succeeded in co-opting at least some women. Whenever I visited a village with Preity, she would point me towards the woman that would at least 'pretend' to share the designer's worldview, one who was loyal and could exploit the discourse to her benefit. Often this would be the supervisor of one of the centres, earning two or three hundred more in a month than other women, and often already coming from either higher caste or a wealthier family than the other women. She would be introduced to me because she and her house were more presentable, featuring better furniture and TV, and because she embodied the designer's success in co-opting the women into the workforce also on the ideological level. These women knew the boundaries between the speakable and the unspeakable and functioned as an extension of the designer in the village. Due to their proximity to other village women whom they were supposed to manage on behalf of the designer, they were in an ambiguous position – they were feared, since they tended to be bossy, they knew that if they did not deliver, it would be them bearing the consequences and getting scolded and so they had a tendency to demand obedience and oppress the other women only to protect themselves; they were despised, mocked but also appeased. Mocked precisely because, as one of the girls working under such a supervisor pointed out, 'they are just acting, it is just theatre for the designer' – and yet there was profit inherent in these women's ironic reproduction of the discourse, profit inherent in the implicit mockery. Indeed, with these women 'in between', it was always hard to tell if they mocked the designer by repeating and invoking the keywords of the designspeak, if they only acted as if, or if they really believed. Some women really learned how to use the craftspeak to their benefit; oftentimes they would play on these sentiments in order to squeeze a little extra cash from the designer (Boyer and Yurchak 2010). But the moment the designer leaves, they laugh at his naivety, making fun of how they managed to trick and fool him. Such acts fall into the parodic genre, akin to the one identified by Yurchak in the late socialist Russia (Yurchak 2006), an irony based on overidentification, mimicry and performative imitation that involves 'such precise mimicry of the object of one's irony that it is often impossible to tell whether this is a form of sincere support or subtle ridicule' (Boyer and Yurchak 2010: 185). Even if such acts of staged parodic overidentification were possibly the most provoking to the designers, who seemed never sure if the women really understand or just made fun of them, at the same time it was precisely these women who would accomplish in the village what the designers could not do themselves. Thus even against their parodic attitude, they functioned as the most effective extension of the designer. As a reward, they acquired a privileged position – it was enough to give power and prestige to one in order to enforce control over the rest. According to Preity, such a woman became truly empowered, because of her hard work of managing and controlling, she would even, unlike the other women who rarely left the village, travel to the city with the orders. By appropriating the authoritative craftspeak and the discourse of work ethics, even if mockingly, such women managed to acquire a position of power and dominance in the local society, and yet, as one of them pointed out, it was not necessarily a happy existence – 'now my life is hassle, full of worries, now I travel all the time, now I have to play the game'. Now she was on the treadmill from which it became impossible to get off. She, too, took up a loan from the designer, which increased her sense of being trapped in this cycle forever.

Dependency and benevolence

Here we must emphasize the crucial difference in the conceptions of dependency among the designers and the embroiderers. Designers, NGOs like SEWA, and even middle-class traders operate with the liberal-individualist post-industrial notion of dependency that imagines dependency as deviant, stemming from individual incompetence or laziness (Fraser and Gordon 1994), and paint the dependency, understood as subordination, of the embroiderers on their male family members as unacceptable; at the same time they present wage labour as emancipatory, as the only path to true independence and liberation, especially for these women. The women on the other hand seem to have a bigger problem with the dependency that wage labour creates than with their economic and social subordination to their male family members. Wage does not make them independent, and in that situation it becomes reasonable to let the men work for them. Not to mention that individual independence does not hold the same seductive appeal as it does for the middle classes and the elites. While the designers get enraged about the position of these women, about the *noneconomic* hierarchy and inequality, the embroiderers get enraged about *economic* hierarchy and inequality, and the dependency, rather than independency that wage labour creates. The self-proclaimed benevolence of the designers, their willingness to help out financially when they could and so on, that peculiar combination of charitable donations through their NGOs and personal loans that would typically cut the wage of the woman to at times a mere 25 per cent of the original wage, only increases the fear of dependency among the women. These turned out to be the less subtle strategies of coercion as opposed to preaching and convincing. Benevolent coercion, a form of (structural) violence, is indeed nothing unfamiliar to India. Benevolence, understood as a virtue, was propagated by the Scottish philosophers, from David Hume to Adam Smith, and the British Empire saw very clearly its own endeavour as profoundly benevolent, claiming that colonization was good for the colonized, benefiting them culturally, economically, while civilizing them. The legitimacy of the Empire was among other things imagined to lie precisely in its 'benevolence'. Benevolence, directly linked to paternalism, was therefore one of the techniques of the Empire which subordinated indigenous people and their culture. Some would argue that these practices could be understood as a legacy of imperial benevolence (Gilbert and Tiffin 2008). The contemporary logic of benevolence, a combination of patron–client relations, 'ethical business practices' and philanthrocapitalism, has to be read in a similar way, as it is used to the same effect – namely subordination. Acts of benevolence are problematic because far too often they mediate economic self-interest under the label of public responsibility, while putting the beneficiary of the benefactor into a position of submission – often by providing help nobody asked for in the first place. At the same time, the notion of benevolence, as a discourse of power, is also related to ideologies of patronage and the positive value of patronage of crafts and arts by former royal elites. Designers, who either come from semi-royal families or like to imagine themselves as such, are all too keen to act like patrons in the name of preservation of heritage and crafts and in order to sell the experience of patronage to their clients. The opulently embroidered dresses for sale embody the power over labour power, the power that forces the artisans into dependency on wages, the power over their lives, the same power that insists on empowering them by subsuming them into the easily manageable 'organized' labour force that does not question nor resist.

We have seen throughout this exposition that 'irony arises in practice and excites the moral imagination by its identification of a gap, contradiction, inconsistency or incongruity' (Fernandez and Huber 2001: 262–263), here an incongruity between the talk of the designers about empowerment and value of nation and tradition and so on, and the realities on the ground. Mocking and irony can thus be understood not only as acts of insubordination but also as ways of retaining meaningfulness of the village women's daily lives. Keeping an ironic relationship to the designers is a viable strategy that keeps the two worlds at a safe distance from each other, while confirming the validity of one's own value systems. Joking relations have been studied by anthropologists before (Mann and Spradley 1975; Radcliffe-Brown 1961; Douglas 1968). Some claim that the function of jokes is to symbolically attack established order without subverting it (Yoshida 2001), to challenge a dominant structure and belittle it (Douglas 1968) or to in fact establish and maintain social equilibrium and order (Radcliffe-Brown 1961), while at the same time keeping too much of order at bay (Radcliffe-Brown 1961; Willerslev and Pedersen 2011). In light of the ethnography above, there seems to be some truth to all of these views. The irony reverses the visible and the invisible; it replaces the possible with the impossible, inverts the way we tend to think about power relations and says the unspeakable; it reveals the dependence of the designers and of the imagined nation on the artisans, who are expelled beyond the internal boundaries of 'society'; excluded from the visions of economic superpowerdom, while at the same time embroidering the attires of the new business leaders of the nation. The village embroiderers show that 'by laughing at power, we expose its contingency, we realize that what appeared to be fixed and oppressive is in fact emperor's new clothes, and just the sort of thing that should be mocked and ridiculed' (Critchley 2002: 11).

Desai observes that 'much of Indian humour is rooted in what Herbert Spencer termed "descending incongruities" – that is humour extracted out of incongruous situations that underlined one's superiority over the type of person who was being made fun of' (Desai 2010: 244). This humour is based on emphasizing the differences between different groups of people as much as between their sources of value and significance to which they attach meaning. The designers laugh at the craftswomen and their approach to life as much as the craftswomen laugh at the designers. They laugh at each other; laughing with each other remains an impossibility. Laughter seems to have both a humanizing and dehumanizing function – laughing at dehumanizes the object of laughter, while laughing with humanizes those who laugh together. The lack of laughter *with* is a sign of a relation of inequality. I was advised by the designers not to 'get close' to the craftswomen and not to laugh with them, as they would eventually 'exploit' me, or so I was told. Laughing with was out of question.

Conclusion

Throughout this chapter we have seen how the female embroiderers resist the rhetoric of the designers infused with pompous notions such as nation, heritage and tradition, and how they mock the designers' attempts at helping them; attempts that systematically position them as vulnerable and powerless. Instead, they show the designers their power, they show them that they do not need them in order to survive. In that way, they are the privileged ones, they are sovereign; they show the designers that it is they who are dependent – without their labour, without timely deliveries, without quality embroidery, they are nothing. In such a scenario, it is no wonder that the charitable organizations set up by the designers often attempt to relocate the labour force from the villages into the city; this means away from the land they own or use, the land that gives them leverage and the ability to say no to having to subject themselves in a factory-like environment. More than so-called 'fair salaries' and a clean working environment, the women, as we have seen, value their leisure time, being with family, friends, roaming around; there is a virtue in laziness rather than in obsessive productivity (especially for others). Wage work is not necessarily seen as empowering; to the contrary, it can be a curse that makes life miserable. But 'poor women' have been turned into a global development project run by the elites and the middle classes. Not only does this project help sell clothes labelled 'ethical' to consumers who have a bad conscience about being complicit in the exploitative capitalist system, or to those who like to visibly demonstrate their moral superiority, but it is also instrumental in reproducing the relations of inequality and, as we shall see in the next chapter, when employed just right – in empowering elite women. As it turns out, carving a space for themselves in the business world or public life, while being good and moral wives, is problematic for the elite women. In order to be both moral and to be able to cultivate their erotic capital, the women displace their morality from their bodies onto an external social cause. As such, they often speak on behalf of the poor, and especially the 'vulnerable' women and create various initiatives in their name. The charitable cause of the poor and vulnerable woman, as we shall see, becomes indispensable to the empowerment of the elite wife and her emancipation from the domestic sphere.

6 EROTIC CAPITAL AND BENEVOLENCE OF VAMPISH GODDESSES

In autumn 2012, an Indian pharmaceutical company released a controversial product called 18 Again, a tightening vaginal gel, 'the new name in women empowerment', as the commercial proudly proclaimed. Not only did the product promise a tighter and cleaner vagina, but also women's rise to social power. The ad featured a plump housewife in a *sari*, dancing joyfully with her husband while singing 'I feel like a virgin'. With a retail price of 2,430Rs per package (and 9,400Rs if purchased online from outside of India), we are talking elite vaginas. Empowerment of the elite woman was meant to happen through her alluring rejuvenated virginal vagina providing her with regained arresting power over men. Connecting sexuality and empowerment, the product's marketing hit a soft spot. 18 Again tapped directly into the anxieties and dilemmas of the married elite urban women of South Delhi, the most devoted clientele of their fashion gurus. Like the vaginal gel, designers too promise to transform and empower women. They promise that their garments will deliver sexual and social power and that the garments will do all the work for them, even act on their behalf. Hence, the women won't have to translate their imagination into daily acts of laborious doing, but can keep the imaginary while delegating the labour onto the material object. In line with the meritocratic ideology, they feed these women narratives of happy self-creation, reinvention, self-innovation, and self-optimization. It helps that most elite women are avid readers of self-help books, India being one of the largest markets in the world for such publications (Figure 6.1).

Everywhere we look these days, commodities are presented to us as solutions to our pressing problems, to our manufactured problems, to our weaknesses, and so on, but are they effective? Investments in acquiring sexual power and allure through latest gadgets, gels and clothes run high as movies, magazines, TV shows, and fashion ramps overflow with images of women who made it because of their erotic

FIGURE 6.1 A model dressed as a virginal beauty at the India Couture Week 2014, design by Varun Bahl

Image courtesy: Nitin Patel Photography.

capital. Catherine Hakim has in her controversial book *Honey Money: The Power of Erotic Capital* (Hakim 2010) argued that investing in cultivating one's erotic capital can be truly empowering and should be used to get ahead in life, the way any other form of capital is used. But while Bollywood overflows with successful beauties that made it due to their carefully cultivated erotic capital, real-life scenarios are far trickier. One of the most obvious reasons for this is the persistent and omnipresent pressure on female morality. Ask any woman or designer and they will tell you that Bollywood fashions have to be 'adjusted' from the 'reel' to the real life – meaning, they need to be re-moralized. And yet, the lowly, the vulgar and the dirty associated with the ambiguous figure of the actress, at once celebrated and scorned, needs to be carefully preserved in the elevated designer version for the elite married client. Hence, intense social pressures on the aesthetics and appearance of female morality complicate any straightforward attempts at empowerment through erotic capital alone. Both morality and sexuality have to be dealt with; for the elite woman this is a balancing act in which fashion plays a crucial role, not least because of its perceived ability to act on behalf of the wearer.

'I like cheap': the allure of the low and the vulgar

Once when shopping with Amrita, a housewife in her mid-thirties, at *DLF Promenade* mall in Vasant Kunj in South West Delhi, it struck me to what degree most stories of post-marital relations, the stuff of the most juicy conversations with designers, revolve around balancing sex appeal and morality (Figure 6.2). The aesthetics of opulent Indianness, so essential to contemporary elitist fashion, often equals displays of women's morality. Even Amrita is always traditionally yet stylishly dressed and has an aura of respectability around her. Probably for that reason I almost spilled my coffee when she suggested we go find some übersexy underwear since her husband needs proper visual stimulation. A long discussion followed and it turned out that the initial source of inspiration for her underwear experiments was the movie *Kabhi Alvida Na Kehna* (Johar 2006), a love drama about two couples stuck in far from ideal marriages, leading up to an extramarital affair between Dev (Shah Rukh Khan) and Maya (Rani Mukherjee). Prior to the film's release, Amrita has never given much thought to her underwear, considering it largely functional. However, the following scene that legitimately brings sexy underwear into the realm of married respectability triggered a shift in her mind. Trying to fix their respective marriages, Dev and Maya become friends sharing tips on reigniting marital passion:

> Dev: You are that teacher type, boring with no personality. You are compulsive cleaner to the point of illness. Basically, you are a loyal maidservant. You

don't have anything womanly in you. You are not sexy, not from any angle . . .
maybe from behind . . . but no man can get excited looking at you.

(Later on Dev takes Maya into a sex store showing her a mannequin in sexy
underwear):

Dev: You need to wear clothes like these for your husband.

Maya: No Dev, if I wear clothes like that type of woman . . .

Dev: Yeah. That's the type men like.

Maya: Dev, but that looks cheap.

Dev: Yeah. Cheap, cheap is nice, I like cheap Maya! If you want to be sexy then
ask me . . . I'm the man!

Amrita noted the point: if you want to have a working marriage, at times you have to
transform yourself into a seductress, masquerade as a hooker and work that sex
appeal. By imitating and appropriating the frivolous attitude of the vamp, domina or
prostitute, Amrita also attempted to challenge the patriarchy's subjugation of female

FIGURE 6.2 The author posing in a wedding *ghagra choli*, wedding attire popular
among the Muslim population, during a fashion shoot for Novelty in Lucknow

Image courtesy: Lill-Ann Chepstow-Lusty.

sexuality. It would be easy to argue, from the classical feminist standpoint, that she merely fell into another patriarchal trap, namely sexual objectification, or self-objectification. But that would not only be too easy, it would also not stand on empirical nor experiential grounds. We need to be wary of the notorious feminist claims about objectification's inherent evils (Frederickson and Roberts 1997), about its moral deplorability. Such claims presuppose an essentially good authentic self that is corrupted by the suspect interests of the Other, the Other, whose badness resides in its externality to those good interior selves. Instead, we need to insist that being good or bad is not inherent to the processes of objectification as such. Rather, the question is, where does the actual once-occurrent objectification push us, or where does it push the objectified and his/her cause? The direction can then prove itself detrimental or favourable to a given cause, but the question is not the moral value of objectification as such, as some feminists would like us to believe. While Amrita was content to turn into the bad girl at home alone with her husband, but remain the good moral girl in the public space, playing the madonna–whore along the public–private distinction, other women demanded more from erotic capital; they wanted power in the public space, too. They did not only want to reclaim individuality, challenge social norms, satisfy their desires, but also to change their position vis-à-vis men in society at large. Like in Katrina Kaif's item number Chikni Chameli in *Agneepath* (Malhotra 2012), where she as the only dancing girl on scene seduces hundreds of men, they too wanted to fly on a chandelier over their heads in a mark of erotic conquest. And they were determined to use the techniques of the low and the vulgar to acquire that power. Since moral virtue is in India traditionally bound to control and suppression of female sexuality (Saavala 2012; Donner 2008), dangers of failure to strike the right balance between sexual power and morality always lurk behind, even among the elites that are in other matters less pedantic and more prone to engage in obscene language and acts, precisely in order to distance themselves from the 'tight-ass' middle classes. Yet, in matters of women, of their sexuality and morality, the attitudes are largely comparable to those of the middle-classes.

Fashion designers present themselves as a solution to this problem of balancing morality and sexuality. They do so largely by aesthetically elaborating on the cultural tropes of (1) sexually liberated courtesans and movie vamps, and (2) of benevolent goddesses. They cater to women who do not aspire to be 'domestic goddesses', even if they are systematically being pushed into such a position (Donner 2008), but want to be public goddesses, recognized and influential socialites in their own right. While in some business elite families, the role of the woman as a socialite is encouraged or at least accepted, most women struggle to achieve such a role, often having to fight both the wishes of the mother-in-law, of their husbands and larger family. Let us first explore the ways in which the tropes of the courtesan and the vamp, or item girl, are used, only to look at the role of ethical fashion and charity as effective strategies of displacing morality from the female body to an external social or ecological cause.

Erotic capital: the power of courtesans and vamps

In India, a married woman's power is imagined to reside largely in her sexual purity, while sex is reduced to its reproductive function and robbed of pleasure, at least for women, who are not only meant not to enjoy it but also to supress any signs of their desire. Even in 18 Again, we see a paradoxical play with regained semi-virginity (morality) meant to reignite the passion of the husband, where the woman's happiness is supposed to derive from the renewed tightness and the pleasure that it can offer to her husband. In such a scenario, reclaiming feminine sexual desire and with it sexualized gaze as legitimate for any woman becomes the core of the struggle between the sexes, at least for the elite woman often relieved from other social problems by virtue of access to almost unlimited financial capital. Things do not seem to have changed all that much since Vibhavari Shirurkar's book *Kalyanche Nishwas* (The Sigh of Buds), published in 1933 in Marathi, which was deemed obscene and scandalous as the author sought to assert women's sexual desire and counter the image of the passive and indifferent woman (Banerji 2008; Das 1991). The same struggle continues today, a struggle no less against the shadow cast by the obsessively celibate Gandhi 'over the Indian psyche', the man who turned his philosophy of nonviolence and asexuality into a 'dictum of modern India's uneasy and confounded outlook on sex' (Banerji 2008: 278). Even though the tendency is to imagine the contemporary elite Indian woman as more sexually open, as she in 2012 enjoyed the Hindi adaptation of Eve Ensler's *The Vagina Monologues* (Ensler 2000), or eagerly defended *Fifty Shades of Grey* (James 2013), reading it as a manual for handling her burnt out, or never ignited, marriage, the reality is still very much driven by duties and obligations. Even her main role is to 'continue the family line and enable it to perform life-cycle ceremonies' (Srinivasan 2006: 165) upon which the *dharma* of the family depends. As Henrike Donner points out, marriage in India, and even more so among the wealthy, is 'still . . . very much defined in terms of collective interests which subordinate individual women's and often men's desires to the socially constructed interests of the family' (Donner 2008: 72), and too often to the business interests of the respective families. The elite weddings have in recent years shifted from luxury locations in India to hotels and villas in Singapore, Thailand, Indonesia, the Gulf and even Russia. Tax-free shopping may play a role, but the main reason is the ability of the families to control who attends the wedding (business) party. In India, thousands would attend an elite wedding, but abroad the numbers are in hundreds. Shifting the location translates into policing the elite boundaries and making sure that only guests with real credentials attend the event, that is guests with whom the families can strike business deals that will not only pay back the wedding's costs within few months, but also establish valuable future alliances. The couple might be in a spotlight and on the ramp, but in reality, it is only part of the theatrical stage set, like a band playing ambient music in a bar, where frontstage and backstage are reversed. Even after marriage, the couple is subordinated to the pressures of the larger family and does not exist as an independent unit; hence even sex is far too often turned into a daily chore aimed at producing preferably male offspring. Elite men often tend to unabashedly engage in sexual affairs outside marriage, claiming that sex at home is a matter of duty (and of *dharma*), not of pleasure, and therefore cannot be enjoyable. Thus, wives tend to be from the outset perceived as sexually undesirable. As in films, so in reality, sexual desire and sexual purity still tend to be bifurcated into the distinction between the devoted wife and a courtesan, item girl, or the cinematic vamp and these are not meant to mix. Moreover, having a mistress is often a strategic act aimed at increasing the man's machismo and status within the circle of men to which he belongs. Hence, the existence of the mistress is to be flaunted rather than to be kept secret and wives are typically encouraged to act as if they do not know. When arguments arise, husbands can go as far as to claim that since having a mistress means increased respect, status and trust among their male peer-group, it also often translates into financial benefits, something that the wife enjoys. In this scenario, being sexually desirable to their husbands and suffusing their gaze with desire rather than duty, is often an important concern for elite women.

Meanwhile, designers love to create for shopping queens with a grand lack, as it allows them to easily present themselves as *gurus* in possession of the magical remedy. Recently, however, this job has become difficult. While in the 1990s, as we saw earlier, it would be enough for the designer to simply strip the woman down a bit and claim to liberate her by undressing (see Chapter 1), the current aesthetic and ideological climate, mirroring the rise of Hindu nationalism and traditionalism, poses a challenge. Namely, how can the designer now insert the power of the vulgar into the image of the opulent, princess-like and benevolent 'Mother India' rocking the ramp? No matter how lavish, this return to the aesthetics of what is imagined or reinvented as traditional morality (Hobsbawm and Ranger 2003) poses a renewed threat to any emancipatory claims to feminine erotic capital raised by the elite women; that is, if they are to be formulated through explicit aesthetics. It is here that the proposed solution of the fashion designers lies. Employing homeopathic or imitative magic, based on the principle of the like producing like (Frazer 2009), the designers advise women to forget regaining virginal tightness through potions, and instead encourage them to imitate the vamps, the courtesans, the mistresses and thus acquire their sexual allure and power by the sheer force of resemblance. Only in such a way, they claim, will the women be able to break with the persistent idea of married sex as a 'mundane chore to be dealt with' (Banerji 2008: 288). Costumes are capable of transforming the actress into her role, present her as the most viable solution. And if imitative magic is not enough, there is always the magical law of contact or contagion (Frazer 2009) which explains the recent popularity of 'antique' embroideries, often between 50 and 90 years old, stitched onto new fabrics and garments. Seen from the perspective of the purity and pollution dichotomy that still governs most of the daily lives in India, these once worn embroideries would be considered polluting and would thus travel down the hierarchy, and yet, here we see that the designers managed to transform them into magical patches. These cut out and stitched on embroidered insignia determine not only the material value of the garment, but are primarily meant to confer power or even erotic capital onto the wearer. Raghavendra repeatedly tried to convince his clients that the given 'antique' simply 'must have been part of lavish wardrobe of a former courtesan; it comes from Lucknow, who else would possess such an elaborate *zardozi* piece!' Hence, the erotic capital of the long-dead past owner contained in the ornament was to infect the new owner with sex appeal. Designers, much like most branding experts, are certainly skilled at combining the homeopathic magic (law of similarity) with contagious magic (law of contact) that, as we know, comprises sympathetic magic (law of sympathy) as identified by James G. Frazer (Frazer 2009) – even in matters of female empowerment, both in private and in public.

While stitching on magical embroidered ornaments and turning to imitation of courtesans' glamour and vampish attitude might feel as an empowering tactics when it comes to sexual liberation, it is not able to address the pressing problem of balancing feminine morality. In another act of imitative magic, designers take here the clue from Bollywood heroins that some of them even design for. On screen, the heroin of the last decade is said to successfully intoxicate the audiences with her moral virtue in equal proportion to her sizzling curves (Qureshi 2011, Babb and Wadley 1998, Dwyer 2000). This is the shared goal of elite women and their designers. And yet, even though the reel heroine is often posited as an example of a victorious merger of morality and sexuality, while the immoral vamp is proclaimed dead as is the asexual moral heroine (Duara 2005), recent movie productions show that claims celebrating the transgression of the dichotomy are premature. The blockbuster *Cocktail* (Adajania 2012) is a case in point. It is a story of three characters set in London; Gautam (Saif Ali Khan), a software engineer and a notorious flirt and womanizer, Veronica (Deepika Padukone) a rich, fearless, free, party girl, always dressed in skimpy clothes and drowning her troubled upbringing in alcohol and men, and Meera (Diana Penty) an introverted, traditional, shy girl with her body always covered appropriately, who ended up in London as a result of a hoax marriage. Veronica accidently meets Meera and upon seeing her crying in the toilets with her luggage, she offers to let her stay at her house. Though an unlikely match, eventually the two become friends. Then Gautam appears in their lives. Veronica starts dating Gautam and he moves into the same flat with the girls. One day, his mother arrives and in panic he pretends that it is Meera with whom he is in a relationship, knowing that compared with the unmannered Veronica, Meera is the ideal Indian girl that every Indian mother would love as a daughter-in-law. When the trio go on holiday to Cape Town together with the mother,

Gautam and Meera fall in love. All the while, Veronica, also in love with Gautam, tries hard to change her 'modern' personality by dressing in Indian suits, appropriating the demure mannerism and masquerading as the ideal Indian woman Gautam's mother wants. Upon seeing this, Meera sacrifices her love and moves away from the two. But even though Gautam stays with Veronica, he is changed, no longer the flirt he used to be. Veronica sees that he is in love with Meera and realizes that she cannot step in between them and decides to travel with Gautam to India, where he proposes to Meera. Veronica, the 'modern' Indian girl, this vamp-like creature, turns out to be good for entertainment and sex, and for initiating the unmarried men into the secrets of pleasure like the courtesans of bygone eras, but when it comes to love, Veronica is not considered worthy. It is the virginal and traditional Meera, who enchants the notorious flirt and makes him fall in true love. While Gautam's sexual history is forgotten, or makes him even more attractive, Veronica's sexual history prevents her from ever finding true love. It is also this disequilibrium that the elite women aim at correcting by reclaiming their sexual desire. While men's affairs can be prestige-enhancing, women's affairs lower the chances of a good match in the marriage market or can outright result in honour killings. The movie also teaches us that love and sex in India are meant to begin for women first with the wedding rite of passage in which 'sexual innocence is ritually transformed into a state of sexuality' (Werbner 1986: 233) – therefore stories of desire, passion and love, are post-marital stories (Puri 1999; Sandhya 2009; Uberoi 2010) rather than pre-marital stories – as is also the case in our investigation. Furthermore, the movie reiterates the boundary between *vamps* and *pativratas* or devoted wives, a boundary that has been yet again redrawn during the recent discussions surrounding the protests spurred by the infamous gang rape and death of the victim in December 2012 in New Delhi, when the chief of RSS (*Rasthriya Swayamsevak Sangh*), Mohan Bhagwat pronounced that such crimes happen only in urban India and not in the rural India, not in the pure *Bharat*, and that only 'where "Bharat" becomes "India" with the influence of Western culture, these incidents happen. The actual Indian values and culture should be established at every stratum of society where women are treated as "mother"', as reported by *The Economic Times* (4 January 2013). Even though condemned by many, Bhagwat still enjoys a large number of supporters. In Bhagwat's world, Veronica would stand for India, while Meera for *Bharat*. Across India, these dichotomies are being played out in many avatars (Nielsen and Waldrop 2014), but what interests us here are their consequences for the lives of elite women trying to transgress them, those who feel the need to masquerade as Veronicas in order to acquire love and passion from their husbands, or in order to gain a place in the male-dominated public realm, but are haunted by the problem of displays of morality.

It is likely that in this struggle, clothes can be equally the woman's best friend as much as her greatest foe, since it is in clothes where matters of aesthetics merge with erotics and concerns for morality. The ultimate question asked from the clothes is: what can this particular garment do for me in terms of aesthetics, erotics and morals? Or else: what act, belief, or virtue (or lack thereof) can I effectively delegate onto the garment? While clothes can certainly help make certain things possible, their power is largely overestimated, no less due to the designers' effective propaganda. The amount of hope for the future Self projected onto them is at times truly remarkable. The following case of Sushmita cuts to the core of the problem of balancing erotic power, sexual desire and morality, a problem that runs as a persistent trope through the narratives of designer elite clientele.

Sushmita arrives to meet me again at Café Oz in Khan Market, the costliest Delhi market. She makes an entrée in her signature miniskirt, high heels, heavily embroidered top and massive jewellery with traditional embellishments; perfect attire for the self-proclaimed career oriented individualist and hedonist. She has been divorced now for three years and lives with her eleven-year-old son in her brother's house in South Delhi. Coming from an upper-class Hindu business family based in Delhi, her marriage was arranged before she could even finish her college degree. Like many other such marriages, it was a match of two wealthy families, a financial transaction. That afternoon in the coffee house she recounted her story of her sexual and fashionable liberation. Being a housewife and a daughter-in-law was a 'hell on Earth' for her; she was 'stuck' with a husband that neither loved her nor desired her. She felt like a servant:

> The only difference was that he could use me for sex too. Even sex became one of my chores, he just commanded me to do it and he was so passive, lying there waiting to be satisfied, he never cared for what I desired. I was a wife to him and wives are not meant to be sexy and desirable, they are there to cook, take care of household and servants and to produce baby boys.
>
> Interview, October 2010

This started her self-proclaimed obsession with attempts at seducing her husband. She spent days shopping for sexy *saris*, underwear and jewellery in hope that they would turn her first into an object of his desire and then of his love. A bunch of her designer friends assisted her in this mission, convincing her that their clothes would do the work for her, that in them she would be whoever she imagined herself to be and that all her dreams could come true, only if she trusted in the power of their dresses. But then, one day she realized it was not going to work:

> Once I bought a red *sari*, a see-through one, with red and golden embroidery. I had a blouse done to match it; more like a bikini bra in fact, very filmi. I wanted to be seductive like the vamp. All men are so crazy for these women. I put it on when we were alone and I came to him. I wanted to show him that I can be sexy

and I started dancing. He got mad, shouted and hit me. He said I am his wife and I should better dress like one and not like a cheap slut.

Later Sushmita found out that he was cheating with several women, which led to their divorce. Today she is enjoying a 'free life' as she calls it, believing that 'there is more to life than these crazy restrictions'. She points out that still she cannot tell her family that she is going to 'Goa with a group of friends just to have fun and sex. But at least I can do it'. Sushmita's experiments with masquerading as the imagined seductive Other turned her 'self, sexuality, and private life into crucial sites for the formation and expression of identity' (Illouz 2007: 44). She tried to reclaim her individuality and the desires suppressed by society by masquerading as 'the other woman', by taking on the clothes and attributes of the vamp. In the end, through masquerading as the other woman, in both imagination and dress, she found out what her life was worth living for. Resorting to the means of the vamp also meant breaking her marriage.

Stories like this seem eternal, even the devoted goddess Parvati is said to have bedtricked Shiva, her husband, on numerous occasions, disguising as 'a seductive foreign woman, a woman of low class, or an Outcaste woman' (Doniger 2000: 17). The low and dirty becomes yet again desirable, a 'dirty sacred' (Pfaller 2008) capable of transforming the dangerous and the polluting into something sacred and sublime, bringing the otherwise dirty sexuality into the realm of the sacred. Through her red *sari*, Sushmita wished not only to 'extend who she was through imagination of someone whose existence was her own creation' (Doniger 2000: 14), but also to bring the dirty into the realm of the sacred, even when the trick did not work with the husband. As Wendy Doniger says, 'when the wife wishes to masquerade as her husband's mistress (or, rarely, the mistress as the wife), she wants to be with one man, but to be a different woman to that man' (Doniger 2000: 13). And this is the crucial struggle here. The social system defined Sushmita as a wife, a mother and a loyal caretaker, whose sexuality needs to be suppressed and controlled. She desired to transgress this role by exploiting the transformative powers of garments, which she imagined would unsettle her structural position, as her designer friends suggested, thus allowing for a more desirable role. Indeed, the dichotomy between dutiful wife and object of sexual desire, ingrained in the Indian cultural codes, has proven to be stronger, manifesting itself in the violent reaction of her husband, who made it clear that these two roles should not mix. Georges Bataille has long ago put words on this more general dynamics, when saying that 'a wife is mainly the woman who bears children and works at home: this is the form in which she is objectified in the manner of a brick or a piece of furniture'. Curiously, he also notes that 'experience has shown us, unambiguously, that when they mean to seduce, respectable women tend to resort to the embellishments of the harlot' (Bataille 1993: 140). Even Sigmund Freud observed that 'a virtuous and reputable woman never possesses the charm required to exalt her to an object of love; this attraction is exercised only by one who is more or less sexually discredited, whose fidelity and loyalty admit of doubt' (Freud et al. 1959: 194).

Female sexuality is dangerous for other reasons as well. If women and their desires had a say in the business of Indian marriage and 'if lovers started pairing up by choice, and women started taking the initiative of deciding who they wanted to have sex with, and whether with or without marriage, it would put the patriarchy's very existence into jeopardy' (Banerji 2008: 305). Normalization of unrestrained and uncontrolled female sexuality would destabilize patriarchy at large. Even individually, men who are considered too infatuated with their wives might lose loyalty to their parents and kin and break out of the joint family, settling down somewhere else, alone with the wife (Uberoi 2010). Also for this reason, mothers-in-law often put daughters-in-law under constant surveillance. Fearing female sexuality is nothing new to Indian men. Already the Vedic man, in the early Indus Valley Civilization, is said to have feared women, whom he imagined as singularly hungry for semen; even their obsession with gold jewellery (representation of semen) was a sign of their greed, these men too viewed the vagina 'with suspicion as dangerous place to pass through' (Banerji 2008: 49). The fear seems to be still with Indian men; only the spectacular fertility rituals and state-owned brothels are gone. And so, as Caplan points out, good females are 'those who are controlled by males. Benevolent goddesses, for example, are those who are properly married and have transferred the control of their sexuality to their husbands. Women who control their own sexuality are seen as highly dangerous, representing both fertility and death, malevolence as well as benevolence' (Caplan 1987: 280–281).

In this sense, the current fashions of theatrical and proud traditionalism can also be understood in terms of the fears of patriarchy triggered by the increasing independence of Indian women and their visibility in the public sphere. When catering to their clients, the designers are trapped in a dilemma partly of their own making – they need to overcome the very fashions that they create. Being the problem and the solution at the same time is the core of the twisted logic of the market. It is therefore no wonder that fashion has always been both part of pushing boundaries and instrumental in conserving them. Maybe that is also why the Indian courtesans, as powerful historical and mythological figures, inspire designers to such an extent. Even private parties increasingly feature staged *mujras*, and so even when Hindu nationalism rules politics and convictions, the Mughal aesthetics of erotics is trending and the seductive Urdu poetry is experiencing a revival, both in everyday life and in pop culture. It seems that the elite, predominantly Hindu, needs the high culture of those it perceives as the 'low Others', the sexualized virile Muslims and prostitutes, in order to claim their power. In the Hindi cinema, too, the often Mughal-inspired courtesan and not necessarily the heroine, 'is the essence of female eroticism' (Dwyer 2006: 118) and as such both desirable and threatening. It is not a coincidence that many item songs have a touch of Islamic culture, either in lyrics, characters, or in the form of *mujra*, even when otherwise the characters are portrayed as Hindus. In the item song *Asalaam-e-Ishqum* ('Salutation of Love') of the blockbuster *Gunday* [Outlaws] (Zafar 2014), the explicitly erotic content is immediately linked to Islamic symbolism, wording, hand gestures and dress. These hand gestures and seductive movements as seen on the screen are imitated by Indian women across social divides, only the elite tend to spice them up with designer robes, exclusive whisky and slim cigarettes. While on the one hand a lot of effort in women's lives is meant to go into controlling their sexuality which is presumed to just be there waiting to spell disaster for men if not suppressed, simply uncovering does not let this mysterious sexuality out, as the men fear. After all, even *mujra* performers can be covered from head to toe in layers of fabrics and jewellery and yet cast their erotic spells. And so, rather paradoxically, revealing sexual power and cultivating erotic capital turns out to be hard work, maybe even harder than hiding that same mysterious power. Again, it is about striking the right balance between what is considered at a given time and space proper and moral and what is considered dirty and immoral. Courtesans have been particularly skilled at appropriating the characteristics of the lady (Gundle 2009), the exact opposite of what elite women are attempting to do.

The fashion industry is a testimony to the power of this merger. Already Rohit Khosla took inspiration in the Mughal aesthetics in his Spring/Summer collection from 1988, quite tellingly called *Purity & Sin*. Muzaffar Ali has brought the famous Lucknow courtesan, *Umrao Jaan* (Ali 1981), on screen in all her seductive glory. From Ritu Kumar, via Abu and Sandeep to Tarun Tahiliani, all have at one point or another played with the idea of the courtesan. Anand Kabra has presented at the Wills India Lifestyle Fashion Week Spring–Summer 2013 a collection based on the seventeenth century love story of Taramati, a forgotten beautiful courtesan, and the sultan Abdullah Qutub Shah, the seventh sultan of Golconda. JJ Valaya has in his collection for the Wills Lifestyle Fashion Week 2010 narrated a story of a fictitious courtesan Alika and her quest for love and great life. At the Lakmé Fashion Week Winter/Festive 2011, Payal Singhal presented a collection, which intended to be an amalgamation of Umrao Jaan, the famous Lucknow courtesan and Lady Gaga, thus merging the bygone era of stage dressing with its vampish futuristic avatar, making the courtesan meet the vamp. Amrapali, a famous jewellery label by Rajiv Arora and Rajesh Ajmera is named after a famous courtesan at whose mango grove Buddha stayed and who later renounced her position as courtesan, adopting the Buddhist way. We could go on; the allure of the fabled Indian courtesans, be they *devadasis* or *tawaifs*, is enormous (Figure 6.3). One reason for *chikan*'s popularity is precisely its connection to the wardrobes of the famous Lucknow courtesans, who invoke the decadent sides of the *nawabi* royal court and its pursuit of sophisticated seduction, sensuality, and other 'morally dubious' pastimes (Oldenburg 2007). Courtesans are one of the favourite stereotypes of female power in South Asian film, fashion, songs and literature; as the other women, they are independent, free,

FIGURE 6.3 Model in courtesan-style attire at India Couture Week 2014, design by Shree Raj Mahal Jewellers

Image courtesy: Nitin Patel Photography.

educated and beautiful professionals and property owners (Gordon and Feldman 2006). The *tawaifs* became part of Lucknow's powerful pre-colonial elite and due to their liaisons with powerful men and the patronage of the *nawabs*, they not only enjoyed luxury, privileges and property, but were also crucial players on the cultural scene of the day; from *kathak*, via poetry, to fashion, they were the trendsetters (Sharar 2005). Srinivasan rightly noted that there were two options of acquiring power 'open to the pre-colonial Indian woman: that of the sexually liberated and educated courtesan or the pure, sexually controlled, uneducated wife' (Srinivasan 2006: 161), the first, a keeper of culture, the second, a keeper of lineage, a split, as we have seen, still very much alive. Lying on the margins of the patrilineal system, and reproductively irrelevant, the courtesans enjoyed a great degree of power and wealth, even to such a degree that she could be said to have reversed patriarchy and posed a threat to the established order (Oldenburg 2006). When the civilizing mission of the British was appropriated by the nationalist leaders of the late nineteenth century, dancing girls became perceived as a social malaise that needed to be eradicated, the dirty sacred turned into mere dirt. At the same time, however, their dance, music and performances were preserved while being dissociated from the polluting activities. Since the high cannot resist predating on the low, the dance of the *devadasis* was turned into *bharatanatyam*, a national dance thought to demure middle class girls in state-run art academies, *kathak* was reinvented in the process of sanskritization as an inheritance of the devotional Hindu past, with men becoming its elite practitioners and the new teachers in the dance academies. In the process, Muslim courtesan *kathak* dancers were sanitized from the official narrative (Walker 2010), even when they survive on the screen and on the ramp. This process runs parallel to the sanitization of *chikan*, the process of turning it into heritage luxury worthy of the elite that we encountered earlier. Some courtesans, like *Begum* Akhtar, reinvented themselves as singers, catering to the market of commodified heritage and culture. Due to these nationalist processes of heritization and sanitization 'the definition of the cultivated woman would enter a new phase: the keeper of culture and the keeper of the (pure) lineage was to become one and the same' (Srinivasan 2006: 178). Sexual desire was censored in the process of this merger, and yet, it keeps lurking even under the most modest of *pallus*. The image of sexual desire, power and erotic capital is not going away, even against the sanitizing efforts of nationalist censorship. Already the *Kamasutra* (Vatsyayana et al. 2009; Doniger 2003), which devotes a chapter to the role of courtesans as bearers of culture, suggests that a courtesan should be proficient in the sixty-four arts that defined a cultured person of the time and if she did and became imbued with politeness, beauty and virtue, she could receive a seat of honour in the assembly of men (Srinivasan 2006). Today, the fashion model, with her carefully cultivated art of walking the ramp with confidence, attitude, and beauty with a hint of arrogance that screams superiority, can be viewed as a continuation of the courtesan performing for selected high net worth individuals. Only this time the audience includes women, who are meant to both emulate her and consider her morally corrupt on a par with a prostitute. The fashion model's carefully cultivated and staged stiff and self-absorbed theatrical arrogance is intended to create an aura of sovereignty and superiority around her. Otherwise a rather appalling quality in our fellow humans, cultivated arrogance is at the core of fashion marketing, and it works; it screams value and worthlessness of the audience at the same time. The intention is obvious – create a lack and a feeling of inferiority and then present your dresses as the solution, and if you emulate the praised 'attitude' you shall be the star.

Designers often instruct the women to learn from the models how to walk with confidence, how to project an image of elevated power. They teach them not to fear theatrics, exaggeration or deception. There is also little concern among the elite women about revealing their 'authentic self' or 'being true to themselves', as we often encounter among the Western clients of the last few decades, who seem to look for clothes that they imagine would match their authentic self or personality. India is still a place where play and social role is not only allowed, but expected and encouraged, therefore, dress is meant to alter, enhance, cover up, deceive, and flatter and so on. Hence, looking for role models and imitating powerful icons or mannerisms of models and Bollywood courtesans comes naturally to most women and men alike. There is a widely shared assumption that imitating the powerful will result in becoming powerful. But as the discussions with the designers show, nuances are crucial. And so as much as the garments are discussed in minute detail – shades, embroideries, cuts, millimetres of cleavage, necklines, levels of transparency, so is the degree to which imitation can be stretched in order to be effective. This reminds of the ways in which some embroiderers draw their own moral lines around as miniature things as different stitches, as if subscribing to Roland Barthes' notion of the importance of the detail in the general economy of clothing (Barthes et al. 2006). One of the most desired details of *chikan* embroidery is the *jali* stitch, not only because it requires great skill, a sign of exclusivity, but also because it shows the skin. In *jali* stitch the thread is never drawn through the fabric, instead the warp and weft threads are carefully drawn apart to create minute buttonhole stitches; the front and the back of this stitch thus look equally delicate. Because of these little holes, some embroiderers refuse to embroider this stitch, claiming that 'it spoils your eyes' by virtue of its immodesty. According to them, such embroidery cannot guarantee the moral status of the woman who wears it. This brings us to the problem of balancing erotics and morality. As we shall see, the most effective strategy is to displace woman's morality from her body, and its purity manifested in demeanour and clothing, onto an external ethical cause. Externalizing morality onto a social cause, such as uplift of the poor, or free medical care or education for children, and then incorporating it into the public persona of the woman, has proven to be one of the most effective and popular strategies of balancing erotic capital with moral capital.

Victories of sexy and benevolent goddesses

Kamini is a jewellery designer based in South Delhi, stylish and sexy at all times. But it has not always been that way. She recounted her life story to me as one of transformation from a modest daughter in-law wearing *saris* and attending *pujas* to a strong business woman and successfully loved wife, a story of lifelong self-cultivation and achievement. Kamini's transformation was triggered by her realization that her husband was indifferent towards her exactly because, in her words: 'I was someone the family wanted me to be, any other woman could be in my place and it would make no difference, I had to change'. She describes herself at that time as lacking personality. First when she began experimenting with clothes, dressing up and exploring her creativity in jewellery design and art, her husband appeared to notice her and fall for her. Today, Kamini believes that appearance is crucial, that expressing her personality through play with clothes and their codes triggered the love for her in her husband and transformed her into a new and more valuable woman. Masquerading as the Other thus appears to be necessary in the process of creating and recreating of self in each moment of reflexive consciousness. Kamini transformed herself from a stereotypical housewife into a stylish modern businesswoman by developing her erotic capital. This helped her gain confidence to face the world outside of the home sphere. Her husband realized that she is a valuable asset and sexually desirable, too. If carefully cultivated, in certain circles of Indian society, the vamp-like qualities are 'rising in social and economic importance', becoming 'a key factor in women's changing status in society and the economy' (Hakim 2010: 14). Kamini's masquerading as the imagined other and play with garments, which she believed to possess the power to transform her into someone else at the same time as helping her find out whom she could be, have in the end changed dramatically her position within the family and within the society at large; she differentiated herself from the stereotypical image of Indian wife and mother. But there is more to Kamini's story. Before she started her jewellery design business, she also got involved in a charitable organization and a trust for the education of women and for improved sanitation facilities (from rapes to education, private toilets are there to rid the world of all evil, an idea recently popularized yet again by Narendra Modi himself) that was owned by her husband's friend and business associate as a part of his corporate social responsibility programme. Her involvement in the programmes of the trust functioned as a stepping stone into the public sphere, but also, as I would argue, a way to displace her morality from her body onto an external social cause, utilizing the impoverished bodies of other women in the process, thus allowing her to be both erotic and moral at the same time. And Kamini's case was not unique. Already Gandhi encouraged women to engage in charitable action, also as a means of entering and participating in the public sphere and in the building of the nation, and recently

Narendra Modi has again emphasized the role of women in charitable foundations, NGOs and CSR programmes (see Chapter 4), claiming that as women they are more sensitive and therefore better suited for such tasks.

Merging erotic or feminine power with public displays of benevolence in the form of running charitable trusts and foundations has been proven as one of the most effective strategies of gaining access to the male-dominated public sphere. Politics might be another option; however, politics demands strict dress codes of simplicity and chastity (possibly more so because politics is considered 'dirty' as they say in India) hence is rarely chosen as the desired path by the elite women. Also, unlike the middle class female activists, who often sport *khadi*, degrees in social sciences and short haircuts along with their semi-radical beliefs, the elite women are keen to exploit their sexual power to get ahead, not to supress it. They often laugh at the thoroughly moral looking middle class activist. One incident made this difference even more obvious. I was watching TV with Kamini and a discussion was going on about the *hijab*, during which an Indian feminist, with the most clichéd short hair, glasses and *kurti* from Fab India, raised the issue of oppression, female subjugation and so on, arguing that *hijab* should be banned as in France and the women liberated. Kamini immediately argued against her:

> Women like her are the problem, is she going to tell me what to wear and not to wear too? I know this type: she would say the exact same thing if you have Botox, sexy clothes, and styled up hair. She would say, look at them, poor things are oppressed by the beauty industry; we must prohibit this or that and liberate them from the oppression. The only way of being a woman according to her is in her way, everyone should be like her. Some women want to cover up and proudly wear their *hijab*, others want to be sexy; nobody should be deciding what is good for them. Ok, if you are being forced and threatened into wearing *hijab* then you should get help, the point is, you should be free to choose your ways.
>
> Interview, April 2011

One of Raghav's clients noted some days later: 'do they have to be so ugly and unkempt, just because they work in some NGO? I prefer doing charity in style.' Women like her do not wish to embody and personify morality, neither of the kind of the middle class activist or of the typical *pativrata*, a stereotype they too are meant to conform to. To the contrary, many wish to visibly stage their sexual liberation. However, this is still not possible without addressing the question of morality, virtue and without staging morality. So the question emerges: how to be at the same time the idealized *pativrata* – the demure, chaste, self-sacrificing, unquestioningly loyal, devoted wife and mother that worships her husband as a god (Obeyesekere 1984), while being the opposite, the *vamp* – the seductive female character of Hindi cinema that calls 'attention to her sexual needs' (Uberoi 2010:

120). Resolving this question of how to be 'the other woman' or how to be like a seductive courtesan to their husbands, while at the same time displaying the necessary morality, means finding ways of insubordination or minor resistance to the oppressive social norms placed on their appearance, demeanour and the very meaning of their existence (Thapan 2009). In such a scenario, commitments to ethical and sustainable fashion, involvement in charitable foundations and trusts, endorsing the cause of uplifting craftsmen and so on, are easily appropriated by these women and provide a solution to the problem of morality, turning individual chastity into social responsibility. The 'ethical' garments present themselves as a solution to the problem: the woman can look sexy, while delegating her morality to the ethical garment, this garment is then, interpassively (Pfaller 2003), moral for her. This is exactly where the popularity of *ahimsa* (nonviolent) silk comes from – the nonviolence here refers to the silkworm not being killed in the process. The concept of *ahimsa* invokes Gandhi and his morality (and no less his celibacy), however, not all customers necessarily know that the talk here is of the silkworm – that is not relevant, the garment is *ahimsa* – enough said. But then again, the problem is, who can really see that the garment in question is labelled ethical? And so while ethical fashion can provide a temporary relief to the dilemma of sex appeal and morality, in practice other measures have to be taken if a woman wishes to succeed at both – the measures that Kamini so skilfully employed. Following and imitating the examples of women like Nita Ambani, the wife of the industrialist Mukesh Ambani, who runs many of the family's philanthropic projects, or of famous socialites and celebrities, or even of the immediate examples of the designers themselves or the designers' female family members who often manage the NGOs attached to the fashion business, the elite women understand that running a charitable foundation is their ticket to recognition in the public sphere, while being at the same time a legitimate display of their morality. If they lead their husbands' foundation for instance, all of a sudden they are no longer left home alone, while their men do their business with other men, but they are taken along, thus entering a space where not all wives, but only wives like them, interact.

Grounded in interviews with elite female customers, who run such smaller or larger charitable foundations, I claim that we need to recognize that the rise of philanthrocapitalism in India that we are witnessing today, and that we discussed earlier, is fuelled to an unprecedented degree by the desire of these women to participate in the public sphere or to at least gain access to other arenas than the home and the shopping mall. Often, these women would tell me of how they initially had to convince their husbands that running such a venture parallel to their business will turn profitable and that it is preferable to giving donations to already existing charities or NGOs, no less because they could invest strategically in the causes that are essential to their business – such as in the case of designers, as we have seen, investing in the effective co-option of the rural workforce into the capitalist system, or in improving the quality of the product, while at the same time for example covering basic health expenses (again in order to ensure the reproduction of the workforce). The elite women tend to typically invest their time and energy in the cause of the uneducated poor, especially women, and create various initiatives in their name. For some, these ventures have become a stepping stone into the world of business. Once they have proven themselves worthy, their husbands would fund their own business, typically in fashion or beauty industries.

Rather paradoxically, the charitable cause of the poor and vulnerable women is indispensable to the empowerment of the elite wife and her emancipation from the domestic sphere and her becoming a vampish benevolent public goddess – something that at the same time leads to the reproduction of the poor, the incompetent or the disempowered. As we have seen, perfectly literate women are constantly represented in the public charitable discourse as illiterate and uneducated. The sad fact being that their education, their literacy, or their competence in not only not acknowledged, but directly denied. Literacy alone often cannot transgress the class and caste background, and definitely not in the way meritocratic ideology promises us. Yet, their perpetuated disempowerment serves the case of the empowerment of the elite woman, who tries to emulate the ideal type embodied by Priyanka Chopra, the Indian Miss World (2000), famous actress, singer and advocate of educational programmes for girls, among others UNICEF supported programmes, perfectly merging her erotic capital with morality delivered by the causes that she benevolently takes under her goddess wing.

Vandana is a case in point. She started her small fashion label in her mid-forties, in 2010, without any training at a fashion college, but with financial support from her husband. The initial negotiation with her husband was a balancing act itself. As the children slowly grew up and went to college, her husband encouraged her to entertain herself and find a small business, possibly home-based, that she would like to do. Since Vandana was a skilled painter, and enjoyed drawing, she thought that fashion might be something for her and so she proposed the idea to her husband. But he was not particularly happy about this choice; the fashion business seemed too frivolous to him, for women of loose morals, no matter how much he could appreciate Vandana's style otherwise. Vandana was not ready to give up on the new dream, and therefore thought of ways to change his mind. Suddenly it occurred to her that venturing into ethical and sustainable fashion might be a way. Around 2008, when she was contemplating the idea, it was fairly new. At that point, there was not as much talk about sustainability, ethical business and CSR as there is today. She envisioned her future fashion label to be exclusively using organic cotton and natural dyes, but in a glamorous way, not holding back on the bling or embroidery for that matter. She argued her case one evening in front of her husband, telling him how many people die young as a result of poisoning and cancer caused by pesticides used in cotton production, how many live in constant poverty, and that the average age of a cotton worker is around thirty-four. She told him that she wanted to change that with her fashion label and create a reputable fashion business, combined with an NGO or a trust to help the workers. She told him scary stories about chemical colours eating up the skin of the workers and so on. Eventually, she managed to sell him the idea. Vandana spent the following two years setting up the business. Soon she realized that her idea was far too ambitious and naïve; organic cotton was extremely hard to get and convincing people to shift to organic production rather impossible. Moreover, she lacked the knowledge, staff and resources to set up an NGO. Furthermore, natural dyes have proven to be too unstable and weak in colour to even compete with the bright permanent chemicals, and so on. In the end, she settled for a compromise, a trust funded largely by her husband's business, where the money went into supporting programmes of NGOs and other organizations that worked in the vicinity of her workshops in Lucknow, Delhi, Varanasi and Jaipur. Four times a year, Vandana holds by-invite-only talks at five-star hotels about the necessity of ethical fashion, served over cocktail and haute snacks, and sponsored by a vodka brand. Following that, she publicly donates to diverse organizations and shows her latest collection; she looks glamourous, her curves sizzling as she small-talks her way through the evening. She is the perfect, benevolent and vampish goddess, who effectively externalizes her morality, by displacing it onto the social cause of ethical fashion, thus liberating her body from the burdens of displaying modesty in clothing.

Conclusion

In this chapter, we have seen how elite women straddled the problematic terrain between the socially defined female roles – on the one hand the devoted wife, and on the other the prostitute – and how, when resisting the role of the asexual but dutiful wife, they resorted not only to the techniques of seduction employed by the notorious courtesans and vamps, but also to techniques of externalizing their morality away from their bodies, attires and demeanours, onto an external social cause. Here their destinies became intertwined with those of the craftswomen we met in the previous chapter. The cause of the poor women came especially handy when the empowerment of the elite woman was at stake. All the upper class Delhi women we met in this chapter, tried to negotiate their position within their relationships with husbands, families and society at large and transgress the socially determined role of a devoted wife, and they did so by fashioning themselves, masquerading as the other woman and taking on the attributes of the vamp – her sexual power, boldness, daring nature, desirability, and seductive appeal. They tried to break free from the notion that good Indian females are 'those who are controlled by males' (Caplan 1987: 280–281) and whose sexuality must be suppressed; they tried to reclaim their sexual desire and display it even to the public gaze. Their masquerading is a form of resistance against traditional notions of marriage that are 'keyed to concepts of duty and domination (social, religious, and/or political) and [that] do not value individualism as an element of eroticism as do stories that privilege desire' (Doniger 2000: 66). The crucial problem for these women, as we have seen, was how to acquire sex-appeal and glamorous style, while at the same time maintaining or even enhancing an appearance of their moral credibility. Displacing morality from the immediate wrapping of the body and its demeanour, onto an external ethical cause, has proven to be the most effective strategy that allowed them to carve out a space for themselves in the public life. But it is not only elite women who have to navigate a tricky terrain of appropriate femininity. Elite men, who excessively indulge in luxury and all kinds of comforts that are considered as effeminizing, also struggle with their masculinity and displays of virility and power. The power mystique of the elites is nothing that comes spontaneously; to the contrary, it has to be carefully designed and mastered. The next chapter investigates how elite men cultivate their image of power and counteract the threat of effeminacy. They too, as it turns out, cannot resist seeking the 'help' of the low classes in the struggle for their own empowerment. In order to counteract the threat of effeminacy and of luxury, they appropriate symbols of low class machismo and incorporate them into elitist aesthetics or they indulge in 'dirty' substances, such as alcohol, meat, and cigarettes and employ the rhetoric of muscularity. Furthermore, the chapter goes on to connect these balancing acts both to the shifts in the political field and the heavy sponsorship of fashion events by the alcohol industry and whisky brands in particular. The concluding discussion of total environments and ambient governance revisits the underlying themes of this book – the power of the fashion rituals and reproduction of (neo-feudal) social order.

7 FASHION, WHISKY AND 'MUSCULAR' NEO-ROYALS

The hero is racing furiously through Mumbai, with the heroine in the passenger seat of his black shimmering Honda. Controlling this beast of a machine between his legs, he looks tenderly at the terrified girl. Flip into dream sequence. He is driving a red Ferrari through the Dubai desert, first slowly to the beat of romantic music, then bursting into dance, showing off his Christian Louboutin *mojri*-like shoes worth €4,000, a phallic extension, conspicuously matched with a Punjabi style *salwar* and *lungi*. These shoes were custom-made for the hero of the *masala* action comedy *Khiladi 786* (Mohan 2012), the popular and muscular actor Akshay Kumar. *Masala* movies often feature strong hypermasculine, typically Punjabi, heroes with criminal ties that enhance their masculinity and impress the heroine. These movies represent one of the most influential emergent fantasies of contemporary Indian masculinity at large, even for the elite men and designers alike, no matter how much they like to claim the opposite. This ideal is ambivalent in its 'vulgarity', no less because of its appeal to the so-called masses, a word strategically employed by the elite and middle classes to construct 'the others, the unknown, the unwashed, the crowd beyond one'. We must keep in mind here that, as Raymond Williams says, 'there are in fact no masses, only ways of seeing people as masses' (Williams 2002: 98). But still, those mocked as dirty masses are imagined to possess something that the elite men lack and therefore desire. Like in the case of elite women, it is the job of the designers to balance the men's masculine act and incorporate that dirty low class heroism into elitist masculinity in order to enhance their 'power mystique' (Cohen 1981). Virile masculinity is essential to the claims of the designers' elite clientele to patriotism, patriarchal power and to their self-fashioning as cosmopolitan muscular neo-royalty. This is why designers often re-use elements of the dangerous, low class, unclean or forbidden and elevate them into a matter of connoisseurship, or even art, turning them into sacred dirt (Pfaller 2008) that makes indulgence in luxury fashion not only legitimate for men, but also necessary if they desire to become men of importance. These phantasmatic masculine ideals are created to overcome the paradoxes of democratic imperialism inherent to the ambitions of the self-proclaimed business leaders. Machismo, politics, gangsterism and big business are increasingly closely intertwined, thus giving rise to a specific type of neo-liberal power mystique and aesthetics that is dramatically gendered and relies on a combination of tropes of sovereign power, benevolent rule, meritocratic achievement and celebration of violence. Here, the sexy women endorsing charitable social causes become displays of both the men's power and of their claims to morality.

Hypermuscularity and neo-liberalism

Classical villains, be they smugglers of the 1950s and 1960s or representatives of the state of the 1980s and 1990s, while thriving in real life, are as good as dead on the screen, and so is any old-fashioned clear-cut distinction between good and evil. Even the successful NRI romantic hero of family dramas of the 1990s is replaced by a bulky, morally ambivalent, and often lower class hero, relying mostly on his libidinal power rather than education or legit achievement. This hero skilfully navigates the shadow terrains of illegality and is prone to excessive showing off. Masculinity in the world of Hindi cinema is no longer associated with rhetorical and physical battles driven by 'virtuous anger' at the ills of the social system, like the iconic battles of Amitabh Bachchan. Earlier we touched on this rise of muscular power and the self-made men, as it manifests itself in the rags-to-riches story of the PM Narendra Modi (see Chapter 1). The fashion conscious Modi has been cultivating his image of virile manhood together with his dressmaker Bipin Chauhan as intensely as his ties with India's corporate tycoons.

Even the new hypermuscular hero of the Hindi cinema, as a function of the ideological apparatus (Althusser 1971), embodies and propagates in his acts and aesthetic form of his masculinity a particular Indian strand of neo-liberal mythology. 'Attributes like ambition, competitive mind-set, earlier associated with the villain are no more considered as evil' (Sarma 2014: 85). To the contrary, worldly power, material wealth and spurious success, achieved by morally ambivalent means, are celebrated. Violence, corruption and street-smartness are cool, normalized and an indispensable macho ingredient of Indian masculinity at large. 'The heroes of production' have been effectively 'replaced by idols of consumption ("great wastrels") such as movie stars and sports heroes' (Ritzer 1998: 5), both on and off screen. Muscular actors such as the cocky Salman Khan, romantic Shah Rukh Khan and the transnational *desi* John Abraham are the living metaphor of this economic and social transformation (Cayla 2008; Srour 2013). They represent the ideal of consumer patriotism, while the muscular politicians function as preachers of neo-liberal policies that systematically intensify the divide between the rich and the poor.

Threat of effeminacy

This shift from production to consumption comes with an inherent threat of effeminacy. Comfortable sedentary life is believed to be the root cause of the crisis of contemporary masculinities, robbing men of their power (Robinson 2000). Even though a sense of crisis is possibly endemic to any attempt to form a coherent identity (Butler 1999), the current crisis of masculinity in India exists both at the level of individually deeply felt, especially among the elite Indian men, who are most threatened by the feminizing effects of luxurious lives, and at the level of the emergent structures of feeling. Modern transnational histories of masculinities are those of struggles to deny and combat weakness, and of the search for virilizing substances, habits and acts (Forth 2008). While luxurious life can on the one hand serve as a symbol of prestige, power and 'civilization', it at the same time threatens masculine identities with its softness, comfort, refinement and passivity. Already colonial psychiatry has connected the luxurious lives of the princes to their pathological effeminacy, sexual indulgence, feminine idleness, onanism, homosexuality, and loss of (self)-control. Shivaji IV, the young Maharaja of Kolhapur, was in the 1870s proclaimed mad by a psychiatrist due to his taste for lower class women and frequent masturbation, and consequently robbed of his power and sent to the Rajkumar College, to embrace Victorian ideals of manliness, such as physical strength, self-restraint and gentlemanly duty. Shivaji's case was in no way unique; many princes shared the same destiny (Kapila 2005). Today, the designers still struggle with this legacy in their continual attempts to reinvent their creations inspired by the wardrobes of the 'effeminate princes' as symbols of powerful neo-imperial manhood. As the character Tyler Durden says in the *Fight Club* movie: 'self-improvement is masturbation, now self-destruction ...' (Fincher 1999). No wonder that guns and dangerous substances such as alcohol, drugs, cigarettes and whores are in such high demand among elite men.

Facing the threat of effeminacy, masculinities need to be repetitively reinforced and men virilized. Indulging in 'fearful things' (Horkheimer and Adorno 2002) or in displaying symbols of such things (carrying revolvers rather than using them), is one of the most widely endorsed strategies of counteracting the feminizing tendencies of consumer lifestyles. The bulking up of the Indian screen heroes, the idealization of the vulgar, rustic, and the brute, of the animalistic muscular power, and the nostalgia for virile Indian manhood of mythological warriors and gods is an expression of the paradoxes that haunt modernity's relationship to masculinity and elite Indian manhood in particular. This rising desire for the raw muscular power, that is, an embodied and essential masculinity somehow lurking behind the veneer of civilization, can be read as a counter-modern impulse (Beck 1997). The phantasmatic true manhood draws on powerful cultural and epic narratives from elsewhere and from other times. These narratives are reworked for the purposes of current and future scenarios, fulfilling the more or less explicit aim of providing a dose of 'the primitive' as an antidote to the effeminacy of 'civilization'. For this reason, some of the younger designers and sons of businessmen and industrialists are great fans of exclusively 'black gangsta hip-hop', with its dominant 'cash, cars and bitches' theme. At the same time, most of them are explicitly racist; they made sure that I understand that even though they listen to the music, they still consider the blacks inferior and even lower in the hierarchy than the local untouchables. For these men, for whom masculinity is a project to be worked on (Orbach 2009), and a matter of constant recreation, transforming the vulgar and 'primitive' into an appropriate dose of manhood is an everyday balancing act.

Nostalgia for charismatic manliness

Fashion designers play a crucial role in both designing appropriately masculine costumes, and in diagnosing and manufacturing the crisis of masculinity; they promise a fashion remedy to a problem they help create. Designers share a pervasive sense of nostalgia for a lost charismatic manhood, a nostalgia that effectively turns such manhood into an ideal. Prahlad Kakar, the leading ad director, has expressed such sentiment in respect to male fashion models, when mourning the 'likes of Milind Soman and Marc Robinson', who 'seem to have disappeared. They were charismatic, distinctive and cut above the rest. Currently, there are hardly any male models worth the recall. Most are simply clones of one another. . . . They look all global but seem to be cast from the same mould' (Kakar 2012). In order to fight this threat of uniformity and rebuild the image of charismatic manhood, one of the most prestigious designers, JJ Valaya, stages actors, industrialists, businessmen, popular historians, CEOs and socialites as models during his fashion shows. By handpicking 'real' people with a distinct aura over generic models, he manages to enhance the power of his garments and seduce the audience into believing that charismatic masculinity is crucially dependent on his garments. Valaya dresses these handpicked men of distinctive character in attires inspired by the pre-colonial royal wardrobes. As such Valaya's designs materialize the trending selective tradition. These selective traditions and what Raymond Williams calls 'residual forms', such as notions derived from a feudal and rural past, enjoy popularity and become incorporated into the dominant culture. They become bound up together with the emergent and novel cultural forms, in which phantasmatic and utopian visions of the future often contain idealized selective traditions and elements of the past (Williams 1973). Within the current neo-liberal muscular climate, the Indian nostalgia for the past is nostalgia for warriorhood, knighthood and brute force, all projected onto the canvas of an imagined global future.

Rhetoric of muscularity

The incorporation of the rhetoric of muscularity, if not of real muscles, into the neo-royal and feudal aesthetics, balances these potential threats of effeminacy. Norman Mailer is a familiar example of the rhetoric of muscularity. Notoriously competitive, he conceived of writing as a blood sport, thus positing danger and risk taking as the path to his success (Sontag 1992). Western male elites of the eighteenth century fell for the same logic as their bodies usually fell short of the overtly muscular ideals celebrated in the neoclassical art. Thus, 'fascinated by muscular bodies they rarely possessed, nobles and bourgeois alike sometimes compensated for this lack by appropriating the language of muscularity as a way of describing their own rather non-physical activities' (Forth 2008: 57).

Rhetoric of muscularity can have its virilizing effects, especially when connected to powerful myths. The same way the Indian elites idealize the Rajput warriors, the Russian elites at the turn of the century romanticized the powerful oppositional manhood of the Cossacks, with their reputation for rape, aggression, and drunkenness, in order to negotiate the tension between the traditional Slavic culture and the models of gentlemanly behaviour imposed by the West as much as the state-sponsored attempts at civilized decorum (Kornblatt 1992; Plokhy 2012). The Cossack myth of powerful manhood has seen a remarkable revival in the 1990s Ukraine that claimed it as the ground for its national self-assertion, thus stripping it of the profound connection to Russia. Then again, the Cossack myth was reclaimed by Russia during the 2014 annexation of Crimea, as the local paramilitary groups of Cossacks came to help Moscow in the hope of being integrated into Russia's primary security apparatus. Contemporary China seems to be undergoing a similar process of powerful self-assertion, as the anthropologist Marc L. Moskowitz has shown in his monograph on the strategic board game *weiqi*. Moskowitz revealed the essential role of this game in the construction of a distinctly Confucian gentlemen and of powerful Chinese masculinity with its rhetoric of muscularity, again a leverage of tradition against the global Other (Moskowitz 2013). Through the game of *weiqi*, men learn to appropriate the language of warfare and muscularity, while comfortably seated at a table. They then strategically employ the same rhetoric in the competitive sphere of business.

The relation between consumer desires, machismo and conspicuous show has been reinforced and acquired a new dynamic in the post-liberalization India. Growing up in Delhi in the 1990s, today's successful designers and businessmen recall gangs of tall, young, and muscular Punjabi men waiting outside the city's night clubs for the party to be over, so that they could rob the rich boys, whom these 'gangsters' notoriously mocked as effeminate, of their imported *Kangaroos*, a US brand of shoes with a little pocket suitable for a condom or some money, in those days a popular status symbol of transnational wealth. While the humiliated rich kids dismissed those macho small-time gangsters as vulgar and low class, they nonetheless confessed to me that all they wanted was to possess that elusive vulgar masculine power, probably as much as the gangsters wanted to possess the shoes. This low class vulgar muscular virility, admired, hated and disdained, exerts an ambivalent power over the elite business circles in Delhi, who, if nothing else, desire to possess at least its rhetorical power.

Elite gyms and sympathetic magic

Muscularity is also closely linked to the appropriation and dissemination of the meritocratic ideal, be it in politics, popular culture or the economy. In fact, the more the meritocratic ideal came to dominate the discursive landscape of business, the more muscles became a way to perform and stage achievement in a clear opposition to hereditary privilege. Muscularity, both physical and rhetorical, is meant to signify achieved status, and all those imaginary battles that had to be fought in order to acquire that privileged place in society. Elite gyms, such as Celebrity Fitness or Ozone Club, with lounges, spas and high membership fees, are booming across India's metropolitan cities. Rather than for cultivation of bodies, these spaces are designed to cultivate relations between young wealthy men, providing an arena for display of belonging to the cosmopolitan elite. In these clubs, muscularity is acquired by membership, by being seen cultivating one's body, rather than by having a hypermuscular body per se. Besides, being hypermuscular is not too desirable either; that is better left to the gym instructor.

The interior of these luxury fitness studios and spas is crafted using the latest strategies in experience design, such as to stimulate an experience of power, strength, wealth, celebrity status and so on, setting the members through this fortified experience apart from the rest of the society (Bodeker and Cohen 2010). Muscularity within such a space exists more as an idea shared among the elite men; membership in these luxury fitness spaces promises to infuse the elite male body with an invisible muscular power. With the exception of one of my elite informants, a dedicated *Brahmin* vegan bodybuilder, none of the men had actual muscular bodies even though they frequented elite fitness establishments. And yet, they managed to stage their muscularity, as an illusory quality; actual muscles, after all, were associated with the low class aspirants attempting to climb up the social ladder. Elsewhere, I have written about aspiring lower middle class men mimicking the fitness and fashion routines of their favourite Bollywood stars in a magical belief that by appropriating these routines they will themselves somehow become heroes (Kuldova 2010). This mimetic relationship to muscular celebrities

(Nayar 2010), who are often worshipped as gods, can be easily paralleled to the relationship of North Indian wrestlers to the monkey god Hanuman, whom they identify with, devotedly worship and imitate in an attempt to appropriate his most desired qualities and divine power (Alter 1992).

The elite men, frowning on the widespread practices of mimicking, are largely content with being exposed to the environment of the fitness studio and to the muscular fitness trainers. They behave as if muscularity could be magically acquired just by their mere presence in the studio, by sharing expert-like knowledge of male health and muscle-building or obsessively purchasing protein powders, supplements and so on. Muscularity takes on the form of sympathetic magic (Frazer 2009). Expensive workout clothes and membership cards function in the same way as objects gifted by the now deceased and controversial spiritual *guru* Sai Baba to his devotees, objects imbued through his personality, wisdom and spirituality with a magical power 'capable of transforming people's bodies and minds from sick to well and from sceptical to devotional' (Srinivas 2010: 294).

Elite fitness clubs, the institutions of the cult of the perfectible body, are increasingly significant spaces of homosociality (Osella 2012), where men libidize each other, admire and insult each other, debate and touch each other, creating an excess of masculine power in an attempt to appropriate it. Even though women are present, they are in a minority, usually socializing with other women or the trainer, who is a particularly seductive attraction of the gym, providing care, compliments and understanding, fulfilling similar needs as the fashion designers and tailors. Women's bodies are notoriously labelled as soft and fragile, demanding different routines and fitness machines; and so it is suggested that they instead join women-only fitness studios, such as Viva Fit, owned by one of my interlocutors.

Fortification of homosociality

Elite fitness clubs in India are partially modelled upon the tradition of elite male clubs, a continuation of the British gentlemen's clubs, as much as boys-only English boarding schools, such as the famous Mayo College and Doon School, founded under colonial auspices in order to teach the sons of Indian aristocracy manly virtues and behaviour (Sinha 1999). While in other realms men tend to switch continually between English and Hindi, in the gym, that hypermodern overdesigned space, they rarely utter a word in Hindi. English is the language of privilege imbued with residual elements of the colonizers virility, who established English in the nineteenth century as the language of social power. Consequently, the 'upper-caste masculine authority came to be yoked to the charisma of colonial English and, with that, subtly coded the English language as masculine' (Chandra 2009: 199). Like in the fancy gyms, so in the elite men's clubs all over India, masculinity and gentlemanly virtues are cultivated, be it the famous MB Club in Lucknow (see

Chapter 2), or others. Fortification, or gating, of these elite masculine spaces, in which women perform only a secondary, far too often decorative role, is the key to understanding the ways in which elite boundaries are maintained and policed (Waldrop 2004). Within these fortified play-spheres, men can stage their masculinity as much as muscularity, rhetorical or physical attributes.

Godly warriors and Hindu nationalism

The Indian neo-liberal ideal of masculinity as hyper-muscularity is partly influenced by the global circulation of popular Hollywood cinema and the images of stars such as Arnold Schwarzenegger, an inspiration to Indian bodybuilders (Black 2013). But more importantly, it builds on Indian wrestling traditions (Alter 1992), ideologically infused by Hindu nationalist movements (BJP and the militant group RSS) of the 1990s and the recent imagination of India as a global superpower. Familiar tropes are reworked under new conditions. We must also not forget the influence of the trope of British hegemonic masculinity, with its aggression, muscularity and militarism. The colonial administrators scoffed at the weak and effeminate Indian men; weak because they were so easily conquered. As Edward Said rightfully pointed out, the Orient was notoriously feminized and positioned as irrational, non-martial and weak (Said 1979). Even the North Indian martial tribes, on the one hand admired for their bravery, were on the other hand projected as irrational, lacking in morality, codes of honour, and national consciousness. In the view of the colonizers, the martial qualities of the Rajputs, Pathans, Marathas or Muslims approximated animalistic bestiality, a far cry from what the British believed in, namely rational militarism driven by codes of honour and ideals of chivalry. Within this logic of legitimization of the colonial power, only the European masculine hero could transform the Indian chaos into order, as Ronald Inden famously remarked (Inden 2000).

In the 1880s, in response to the British devaluation of Indian masculinity, Swami Vivekananda preached a Hindu identity masculinized according to the hegemonic ideas of manhood, a combination of Hindu spirituality with Western emphasis on physical strength (Sinha 1999; Banerjee 2003). He dreamt of 'muscles of iron and nerves of steel, inside which dwells a mind of the same material as that of which the thunderbolt is made', of 'strength, manhood, *Kshatriya-Viriya*' (warrior courage) and he demanded: 'No more weeping, but stand on your feet and be men ... take away my weakness, take away unmanliness, and make me a man' (Vivekananda in Jyotirmayananda 1986: 26). Influenced by the revival of virile Hinduism of the last three decades, the Hindu pantheon has become victim to an aesthetic makeover. Gone are soft chubby bellies and androgynous depictions of gods. Vivekananda's urge for masculine power culminates in this age of hard six-pack abs, acquiring a new layer of meaning. Virile Hindu masculinity has become a repetitive standard trope of Indian mass movies and soap operas. As in the case of the movie *Singham*, or Lion (Shetty 2011). Roaring like a lion, this last just policeman from Shivgarh fights criminals with unscrupulous means. Embodying the power of Shiva, he possesses otherworldly muscular power, which he displays in the exaggerated action scenes; ten men fly high into the air when one is slapped. In the title song of the movie, we see Singham (Ajay Devgan) rise from the holy Ganges to the sound of Shiv *mantra*, against the backdrop of a sun rising behind a Hindu temple and crowds of devotees performing a *puja*; muscular and bare-chested, his hands in *namaste*, and opening his eyes to the sound of a lion roar, he walks through the crowd displaying all his power and determination, celebrated like a godly incarnation.

This 'local' masculinity of Hindu nationalism is consequently turned into an element of elitist Indianness directed at the 'global' Other, as is the case of recent popularity of the *Shiva Trilogy* by Amish Tripathi (Tripathi 2010, 2011, 2013), the fastest selling book series in the history of Indian publishing. The heroic Shiva in his muscular warrior avatar created by the marketing and finance *guru* turned writer perfectly taps into the desire for national pride. Most of my interlocutors own this book, but none of them have read it. The book is merely a symbol demonstrating their proclaimed belief in the power of Indian culture, Shiva epitomizing the superior warrior God and Amish Tripathi India's success story. It is a source of their pride. In promoting the book, the marketers employed strategies of experiential design, akin to those used in luxury fitness studios. They used theatrical trailers screened during commercial breaks in cinema halls, and even recorded a special music album with ambient songs by multiple popular Indian artists, intended to enhance the reading experience. Listening to the music, a remixed pop version of adapted chants (or chant-like lyrics), was described by several men to me as 'profoundly empowering', a libidizing experience of 'merging with the Shiva-energy'. Trailers have become common also for comic books, whose collecting is becoming increasingly popular especially in the metros. Comic books, novels such as the *Shiva Trilogy*, Bollywood movies or soap operas like the *Devon ke Dev ... Mahadev* ('Lord of the Lords ... Mahadev') based on popular tales of Shiva and featuring the muscular Mohit Raina as the Mahadev, mark a rising proliferation of the rhetoric and aesthetics of muscularity that is eagerly consumed by men as much as women.

Gangsters, wrestlers and muscular politics

By transforming the divine mass-cultural icons, the Shivas, Rams and Hanumans, into muscular warrior-like heroes (Jain 2007, 2001; Kapur 1993), the Hindu

FIGURE 7.1 A group of Punjabi wrestlers in Oslo
Image courtesy: Lill-Ann Chepstow-Lusty.

nationalist movement invariably connects muscularity not only to Indian masculinity and sexuality, but most importantly to state power (Figure 7.1). Oversized statues of muscular gods are popping up all over India, sponsored by politicians and businessmen. Chief ministers are building god-like memorials and statues of themselves. Indian political culture cultivates virile masculinity as a strategy to usurp social and political power. Mulayam Singh Yadav, the leader of the Samajwadi Party (SP) and former chief minister of Uttar Pradesh, is a wrestler-turned-politician, and he is not alone. North Indian politicians are often referred to as *goondas*, a label suggesting criminal ties and a style of doing politics that relies heavily on the imagery of aggressive and violent masculinity (Hansen 2001), accompanied by ostentatious consumption of whisky, meat, cigarettes (Michelutti 2010, 2008) and other dirty and dangerous substances.

Elite fashion designers, as well as elite businessmen, have as ambivalent a relation to *goondaism* as to actual muscularity. They both know the importance of designing and aesthetically displaying a certain degree of *goonda* power, after all many are involved in one black market dealing or another. However, the criminal and political ties, common in business circles, have to be both undercommunicated and communicated. If overdone, one risks, if not falling into the *goonda* category, a loss of face. Still, a fair amount of *goonda* power is essential for business as much as for politics, demonstrating the ability to deliver, to flex the muscle and provide resources, protection, networks, brute force and cash when needed. The support of my business interlocutors for politicians like Narendra Modi, who has shown that he does not shy away from using police force and Hindu militant volunteers against India's own citizens, is symptomatic of the business oligarchy's desire for neo-imperial exploitative power and the rule of business and money over the rule of law.

The figure of the gangster who can work himself up to become the ruler of the underworld and lord of the city, the ultimate Indian self-made man, has become central to the current hegemonic fantasy of masculinity. No matter how morally ambivalent, the gangster is a hero and an achiever, immortalized in movies such as *Shootout at Wadala* (Gupta 2013) that portray the complexity of his character rather than passing a final moral judgement. This meritocratic hero is particularly seductive for the business elite who like to identify with his power. The don's masculine traits and overachiever's spirit are easily turned into desirable symbolic goods that can, paradoxically, legitimize one's far too often illegitimate or hereditary wealth. As such, the gangster holds a particular allure for the world of glamour (Gundle 2009), where his exterior signs of success are re-elaborated such as to produce an aura of achievement and power. Designers for instance recreate the Bollywood 1960s and 1970s costumes of the Mumbai underworld gangsters, known for their bling detailing, colourful prints, extravagant shirts, unique styling and so on, and match them with luxury shoes and *bandhgala* jackets of Rajput royal inspired cuts. Consumers then indulge in the thievish joy of interpassive masculinity, while the magical gangster paraphernalia are being manly on their behalf. Sleazy elegance matched with democratic elitism mixes meritocratic symbolism into the dominant neo-royal style, creating a peculiar aesthetic of contemporary elitist masculinity.

Within the aggressive business circles, the desire for symbols of virile manhood is both a matter of claiming individual social power and of claiming the power of the nation. No matter how much the Punjabi machismo or the presumed uncontrollable sexual drive of Muslim men may be frowned upon and feared, they are at the same time desired; and proudly displayed in the theatrical public sphere. Even Vivekananda argued for the incorporation of what he took to be the 'base' animalistic Muslim virility into the spirit of the spiritually superior Hindu warrior (Banerjee 2003) in order to acquire social power. Contemporary designers, too, instruct their clients to deliberately display these qualities in appropriate measures, but rather than being displayed through acts, they are expressed through specific aesthetic forms. Even though men generally have a fairly good understanding of how the balancing acts of masculinity work in practice, the designers again claim superior expert knowledge in these matters. To them, masculinity must be in the first place effectively designed; it must acquire an appropriate aesthetic and experiential form. The elite men in particular tend to be preoccupied more with their narcissistic display of aesthetic symbols of heroic acts than with the acts themselves.

Interpassive masculinity and muscularity

Masculinity takes on an interpassive (Pfaller 2014) structure as men delegate their masculinity to whisky, cigarettes, revolvers, protein powders and power clothes. These items are masculine for them and on their behalf, so that they can be insecure and weak while objectively appearing masculine. Revolvers and power clothes are objects that also strategically set these men apart from the white collar middle class men, whom they stereotypically mock as weak, submissive, or overtly moralistic. The frightening figure of the emasculated middle class man is a common enemy of both low class men and their elite counterparts. It is not a coincidence that low caste politicians from deprived socio-economic backgrounds mingled well with business elites and rose to power. Squeezed in between, the middle class man is mocked from both ends of the hierarchy for being effeminate. Even in the West, the clerk has been a stigmatized figure, a symbol of the anxieties about modern society's impact upon male bodies, of the sedentary muscular decay caused by the comforts of everyday luxuries (Forth 2008). This common enemy therefore effectively facilitates the overlaps between the idealized low class machismo and the elitist displays of masculinity.

By possessing and displaying all the necessary symbols of powerful masculinity, the elite businessmen do not really have to fight or get their hands dirty. After all, even if some are really involved in criminal activities, there are always men who can be hired, rather cheaply, even to kill and become an accessory of power. Revolvers, conspicuously carried around during private parties, fire shots mostly only into the air during whisky infused night drives on national highways or at Coca-Cola cans in the fields. Most of these guns have expired licences. Not because these men would be unable to renew them, but, as one petrol pump chain owner told me, 'what fun would there be in shooting with legally held weapons'?

Over a glass of whisky, these men also proudly told me stories of their 'hunting expeditions'. This is what they called their male-only trips to national reservations and wildlife resorts; places that are built to protect tigers, leopard, rhinos and so on. Hunting in India is illegal (with the exception of man-eating tigers), but again, illegality stimulates the desires of these rich men. At least they claim they bribed their way to attempting to shoot a tiger. Most of the time their pleasure derives from driving around in a jeep loaded with rifles looking for a tiger that keeps notoriously hiding. Illegal hunting is the surefire way to counteract effeminacy, after all the intellectual 'Bengalis scared of the tiger' (Sramek 2006) are stigmatized as the example par excellence of effeminacy in men.

Even among the Bollywood celebrities, illegal hunting is a popular virilizer. Salman Khan was accused of hunting and killing the endangered chinkara and blackbuck (in 1998 and 2007), and was handed sentences of two and five years. Appeals against these sentences are still pending in the High Court. To counteract these trends, Raghavendra Rathore, famous fashion designer and cousin of the

Maharaja Gaj Singh from Jodhpur, participated in an awareness campaign called Save the Tiger in 2013. On that occasion, Rathore released a black and white image of a model dressed in RR's signature *achkan* and Jodhpuri breeches, looking down at a tiger. This image uncannily resembles photographs of Indian royalty and the British after their hunts. The British especially emulated the Mughal emperors such as Jehangir, who claimed to have killed personally 17,167 animals (Ali 1927) and for whom hunting was a crucial element of his kingship. Through such photographs, the British wished to represent themselves as the 'new Mughals' conquering Indian nature by means of their virile imperialism (Sramek 2006). The tiger was their fearful thing (Horkheimer et al. 2007) necessary in order to prove their manliness and fitness to rule over Indians (MacKenzie 1997). Hunting was also essential in keeping men away from indulgences in effeminate pleasures and debauchery and in building their Victorian manly character. When I showed the image from the fashion shoot to some of the elite men, their first reaction was nostalgia for real men and their tiger hunts. In the end, I had to tell them that the image comes from the Save the Tiger campaign. They reacted with cynical laughter; we all knew that the underlying message was exactly the opposite. Even today, though far less successful, the hunting trips are meant to express the rich businessmen's neo-feudal power. They show off their ability to bribe and pay enough to never be punished by law for such transgressive acts. George Bataille once pointed out that transgression of secular norms, societal rules and taboos provides human beings with access to the sacred itself (Bataille 1993). The dirty sacred certainly depends on acts of transgression, even if playacted. We must also not forget that, as Julia Kristeva rightly pointed out, transgression of one regulation often means that the transgressor is following another rule or societal law (Kristeva 1982). There is a limited number of transgressive acts that are generally appreciated as acts demonstrating masculine prowess. Transgressive playacting is necessary in order to balance the obsessions with excessive luxury consumption and visits to designer studios. Most of the elite men I ever encountered had a tendency to be rather finicky and insecure, and were looking for constant validation of their masculinity. Fashion designers share a widespread belief that the emerging market for men's fashion is merely pretending to cater to the newly aware male fashion consumer; whereas in reality, it caters to men deeply insecure about their masculinity.

Whisky, meat and other powerful substances

Whisky is India's number one drink. More than mere liquor in a bottle, whisky is an idea with a noble spirit and pedigree, connected to powerful social myths.

Whisky evokes elite gentlemen's clubs, power and white male privilege. Whisky is also categorized within the popular ethno-medical knowledge system, together with for instance meat, as a hot substance. Hot substances increase sexual drive, as opposed to milk or bananas that are perceived as cooling substances (Pool 1987). Even though women also often indulge in whisky, it is frowned upon, especially in the case of unmarried women. After all, women should stay cool, that is, non-sexual or even better, asexual. Whisky brands are therefore endorsed by powerful and successful celebrities, such as Shah Rukh Khan, the prototypical new Indian self-made man, and a globally oriented patriot, whose ads for Royal Stag whisky can be seen on almost every city corner.

Whisky and meat are important ingredients of the North Indian muscular political culture as well. This is a result of remixing of three influential ideas often cited by members of the political elite. First, the aforementioned overlap between the practice and aesthetics of *goonda* machismo. Second, the forged links with the idealized Rajput warriors and royals, represented as vigorous meat-eaters, who offer themselves as sacrificial victims on the battlefield and whose turbans are the symbol of their *Kshatriya*-hood. Warriors and kings have according to many of my elite interlocutors eaten meat and drunk alcohol 'since time immemorial' and imitating them translates for these men into appropriating those kingly powers. And third, there is the undeniable influence of the English gentlemen and of his power to colonize, dominate and act as culturally superior.

The Yadav political elites in North India nicely exemplify all these currents, while their practices resonate with those of the elite businessmen. The Yadav politicians engage in transgressive and excessive chicken and whisky picnics on the riverbanks of Yamuna, followed by nights with prostitutes; all of that only to prove their virility. At the same time, they claim to be vegetarians, something that precisely makes the meat effective as a virilizing substance. They need 'chicken and whisky not to get too dangerously cold and feminised' (Michelutti 2008: 92); alas they could be mocked as effeminate and weak, a stereotype that is attached to *Baniyas* and Bengalis, to whom they refuse to be compared because of their vegetarianism. For the same reasons, it seems, most of my younger *Baniya* interlocutors, coming from purely vegetarian business families, embraced meat eating and whisky drinking when with other men, when reclaiming their masculinity in public was at stake. Sometimes they would even themselves use the word *baniya* in a derogatory way, when attempting to emasculate other men. So, while on the one hand these non-muscular chubby bodies needed to be virilized by the consumption of meat, on the other hand, we can recall the case of the elite vegan bodybuilder that points to the tricky balancing acts of elite masculinity. The elite bodybuilder can display his real muscles only because he is vegan, his veganism prevents his raw animalistic muscularity from being low class and vulgar. He prided himself on every occasion that his muscles were pure, and not built on dirty habits of meat eating, steroids, and alcohol. Only such repetitive insistence on complete purity and abstinence could prevent his muscularity from being vulgar. The fashion industry readily taps into this need to balance masculinities though powerful substances, collaborating in the process with its most prominent transnational sponsor, the alcohol industry.

Fashion and the alcohol industry

Liberalization and privatization in the 1990s attracted international alcohol brands to India, and since then alcohol consumption keeps rising every year (from 2009 to 2010 by 8 per cent), as compared with the stagnating old European and US markets. India is the largest whisky market in the world (Argenti 2007); whisky is the first choice of drink you are served when you enter an upper class home. Alcohol brands sponsor the majority of fashion events (Blender's Pride Fashion Tour, Lakmé Fashion Week, Smirnoff International Fashion Awards), sport events (Chivas Regal Polo Championship, Royal Challenge Indian Open, Chivas Regal Invitational Golf Challenge, while Royal Stag regularly appears as a sponsor at cricket events), music events, movie productions (e.g. the Bollywood movie *Fashion* from 2008 featured direct shots of Smirnoff vodka) tourism and so on (Das 2007). Most of these whisky brands (Blender's Pride, Royal Challenge, Chivas Regal, Royal Stag etc.) are manufactured and distributed by Pernod Ricard, the world's largest spirits and wine company. Since liquor brands are global and are globally avid sponsors of elite events of all kinds (Argenti 2007), by participating in these events, the Indian local elite connects to its counterparts elsewhere, indulging in the fantasy of transnational elite belonging.

Alcohol brands enhance the value of the drink by their association with fashion. Turning alcohol bottles into designer objects and their content into a matter of connoisseurship, they emphasize the parallels between the craftsmanship of a master distillery and that of a designer. The trend of alcohol brands associating with fashion and art is booming as alcohol brands are becoming increasingly aggressive in the emerging markets. Collaborative ventures that permeate the cultural industry are as profitable for the corporations as they are for the governments. The revenues of the Indian government from the alcohol industry amount to around 10 per cent of its total revenues. At the same time, 'the alcohol industry is thought to create an approximately equal sum in "black money" that takes the form of bribes, protection payments, and profits from illicit alcohol. This gives the alcohol industry enormous political power and clout, which may be used to help influence and maintain government policies beneficial to the industry' (Saxena 1999: 42).

Artification of alcohol and fashion

Fashion designers and artists are interesting to the alcohol industry due to their ability to enchant (Gell 1994) the bottles by seductive surfaces, designs and the all-round magical and affective atmospheres of prestige (Böhme 1993, 2003). Alfred Gell has argued that art can function as a technology of enchantment, as a dazzling weapon in psychological warfare, endowed with magical efficacy. The aesthetics, shapes and colours of the canoe-prows of the Trobrianders were supposed to charm their Kula partners, weaken them, demoralize them and thus trick them into offering even more valuable shells and necklaces than they would otherwise (Gell 1994). Local and international alcohol brands look to fashion designers and artists precisely in the hope that they will re-enchant their powerful alcoholic substances, so that they retain their magical appeal and the quality of the everyday sacred.

Once, during a fashion event sponsored by Blender's Pride at one of Delhi's luxury hotels, the designer sent off the beautifully dressed and styled female models to mingle with the customers and serve them whisky, calling them his mermaids. 'They are not just models', he said, 'in my designs and with all that make-up, they become mythological creatures'. And like the mermaids, they are there to seduce and attract the men to the rocky shores, or, in this case, whisky on the rocks. The male models, on the other hand, just sat around the bar, holding their whisky glasses, playacting powerful manhood, furiously imitated by the male attendees, who have by now sent their wives off to another table, so that they could sit at the bar freely gazing at those mythological creatures.

Facing the disenchantment of alcohol consumption that pervades society, from the middle class moralism, via social and health awareness campaigns to statutory warnings in Bollywood movies informing viewers whenever an actor pours a glass that 'alcohol consumption is bad for health', the alcohol industry feels an increased need to devise more powerful and seductive strategies to re-enchant their products. Appropriating the language of art becomes in this context an effective way of elevating whisky into the realm of gentlemanly connoisseurship and self-control, while at the same time retaining the elements of dirt, power and muscularity inherent in this hot substance. The language of art balances the language of muscularity. Artification (Shapiro and Heinich 2012; Shapiro 2004; Shiner 2012) in and of fashion is profoundly connected to branding strategies of transnational alcohol corporations. The residual aura of art elevates both fashion and alcohol. Except, no matter how much the Indian designers like to portray themselves as free creative artists, unconstrained by any social or economic forces, their dependency on and willingness to please the sponsors tells a wholly different story. More and more designers are jumping on the bandwagon of designing bottles for famous brands. Rohit Bal has designed a special edition of Chivas Regal and by using a lotus and peacock symbolism infused the bottle with 'Indianness'.

Raghavendra Rathore has designed limited edition packaging for Johnnie Walker, in his words 'capturing the nostalgic impression of the glorious past that blends seamlessly with a contemporary feel'. While Glenfiddich has funded JJ Valaya's foray into the world of art proper.

For JJ Valaya, India's king of designer trousseau wear, Maharajas have been a lifelong fascination and source of inspiration for most of his collections, as we saw earlier. Glenfiddich patronized the production of his exhibition of art photographs (published as a book *Decoded Paradox*), and invited Valaya for three months to their distillery in Scotland in order to participate in the Artiste Residence programme, where selected artists from all over the globe work under the inspiration of single malt whisky and Scottish culture in order to capture the essence of the brand in their art. And, eventually, not only strengthen the bond between creativity and alcohol, but also transpose the value of art onto the brand. Valaya's photographs aim to re-establish Delhi as the city of rulers, while reinventing feudal charismatic masculinity. In the photographs, Valaya juxtaposes the histories of the royal capital with modern-day Delhi and in the process recreates the wardrobes of the Mughals and Rajputs, which he later turned into a Vintage Valaya collection. And as the media reported, 'Valaya presented his Decoded Paradox photo exhibition here with a hearty little talk over a glass of Glenfiddich whisky' (Fernandes 2011). Those photographed as the fictitious characters from the nostalgia-evoking past are largely members of contemporary Delhi's business elite. We can for instance see Aman Nath, a historian, owner of Neemrana Hotels and founder of the heritage hotel movement, dressed up as a Maharaja and others modelling on a throne, which as a symbol of power and authority runs through a number of these photographs. Interestingly, the modern-day Delhi of Valaya, onto which these Maharajas are juxtaposed, is that of poverty ridden neighbourhoods and, as he calls it, street-smartness rather than the South Delhi of luxury shopping malls and five-star hotels to which his models belong. More than a paradox, Valaya captures the present moment, using the backdrop of dirt and filth to effectively set the neo-royalty apart yet clearly feeding off it. The business elite portrayed in the photographs has turned into the rulers of modern India; Glenfiddich connects them to the world's elite while Vintage Valaya visibly roots their identity. Valaya's photographs have been exhibited in galleries in Mumbai, Delhi, Paris and New York. As James Clifford says, the 'treatment of artefacts as fine art is currently one of the most effective ways to communicate cross-culturally a sense of quality, meaning, and importance' (Clifford 1997: 121).

'Art is life is art' is whisky

More bombastic in scope, is the Chivas Studio, a platform created by Chivas Regal, the famous Scottish whisky, that brings together performance art, visual art, fashion design, music, film and no less mixology – 'the art of making cocktails'. A global concept, it was launched in India in 2010, following New York, Sydney, Paris, Madrid and Hong Kong. Similarly to elite Indian fashion designers, Chivas Royal capitalizes on its utilization of the phantasms of royalty and aristocratic lifestyles, which reinforce its luxury status, and bringing in art is only the next logical step. Max Warner, the global ambassador of Chivas Regal, who travelled all over India to promote the 'art of mixology', says the following about Chivas in *Urban Male Magazine*:

> We've got a legacy. John and James Chivas originally pioneered blending; these guys were visionaries. They were artists and they provided goods and services to the royal family in Scotland, hence the name Chivas Regal or Chivas Royal. I am continuing their legacy in providing the aristocracy of the world with the finest information about Scotch whisky and associating the right brands.
>
> **WARNER** 2010: 102

Visionaries, artists, legacies, aristocracy and timeless appeal, these are identical notions to those exploited by India's elite designers, who, as we saw earlier, struggle to teach the elite how to turn life itself into art. Chivas claims to stand for 'exuberance perfected to an art and a way of life', with its *mantra* (Keller 1999) – 'art is life is art'. Chivas life not only refers to living life with chivalry, brotherhood, honour, gallantry, prestige, loyalty but also living a life of aristocracy, a life that is itself turned into a masterpiece, perfected to the last detail through the most luxurious and sensuous experiences, garments, tastes, smells, ideas and movements. The elite businessmen all nostalgically invoke the Mughal emperors who transformed wine drinking into a refined courtly art. They talk of the poetry and miniature painting, which depicted wine as the realization of the divine world, of the sacred. In those days, a cup of wine equalled a life of joy, power, wealth and success, as they say. It is well-known that the great majority of 'the Mughal kings, princes and nobles were hard drinkers and drug addicts' and that Jahangir 'used to mix wines and drank cocktails' (Lal 1988: 162), a fact that has been brought up several times during our conversations, but that appeared to emasculate Jahangir in the eyes of my contemporary interlocutors; possibly only his ferocious hunting expeditions could prevent him from being perceived as effeminate. Even today, the ambivalent Mughal rulers are the trendsetters. Even though drinking was referred to as evil in many religious scriptures and among commoners, much like in contemporary health propaganda, the power of its glamorization by the ruling classes and association with a life of lavishness, exuberance, luxury and wealth (Singh and Lal 1979) proved to be stronger; even today it promises miraculous moments of sovereignty. Chivas Studio attempts to do just that and provide the elite with a feeling of sovereignty and a total experience that would transform life itself into art, one where haute couture goes hand in hand with haute cuisine and haute cocktails, all served on a plate of interpretation and artspeak, where phantasmatic images of the past and present intermingle. The vulgar habit of drinking is turned into an art form worthy of kings. Artification also legitimates what otherwise would be considered conspicuous consumption (Veblen 1970) by transforming it into an investment in art or life as art. Within the reality of capital, it is the artified commodities that bear the promise of an experience of sovereignty and the miraculous. 'The thing is elevated to the status of the sovereign, in the sense of sovereign value, and human beings abrogate their subjectivity ... in making the object the measure of their dignity and worth' (Lamarche 2007: 65). Such 'things can occasion sovereign moments, but they are neither the form nor the expression of sovereignty' (Lamarche 2007: 67).

Brand essence of Chivas

The miraculous and the sovereign are carefully planted into the brand phantasm (Favero 2005) of Chivas. Its mythology is narrated as follows. In 1801 the Chivas brothers opened a grocery store in Aberdeen, where they sold luxury foods, such as exotic spices, coffee or Caribbean rums and began producing a smooth blended whisky. In 1843 they were granted a Royal Warrant to supply goods to Queen Victoria and finally in 1909 they launched Chivas Regal. In 2003 Chivas launched Royal Salute 50 Year Old, a special edition to celebrate Queen Elizabeth II's fifty years on the throne. The power of Chivas relies on its connection to aristocracy and the cultivation of a tacit belief among its consumers that the whisky has an essence that has the power to transform any drinker into a member of an exclusive club. The branding *gurus* exploit our human propensity to animate material objects, knowing very well that are 'lost without the capacity to appreciate that a liquid looks like wine but is really the blood of Christ' (Bloom 2010: 219).

There is an expression in pop economics – the Chivas Regal Effect; it refers to a product selling in larger quantities because its price has been increased (Martin 2011). It is said that this was the case of Chivas Regal, initially a rather obscure Scottish whisky, which turned into one of the most luxurious whiskies in the world because of its exaggerated price tag. People tend to equate quality with price; the more expensive the better and the more valuable. Studies by neurophysiologists show that the actual experienced pleasantness of wine is higher when the wine tasted is believed to be expensive. These studies show that the experience pleasantness 'depends on non-intrinsic properties of products, such as price at which they are sold' (Plassman et al. 2008: 1052). Our belief that a more expensive wine or whisky are essentially tastier, even if we cynically dismiss it as illusion, in fact alters our sensory expectations which in turn alter our perceptual interpretations and so it happens that we experience what we expect to experience.

Brotherhoods of luxury whisky drinkers

Fashion designers who forged an alliance with Chivas had to capture in their phantasmatic neo-royal designs also the idea of knighthood, honour and brotherhood. Chivalry, this peculiar medieval concept revived in the Victorian era and, combined with imperial ambitions, provided one of the many additional moral justifications for England's rule in its colonies (Girouard 1981). But this neo-royal sentiment again smoothly blends with a meritocratic one. Chivalry namely also appeals to achieved status. It is said that even when chivalry 'formed and authorized the class, gender and racial/religious superiority of the knight' it 'also provided a young male of the lower aspiring aristocracy with the means of upward social mobility' (Rajan 2004: 41). Chivas embodies both the idea of muscular meritocratic achievement and of belonging to aristocracy, thus mimicking the structure of the balancing acts of elite masculinity, and the logic of Indian luxury fashion at large. Chivalry in colonial India was a value ascribed both to the British and to the Indians. Rescuing of Indian brides from *sati* was often quoted by the British as the example par excellence of their chivalry and humanitarianism, intended to legitimize their superiority. Though *sati* was abolished in 1829, it continued to preoccupy British minds long after. In their imagination, *sati* was connected in particular to the area of Rajputana on the periphery of the controlled British India, an area populated by the martial race of Rajputs, deemed to be notoriously obsessed with questions of status, rank and honour. At the same time, the British wrote down stories that portrayed the Rajputs as chivalrous; an imagination that persists until today and inspires fashion collections, such as Samant Chauhan's popular line Rajputana, while tourist brochures still brand Rajasthan as 'the land of chivalry and romance'.

Chivas, in the good old British tradition, exploits the exact same logic of seduction and promise of rank and honour, as did Queen Victoria, who institutionalized the orders of chivalry, promising an elite membership. From the *Order of the Star of India* (1861), to the *Imperial Order of the Crown of India* (1878) and *The Most Eminent Order of the Indian Empire* (1878), the aim of these orders was to 'rank, reward and reconcile the British proconsular elite and the Indian princely elite' (Cannadine 2002: 88). The British understood very well that what mattered and still matters in India, is rank, status, honour, and respect. Precisely by exploiting the status obsession of the princely rulers and their desire for imperial honours, the British managed to unite the elites. Yet, paradoxically, 'the acceptance of an honour did not merely elevate someone in the social and imperial hierarchy; it also put them formally in a direct and subordinate relation to the monarch. For as the "Fountain of Honour", British kings and queens were, among other things, sovereigns of all the orders of chivalry' (Cannadine 2002: 100). Today it is the transnational corporations that distribute the privilege to feel privileged and to experience privilege. As the Chivas Regal campaign claims, life is not about having more, 'the new luxury is about being more'. Having becomes the precondition for being, rather than the other way round, as the underlying logic of celebrity narcissism leaves no space for doing and acting.

Excursus into Chivas life

Returning to New Delhi, I receive a text message from Arjun: 'get me two bottles of Chivas 18 from duty free'. Over the next few hours more messages like this one arrive. Landing at Indira Gandhi International Airport, I am greeted with Chivas commercials promising a lucky winner a luxury stay at the Cannes film festival. Soon after my arrival, I am invited to Arjun's secret flat (his immediate family is not aware of its existence) in South Delhi to join him and his fellow fashionable gentlemen for some drinks, before we head out for a fashion party. The flat is a peculiar play-sphere (Huizinga 1955) designed for staging masculinity and cultivation of homosocial bonds, as women are as a general rule not allowed and my presence is enabled largely due to my whiteness. The flat is a meeting place for his friends and business partners, largely sons of politicians and industrialists, businessmen, restaurant, bar, club and factory owners and, more practically, some lawyers. Nobody lives there, except for a bar stuffed with the world's finest whisky, liqueur and wine, a fridge with Corona beer, limes, ice cubes, juices and sofa, king-size bed, flat screen TV and three ACs. Once, I commented on Arjun's taste for extremely expensive whisky and suggested that it may not be really necessary to waste so much money on it. He just replied, 'so what do you suggest, that I buy some cheap whisky, like some middle class *mamuli aadmi* having a little fun once in a month, or maybe I should not drink at all, right? For your information, I am a Jat guy and we Jats drink, we are aggressive men and we drink only the best and we also give our guests the best, that is how we are. You should know by now that I am no cheap middle class clerk'. The cheapness of the whisky is easily transposed on the middle class 'worthless' man; the 'real manhood' is transposed onto the expensive and the exclusive. At the same time, however, the drinking of both cheap booze and whisky by low class gangsters serves as an inspiration, and these underlying connotations provide the 'primitive' core of its 'Indianness' and make it desirable. They drink and in between the practical matters of business, they show off their knowledge of the world of liquor and cocktails, brands, and big names in business and politics. The meetings follow the same pattern each time, and each time the men overplay their real power, claim to be able to deliver more than they can, claim to be able to take more alcohol than they are, and so on. It is not all fake; rather, these well-orchestrated acts serve the continuation of their mutual bonds, making them feel powerful and good around each other, increasing their confidence as men.

Later on, I am headed with Arjun and Rajesh, the upcoming designer from an upper class semi-royal family in Jodhpur, to a by-invitation-only fashion party sponsored by Blender's Pride at one of Delhi's five-star hotels, while the other men continue drinking in the flat. Arjun is dressed up in R. Rathore's Jodhpur *bandhgala* jacket, in the style worn by the young princes and rulers during the birth of new India. Rajesh wears his own creation, decorated with heavy embroidery, both of them matching these jackets with casual jeans and Dior shoes. We are driving an SUV, Mayawati's flag is spinning around the front bonnet, and the men continue drinking whisky. It does not bother them that the punishment for drunken driving has been increasing over the last years, as the death tolls and injuries on the roads keep rising. Since March 2012, the penalty for drunk driving depends on the levels of alcohol found, but can lead to imprisonment from six months to four years, 10,000Rs fine and cancellation of the driving licence. Still, drunk driving is about the most commonplace pastime among young wealthy men, a way for them to assert both their masculinity and power, as it usually does not take them more than a bribe if they are caught. And if they happen to bump into an honest policeman, it will merely take a call to a distant relative in a higher post, some shouting and arguing, something they actually desire to happen. To handle such situations, Arjun even has multiple fake driving licences in his car ready to throw at the perplexed policemen and drive away. Encounters with police are common, and the thrill is sought after; after all these games of humiliating the police, the system and the law by the power of capital, financial and social, are considered the greatest proof of *goonda* manhood; not to mention the thrill of transgression.

We reach the hotel, the car is checked by security guards, and we are as usual greeted with a *namaste* from a man dressed in a traditional Rajasthani outfit, with a large red turban and an enormous moustache. We pass through another airport-like security check at the entrance and smell the fragrance of luxury spreading through the air of the hotel, the oasis of sensory branding (Lindstrom 2009), relieving us from the filth and heat of the streets. On the top floor of the hotel, we are checked again. Since we arrive late, we miss the official part of the event, a small fashion show that took the form of performance art. The artsy atmosphere still fills the air, the models, dressed in the collection pieces featuring a mixture of fabric prints inspired by Indian miniature art and pop art, are mingling among the guests, alternative music and light projections are still in full swing, the bartenders are juggling with bottles of Smirnoff. Then there are the models, beautiful, tall, dressed up mostly in Western branded clothes. They are paid by the sponsors to attend the event and just mingle. They sit around with older wealthy men, drinking cocktails; some smile, some dance, some just sit and stare at the crowd. This has become a regular part of their modelling jobs in Delhi, a way to make extra money and get free drinks. They are paid to beautify the event. Their beauty is, much like the beauty of art, intended to elevate the aesthetic as much as commercial value of the event and of the fashionable objects on sale, while attracting the attendance of men. In between, a few invited page 3 journalists are trying to get the right pictures of the right people.

Ambient governance and manhood

Art and fashion events sponsored by alcohol brands play into the muscular and elitist desires of men like Arjun and Rajesh, while exploiting the residual aura of high art and drawing credibility from reputable personas of the Indian art world. The connoisseurs of whisky cocktails become one with connoisseurs of art. The environment screams masculine superiority without ever explicitly saying it. During these events, the brand message is at once everywhere and nowhere (Tosh 1994), exemplary of the logic of ambient governance. The experience design of Chivas and similar events, often taking place in lavish ambient luxury hotels with interior design and architectonical elements evoking the palaces of the Maharajas, with waiters and guards in traditional attires, cultivates a sense of wonder and resonance, much like a museum does (Greenblatt 1991). The decorated space with its dressed up models, luxurious products, antiques and art objects, is designed as such to resonate with the visitors and evoke in the viewers the phantasmatic lifeworlds of the royals, as well as the dynamic and cultural forces from which these objects have emerged (Greenblatt 1991). The fashion designs turned into art pieces are there to create a sense of wonder, stemming from the power of these objects to 'convey an arresting sense of uniqueness, to evoke an exalted attention' (Greenblatt 1991: 42). Clothes displayed within such a resonant ambient setting enchant the viewers, triggering a desire in them to possess these objects with all their magical power, one that Chivas hopes will transpose onto the brand. Authenticity, which all brands claim in one way or the other, that is, 'that quality that somehow connects the commodity to a place or time with special significance, often rooted in notions of tradition' (Smith 1996: 506), is also effectively manufactured through designing of resonance and wonder. Sentiment, emotions, morality, both individual and collective, qualities such as prestige, manhood, or Indianness, are all becoming inseparable from the realm of consumption – it is no longer what you are buying, but what you are buying into, be it purchasing designer garments to help elevate the poverty-stricken artisans, the lifestyle of the privileged of the bygone era projected on the canvas of India's confident phantasmatic future as a global economic force to be reckoned with or manhood itself (Figure 7.2). This creation of total ambient atmospheres is symptomatic of a shift in advertising strategies. Direct advertising of the Uncle Sam type, pointing at you to join the army, is being replaced by a fundamental self-effacement of advertisers, leading up to proliferation of strategies of subtle, invisible consumer governance in which desire is managed and subjects disciplined to shop (Serazio 2013). So for instance, the US army, following this logic, developed a computer game that can be downloaded for free, a game without any explicit injunction to join the army and yet screaming 'join', demanding participatory agency, teaching the player the army codes.

FIGURE 7.2 Models posing backstage at India Couture Week 2014, designs by Sabyasachi Mukherjee

Image courtesy: Nitin Patel Photography.

Conclusion: you are inside the game

Chivas-sponsored events function in the same way as the US army game. Those who attend these events find themselves within a carefully designed game, in which they are active players, reproducing in their everyday acts willingly the myths of our days and endorsing the brand values. It is said that the most powerful PR is one of the invisible kind (Cutlip 1994). The increasing importance placed upon engagement rather than impression alone means that people both act and are acted upon, that participation is engineered and that persuasion is achieved in a naturalized and even invisible way to the subject. In a media-saturated and manipulated world ambient governance becomes one of the dominant forms of influencing definitions of reality, desires and beliefs. The atmospheres produced in these settings are not only performative, as we saw earlier, but also disciplining. The practice of astroturfing, that is, the use of paid agents in order to manufacture public opinion and create an illusion of popular, or grass-root sentiment, is becoming widespread. Even though astroturfing most commonly refers to online manufacturing of fake profiles, opinions, and 'independent' blogs, it has also a strong presence during real events, for example among the socialites, designers, or fashion and art critics and others who pose as independent subjects expressing private opinions. For instance, most commonly, fashion bloggers are paid by the sponsors to show up and write about the events, often mingling with the crowd, turning over time into socialites and opinion makers, who at the same time claim to be unbiased and so on.

These guerrilla tactics create an ambivalent terrain, where it becomes close to impossible to distinguish 'fake' from 'real', where brand messages tapping into the core of people's identities, be they related to 'being Indian' or a 'real man', become connected to products and designed experiences, passionately endorsed by the consumers themselves, where people are persuaded in invisible ways and governed without feeling any disciplinary measures. The same guerrilla tactics we see in the fashion business are used in Indian politics. After all, fashion events at luxury venues are increasingly also spaces where Indian political elites mingle with business elites and develop their own strategies of invisible seduction and ambient governance combined with increasing online and offline astroturfing. Sponsorships by the alcohol industry have in recent years effectively transformed elite fashion events into alternative spaces where elite men gather, interact and display their masculinity, while at the same time legitimately indulging in fashion. Whisky turned out to be the perfect balancing substance that has clearly stimulated the rise of the market with elite men's fashion.

The intensified return to Indianness, feudal aesthetics, and the reinvention of tradition and heritage, combined with the *goonda* power and machismo, is symptomatic of the desire of the elites to reinforce the shared illusion of the rise of India as a global power. Global, gendered as masculine, in opposition to the feminine local, calls in the view of my business interlocutors for strong masculine power (Freeman 2001) or at least its aesthetic theatrical displays. As one of them fittingly put it, 'there's been enough talk of India's soft power, now it is time to show the world India's balls', a widespread popular sentiment both among the designers and their clients. The individual management of the balance of masculine power translates into the management of the power balance of India at large, at least among the cosmopolitan business class. Earlier we saw how spiritualism, philanthropy and ethical business are constructed as part of India's soft power, here we see how this construction is circumvented and balanced out by recreating the powerful Indian manhood. Events such as Chivas Studio, popular with the media, as well as cinematic portrayals of the world of the rich and successful, be they businessmen, politicians or gangsters, sustain the ideals of neo-liberalism (Sarma 2014) and spectacular capitalism (Gilman-Opalsky 2011).

CONCLUSION

India often appears as if clearly bifurcated into two parallel and disconnected worlds, into the world of formal and informal economy, the massive world of the poor and the gated world of the rich and the middle class, into the worlds of opulent luxury and dirt. Throughout the book, we have seen that this disconnect is a carefully cultivated illusion that requires great amounts of social labour in order to be maintained, precisely because the mutual networks of dependency are so dense and because traditional caste hierarchies are being increasingly questioned and opposed. The opulent neo-feudal aesthetics comes to rescue and to reclaim the social order that the elites deem necessary for their own joyful flourishing. The maximalist neo-royal fashion does not only visually insist on the imagined traditional hierarchies, providing the elite with an unmistakable aesthetic of social distinction, but it goes hand in hand with new strategies of claiming power, such as the charitable non-love that perpetuates poverty and misery rather than relieving it, as it claims. Everything that is worn by the elites has passed through numerous hands of the underprivileged, the more hands the more luxurious the piece and the more power over others the attire embodies; the artisans are pain-stakingly embroidering these neo-feudal symbols of their own subjugation, while they should be thankful for their 'fair wage'. The current philanthrocapitalism that has taken elite India by storm is deeply neo-feudal in its nature while being wrapped up in rhetoric of good intentions; it is a telling sign of the times of rising socio-economic inequality. It goes hand in hand with the rise of Hindu nationalism, communalist politics, and brutal insistence on traditions that may never have been. But the privileged and often wealthy fashion designers, selling to the very rich, while managing the impoverished workforce, know better than to invoke a singularly Hindu nationalism; they aim higher, namely at designing a distinctly Indian neo-aristocracy, yet of a transnational calibre. Belonging to the very new class of creatives that emerged during the last three decades and that had to legitimize its own existence by claiming its value, creativity, prestige and unique expertise, the fashion designers have turned into practical ideologues of the elite capitalist class; they have developed not only a seductive rhetoric for the elites but also effective strategies of co-opting even some of the most reluctant villagers in the merciless capitalist system of production, while making sure that the artisans do not even think of competing with them. Catering to the transnational business elite, where money matters more than caste background, and where social awareness has to be displayed together with fancy clothes, they have learned never to use communalist or casteist rhetoric; that, they relegate to the domain of corrupt and 'dirty' politics. No, they never talk of caste, they never talk of structural constraints either, but they talk of illiteracy, of uneducated masses, of individual failure, and of the need to empower, educate, and so on. Here, they team up with their heroes, the self-made businessmen and benevolent philanthropists, the same men that are meant to be the heroes of the future Indian superpowerdom, of the land of futuristic smart cities and special economic zones. The designers have learned that dealing in 'ethical business', and running an NGO on the side, can be a powerful tool not of only value creation, but more practically of exerting control and power over their current and future workforce. In line with the meritocratic ideology they worship, they preach hard work and claim that individual incompetence, laziness, lack of drive and of dreams and so on, is the true root cause of all social evil in India. And yet, when it comes to the artistry and knowledge of the artisans, they are quick to dismiss the artisans as members of a collectivity stuck in some traditional past, and to deny any possibility of their individuality and originality. Individual ability in the artisan is out of question, yet his individual failure is to be blamed.

Even when the rich live in carefully curated and gated echo-chambers from which much of the world outside of the luxury venues has been photoshopped, they not only depend for all their wealth, luxuries and social power on those they despise as 'low Others', but they also seem utterly unable to keep away from the lowness and dirt they claim to despise so much. Ironically, as we have seen, endorsing the cause of impoverished low class women can become indispensable for the empowerment of the elite woman, who literally depends for her own social power on maintaining the status quo, while claiming to want to change it. Without (re)producing the poor, vulnerable and weak, the elite women would have nowhere to delegate their morality, while parading in their sexy designer *saris*. But even the elite men seem painfully drawn to what they imagine as the vulgar machismo of the low class Others. They want it and they want it badly, if only to counteract their effeminate indulgences in luxury and to feel like the invincible rulers of the world. Without the powers of those imagined and desired as low and dirty, there would be no designers, and no elites. So laughs the craftswoman, when she prefers to enjoy the everyday luxuries of her anti-work ethic and refuses to embroider anymore symbols of elite distinction. She laughs even more as she drives the designer dependent on a timely delivery crazy. We have a thing or two to learn from her; the political consequences are left to the reader to contemplate.

FIGURE 8.1 Back *lehenga* design by Sabyasachi Mukherjee, a piece that was on show at the Historical Museum in Oslo, during the *Fashion India: Spectacular Capitalism* exhibition curated by the author

Image courtesy: Kirsten Helgeland.

GLOSSARY

All Hindi words throughout this book are italicized, with the exception of personal and place names. Common English spelling has been favoured and Hindi words can appear in plural with the English 's' ending. This more colloquial transliteration has been chosen because it more closely mirrors the dynamic playfulness of the everyday use of Hindi, with its mixing and remixing of Hindi and English terms, as well as the way my interlocutors themselves transliterate Hindi words. All italicized words are explained in this glossary.

Aaraam (se) at leisure, at ease, comfort, luxury, rest, pleasure, repose, inactivity.

Achkan originally a court dress of North Indian royalty and nobility of the princely states; today worn on special occasions instead of Western suits; also worn by the groom, especially in Sikh, Rajput and Maratha wedding ceremonies. It is a knee-length coat with a Nehru collar similar to *sherwani*, but has only one breast pocket on the left side.

Adhurapan imperfection, incompleteness, lack.

Ahimsa translates as not to harm or injure and refers to the idea of nonviolence, occurring already in the Vedic scriptures, and particularly connected to the ethical philosophy of Jainism and to Mahatma Gandhi's movement of nonviolent resistance, Swami Vivekananda and others.

Aina khana glass house or mirror house, or room covered with glass deco in various shapes; in our case a treasure house of the late Asaf-ud-Daula (1748–1797), the Nawab Wazir of Awadh.

Anarkali knee-length or long kurta fitted in the waist, with number of panels, often but not always multi-layered, with long sleeves and embroidery.

Bandhgala closed neck or collar jackets, can also refer to Jodhpuri formal evening suit, or Nehru-style jackets.

Baniya traditionally a caste of merchants, bankers and money-lenders; the word *baniya* is also widely used as a derogatory term for business people who are considered stingy.

Bazaar local market.

Begum an honorific for influential Muslim women of high social status.

Bhang an intoxicating beverage prepared from a cannabis plant mixed with spices, milk and ghee, commonly used during Hindu festivals like Holi in India and Nepal, but it is also believed to have healing properties; Sadhus and Sufis are also known to use bhang to reach transcendental states.

Bharat official Sanskrit name of the Republic of India.

Bharatanatyam classical Indian dance with its origins in the temples of Tamil Nadu where it was danced by the *devadasis*; typically a solo dance, where the dancer incorporates different masculine and feminine characters; it was revived in the twentieth century by several famous performers, such as Rukmini Devi.

Brahmin traditionally a caste of priests.

Chikan traditionally a white on white embroidery from Lucknow, North India.

Chikankaar chikan embroiderer, today typically a female; in the eighteenth century men dominated the chikan courtly art.

Churidar pajama tight fitting and extra long *salwar* that allows for the creation of decorative folds at the ankles.

Crore ten million; commonly used unit in the Indian numbering system.

Darshan auspicious sight, vision of the divine in Hindu worship.

Desi derives from the word *desh* or country, often in diasporic context it refers to something hip, urban, trendy and of South Asian origin.

Devadasi literally servants of god, South Indian temple dancers, who enjoyed high social status in the past; during British rule the networks of patronage broke down as the kings became powerless, while the British insisted on outlawing the *devadasi* system, claiming that it fuelled prostitution; the *devadasi* system was outlawed in 1988 across India.

Dharma a broad concept referring the (natural) law, to that which upholds the whole of the universe, while encompassing ideas such as duty, balance, morality and so on, thus offering a complex set of interpretations depending on the given tradition.

Dhobi a traditional Hindu occupational caste of washermen.

Dupatta scarf worn together with salwar suit, either around the shoulders or over the head.

Gali narrow passageway or lane.

Ghazal poetic form with rhyming couplets.

Goonda from the word rascal, refers to criminals and hired thugs, *goonda* tax refers to extortion money.

Guru teacher or master from the Hindu tradition.

Hijab veil covering head and chest, worn by Muslim women.

Holi ancient Hindu religious festival, also known as the spring festival or the festival of colours and love.

Imambara congregation hall for Shia commemoration ceremonies, especially for the mourning festival of *Muharram*.

Jali a stitch in chikan, where the thread is never drawn through the fabric, instead the warp and weft threads are carefully drawn apart to create minute buttonhole stitches.

Kala concept referring to art, appearing for instance in the Kamasutra of Vatsyayana, where Lord Krishna is said to have possessed sixty-four different kinds of art, which included for instance singing, dancing, theatricals, painting, jewellery making, juggling, applying colours, dressing up, applying ornaments, needlework, weaving, solving riddles, enacting plays and anecdotes, spinning, carpentry, metallurgy, use of amulets, enforcing discipline, achieving victory, mineralogy, or art of conversation.

Kalakaar artist.

Karigaar craftsman.

Kathak a North Indian classical dance, revitalized in post-Independence India.

Khadi handwoven cloth.

Khalipan emptiness, vacuum, void.

Kurta a shirt akin to a tunic, short, medium-length or knee-length.

Lakh one hundred thousand; commonly used unit in the Indian numbering system.

Lakhnawi tehzeeb Lucknow culture.

Lakhnawiyat the essence or quality of belonging to Lucknow, or Lucknowness.

Lehenga long, embroidered and pleated skirt.

Linga representation of the Hindu deity Shiva.

Lungi fabric sewn into a tube like a skirt and then wrapped around at the waist and worn as a lower garment, mostly worn by men.

Mamuli aadmi ordinary, undistinguished or insignificant person.

Mantra sacred utterance, syllable or sacred words, endowed with spiritual value, and power, especially when repeated; common to Hinduism and Buddhism.

Masala mixed spices, remixed.

Mojris traditional flat handmade camel leather shoes for both men and women originating from Rajasthan but widely worn in Punjab, Uttar Pradesh and Gujarat.

Muharram first month of the Islamic calendar, and month of remembrance, beginning with the first night of Muharram when Shia Muslims start mourning for ten days, in remembrance of the Battle of Karbala, where Imam Hussain and his seventy-two followers were killed.

Mujra a form of dance practised by courtesans in the Mughal era, incorporating elements of *kathak*.

Mukeish metal wire embroidery; small rectangular pieces of metal are pressed around fabric threads.

Nafaasat sophistication, refinement.

Namaste customary Hindu greeting with a slight bow and hands pressed together.

Nazaakat delicacy, softness, distinction.

Paan betel leaf, sometimes mixed with tobacco, and chewed as stimulant.

Padshah superlative royal title, a combination of the Persian titles of master and king, appropriated by rulers claiming the highest rank.

Panchayat local assembly of elders, typically settling village disputes.

Pativrata devoted wife, who worships her husband as a god, dresses modestly and never looks at another man.

Puja a Hindu religious ritual; an act of worship.

Purdah religious and social practice of female seclusion; segregation of sexes that prevents men from seeing women to whom they are not related in terms of kinship.

Rani pink or queen pink, a popular shade of pink for festive attire.

Rastogi a Hindu caste, belonging to merchant castes.

Rupee currency of India.

Salwar loose trousers, fitted at the ankles with drawstring at the waist.

Salwar kameez *salwar* matched with *kurta*; *salwar* suit.

Sari from Sanskrit, meaning strip of cloth; South Asian female garment consisting of a drape from around five to eight metres long, and 60 to 120 centimetres broad, worn over a petticoat and blouse.

Shahtoosh from Persian 'king of fine wools', ring shawls woven from the hair of Tibetan antelope, often hunted down and killed in the process; trade in *shahtoosh* is illegal.

Sherwani long, coat-like garment, traditionally associated with aristocracy.

Taluqdar members of landed aristocracy; Indian land holders in the Mughal and British era, who were also responsible for collecting taxes.

Tawaif courtesan, whose clients and patrons belonged to the nobility, especially during the Mughal era.

Tehzeeb culture, spirit.

Zamindar South Asian hereditary aristocrat, who held vast amounts of land and controlled peasants, had the right to collect taxes; eventually, many appropriated royal and princely titles.

Zardozi today a metal wire embroidery, often done with crystals or Swarovski stones, in the seventeenth and eighteenth century *zardozi* was also done with gold and silver threads and semi-precious and precious stones.

Zenana part of house reserved solely for women.

BIBLIOGRAPHY

Adajania, H. (2012), *Cocktail*, 144 min, India: Eros International.

Ali, M. (1981), *Umrao Jaan*, 145 min, India.

Ali, M. (2007), 'Shahr e Nigaaran', *Seminar 575: Between cultures – a symposium on the changing face of Lucknow*, 58–61.

Ali, M. (2009), available online: http://muzaffarali.com/html/fashion.htm, (accessed 17th September 2015).

Ali, S. A. (1927), 'The Moghul Emperors of India as Naturalists and Sportsmen', *Journal of the Bombay Natural History Society*, 31, 833–861.

Alter, J. S. (1992), *The Wrestler's Body: Identity and Ideology in North India*, Berkeley: University of California Press.

Althusser, L. (1971), 'Ideology and Ideological State Apparatuses', in B. Brewster (transl.) *Lenin and Philosophy, and Other Essays*: 127–188, London: New Left Books.

Amrohi, K. (1971), *Pakeezah*, 126 min, India.

Anderson, B. (2009), 'Affective Atmospheres', *Emotion, Space, Society*, 2, 77–81.

Anton, C. (2001), *Selfhood and Authenticity*, New York: State University of New York Press.

Anton, C. (2011), *Communication Uncovered: General Semantics and Media Ecology*, Forth Worth, TX: Institute of General Semantics.

Appadurai, A. (1990), 'Disjuncture and Difference in Global Cultural Economy', *Public Culture*, 2:2, 1–24.

Appadurai, A. (1995), 'Public Modernity in India', in C. A. Breckenridge (ed.) *Consuming Modernity*: 1–22, New Delhi: Oxford University Press.

Appadurai, A. (1996), *Modernity at Large: Cultural Dimensions of Globalization*, Minneapolis: University of Minnesota Press.

Appadurai, A. (2000), 'Grassroots Globalization and the Research Imagination', *Public Culture*, 12:1, 1–19.

Appadurai, A. (2008), *The Social Life of Things: Commodities in Cultural Perspective*, Cambridge: Cambridge University Press.

Argenti, P. A. (2007), *Strategic Corporate Communication*, New Delhi: McGraw-Hill Education.

Armitage, J. and J. Roberts (2015), *Critical Luxury Studies: Art, Design, Media*, Edinburgh: Edinburgh University Press.

Arora, T. (2012), 'India's King of Couture', *Bangkok Post*, available online: www.bangkokpost.com/business/economics/306234/india-s-king-of-couture (accessed 14th September 2015).

Arvidsson, A. (2006), *Brands: Meaning and Value in Media Culture*, London: Routledge.

Arya, P. and S. Sadhana (2001), *Diagnostic Study: The Chikan Embroidery Cluster, Lucknow, Uttar Pradesh*, New Delhi: UNIDO, Cluster Development Programme, India.

Aziz, N. (2007), 'A Mesh of Memories', *Seminar 575: Between cultures – a symposium on the changing face of Lucknow*, 46–54.

Babb, L. A. and S. S. Wadley (1998), *Media and the Transformation of Religion in South Asia*, New Delhi: Motilal Banarsidass Publishers.

Balaram, S. (2005), 'Design Pedagogy in India: A Perspective', *Design Issues*, 21:4, 11–22.

Balaram, S. (2011), *Thinking Design*, New Delhi: Sage.

Banerjee, S. (2003), 'Gender and Nationalism: The Masculinization of Hinduism and Female Political Participation in India', *Women's Studies International Forum*, 26:2, 167–179.

Banerjee, S. B. (2008), 'Corporate Social Responsibility: The Good, the Bad and the Ugly', *Critical Sociology*, 34:1, 51–79.

Banerji, R. (2008), *Sex and Power: Defining History, Shaping Societies*, New Delhi: Penguin Books.

Bansal, R. (2008), *Stay Hungry, Stay Foolish*, Ahmedabad: IIM.

Barth, F. (1969), *Ethnic Groups and Boundaries: The Social Organization of Cultural Difference*, Bergen: Universitetsforlaget.

Barthes, R. (1977), *Image-Music-Text*, London: Fontana.

Barthes, R. (1983), *The Fashion System*, New York: Hill.

Barthes, R., A. Stafford and M. Carter (2006), *The Language of Fashion*, Oxford: Berg.

Basole, A. (2012), 'Knowledge, Gender, and Production Relations in India's Informal Economy', PhD Thesis, University of Massachusetts, Economics.

Basole, A. and D. Basu (2009), 'Relations of Production and Modes of Surplus Extraction in India: An Aggregate Study', *Working Paper 2009–2012*, Department of Economics, University of Massachusetts, Amherst.

Bataille, G. (1993), *The Accursed Share: Volumes II and III*, New York: Zone Books.

Baudrillard, J. (1975), *The Mirror of Production*, New York: Telos Press.

Beck, U. (1997), *The Reinvention of Politics: Rethinking Modernity in the Global Social Order*, London: Wiley.

Berman, M. (1983), *All that is Solid Melts Into Air: The Experience of Modernity*, London: Verso.

Berry, C. (1994), *The Idea of Luxury: A Conceptual and Historical Investigation*, Cambridge: Cambridge University Press.

Bhabha, H. K. (1994), *The Location of Culture*, London: Routledge.

Bhachu, P. (2004), *Dangerous Designs: Asian Women Fashion the Diaspora Economies*, New York: Routledge.

Bishop, M. and M. Green (2008), *Philanthrocapitalism: How the Rich Can Save the World and Why We Should Let Them*, London: A&C Black.

Black, J. (2013), *Making the American Body: The Remarkable Saga of the Men and Women Whose Feats, Feuds, and Passions Shaped Fitness History*, Nebraska: UNP.

Blau, P. (1974), 'Parameters of Social Structure', *American Sociological Review*, 39:5, 615–635.

Bloch, E. (2000), *The Spirit of Utopia*, Stanford, CA: Stanford University Press.

Bloom, P. (2010), *How Pleasure Works: The New Science of Why We Like What We Like*, New York: Norton.

Bodeker, G. and M. Cohen (2010), *Understanding the Global Spa Industry*, London: Taylor & Francis.

Bornstein, E. (2009), 'The Impulse of Philanthropy', *Cultural Anthropology*, 24:4, 622–651.

Bourdieu, P. (1996), *The Rules of Art: Genesis and Structure of the Literary Field*, California: Stanford University Press.

Boyer, D. and A. Yurchak (2010), 'American Stiob: Or, What Late-Socialist Aesthetics of Parody Reveal about Contemporary Political Culture in the West', *Cultural Anthropology*, 25:2, 179–221.

Brosius, C. (2009), 'The Gated Romance of "India Shining": Visualizing Urban Lifestyle in Advertisement of Residential Housing Development', in K. M. Gokulsing and W. Dissanayake (eds) *Popular Culture in Globalized India*: 174–191, London: Routledge.

Brosius, C. (2010), *India's Middle Class: New Forms of Urban Leisure, Consumption and Prosperity*, New Delhi: Routledge.

Brown, S. and P. MacLaren (1998), 'The Future is Past', in S. Brown, J. Bell and D. Carson (eds) *Marketing Apocalypse: Eschatology, Escapology and the Illusion of the End*: 260–277, New York: Taylor & Francis.

Brubaker, R. and F. Cooper (2000), 'Beyond "Identity"', *Theory and Society*, 29:1, 1–47.

Burawoy, M. (1979), *Manufacturing Consent: Changes in the Labor Process Under Monopoly Capitalism*, Chicago, IL: University of Chicago Press.

Butler, J. (1999), *Gender Trouble*, New York: Routledge Press.

Böhme, G. (1993), 'Atmosphere as the Fundamental Concept of New Aesthetics', *Thesis Eleven*, 36, 113–126.

Böhme, G. (2003), 'Contribution to the Critique of Aesthetic Economy', *Thesis Eleven*, 73, 71–82.

Böhme, G. (2010), 'The art of the stage set as a paradigm for an aesthetic of atmospheres', available online: www.cresson.archi.fr/PUBLI/pubCOLLOQUE/AMB8-confGBöhme-eng.pdf (accessed 10th May 2012).

Calefato, P. (2014), *Luxury: Fashion, Lifestyle and Excess*, London: Bloomsbury.

Cameron, A. and R. Palan (2004), *The Imagined Economies of Globalization*, London: Sage.

Cannadine, D. (2002), *Ornamentalism: How the British Saw Their Empire*, Oxford: Oxford University Press.

Caplan, P. (1987), 'Celibacy as Solution? Mahatma Gandhi and Brahmacharya', in P. Caplan (ed.) *The Cultural Construction of Sexuality*: 271–295, New York: Tavistock Publications.

Carey, J. (1999), *The Faber Book of Utopias*, London: Faber & Faber.

Caroli, A. (2012), 'JJ Valaya Brings Ottoman Empire to the Ramp', *Hindustan Times*, New Delhi.

Cayla, J. (2008), 'Following the Endorser's Shadow: Shah Rukh Khan and the Creation of the Cosmopolitan Indian Male', *Adveritising and Society Review*, 9:2.

Chandra, A. (2012), 'Manjari presenting Ganga-Jamuni tehzeeb on stage', *The Times of India*. Washington DC, available online: http://timesofindia.indiatimes.com/entertainment/hindi/music/news/Manjari-presenting-the-Ganga-Jamuni-tehzeeb-on-stage/articleshow/16769810.cms (accessed 14th September 2015).

Chandra, S. (2009), 'Mimicry, Masculinity, and the Mystique of Indian English: Western India, 1870–1900', *The Journal of Asian Studies*, 68:1, 199–225.

Ciotti, M. (2012), 'Post-colonial Renaissance: "Indianness", Contemporary Art and the Market in the Age of Neoliberal Capital', *Third World Quarterly*, 33:4, 637–655.

Citton, Y. (2010), *Mythocratie: Storytelling et Imaginaire de Gauche*, Amsterdam: Editions Amsterdam.

Clifford, J. (1997), 'Four Northwest Coast Museums: Travel Reflections', in J. Clifford (ed.) *Routes, Travel and Translation in the Late Twentieth Century*: 121, Cambridge: Harvard University Press.

Cohen, A. (1981), *The Politics of Elite Culture: Exploration in the Dramaturgy of Power in a Modern African Society*, Berkeley: University of California Press.

Comte, A. (1973), *System of Positive Polity*, New York: B. Franklin.

Conley, L. (2008), *OBD: Obsessive Branding Disorder: The Illusion of Business and The Business of Illusion*, Michigan: University of Michigan: Public Affairs.

Coomarswamy, A. K. (1966), *Introduction to Indian Art*, Delhi: Munshiram Manoharlal.

Crafts Council, D. (2007), 'Reviving the Embroidered Art of Chamba Rumal', *Craft Revival Quarterly*, June.

Crane, G. (1999), 'Imagining the Economic Nation: Globalisation in China', *New Political Economy*, 4:2.

Crill, R. (1999), *Indian Embroidery*, London: V&A Publications.

Crill, R. (2006), *Textiles from India: The Global Trade*, Calcutta: Seagull Books.

Critchley, S. (2002), *On Humour*, London: Routledge.

Cutlip, S. M. (1994), *The Unseen Power: Public Relations, A History*, Hillsdale, NJ: Lawrence Erlbaum Associates.

Das, G. (2000), *India Unbound*, New Delhi: Viking.

Das, P. (2007), 'A Conceptual Review of Advertising Regulation and Standards: Case Studies in The Indian Scenario', Paper presented at *International Marketing Conference on Marketing and Society*, IIMK, available online: http://dspace.iimk.ac.in/bitstream/handle/123456789/597/743-752.pdf?sequence=1&isAllowed=y (accessed 13th May 2011).

Das, S. K. (1991), *History of Indian Literature: 1911–1956, Struggle for Freedom: Triumph and Tragedy*, New Delhi: Sahitya Akademi.

De Neve, G. (2012), 'Fordism, Flexible Specialisation and CSR: How Indian Garment Workers Critique Neoliberal Labour Regimes', *Ethnography*, November 22, 1–24.

Dé, S. (2012), available online: http://shobhaade.blogspot.no/2012_08_01_archive.html (accessed 21st March 2013).

Demossier, M. (2011), 'Beyond Terroir: Territorial Construction, Hegemonic Discourses, and French Wine Culture', *Journal of the Royal Anthropological Institute*, 17, 685–705.

DeNicola, A. O. (2004), 'Creating Borders, Maintaining Boundaries: Traditional Work and Global Markets in Bagru's Handblock Textile Industry', dissertation, New York: Syracuse University.

Desai, S. (2010), *Mother Pious Lady: Making Sense of Everyday India*, New Delhi: HarperCollins Publishers India.

Deshpande, S. (1993), 'Imagined Economies: Styles of Nation-building in 20th Century India', *Journal of Arts and Ideas*, 25/26, 5–35.

Doniger, W. (1999), 'Presidential Address: "I have Scinde": Flogging a Dead (White Male Orientalist) Horse', *The Journal of Asian Studies*, 58:4, 940–960.

Doniger, W. (2000), *The Bedtrick: Tales of Sex and Masquerade*, Chicago, IL: University of Chicago Press.

Doniger, W. (2003), 'The "Kamasutra": It Isn't All about Sex', *The Kenyon Review*, 25:1, 18–37.

Doniger, W. (2010), *The Hindus: An Alternative History*, Oxford: Oxford University Press.

Donner, H. (2008), *Domestic Goddesses: Maternity, Globalization and Middle-Class Identity in Contemporary India*, Farnham: Ashgate.

Donner, H. (2011), *Being Middle-Class in India: A Way of Life*, Abington and New York: Routledge.

Douglas, M. (1968), 'The Social Control of Cognition: Some Factors in Joke Perception', *Man*, 3:3, 361–376.

Duara, A. (2005), 'On The Verge of Exctinction', *The Hindu: Magazine*, New Delhi: The Hindu.

Dundes, A. (1997), *Two Tales of Crow and Sparrow: A Freudian Folkloristic Essay on Caste and Untouchability*, Lanham: Rowman & Littlefield Publishers.

Durkheim, É. (1965), *The Elementary Forms of the Religious Life*, New York: The Free Press.

Dutta, J. P. (2006), *Umrao Jaan*, 189 min., India: T-Series.

Dwyer, C. and P. Jackson (2003) 'Commodifying Difference: Selling EASTern Fashion', *Environment and Planning D: Society and Space*, 21, 269–291.

Dwyer, R. (2000), 'The Erotics of the Wet Sari in Hindi Films', *South Asia*, XXIII:1, 143–159.

Dwyer, R. (2006), *Filming the Gods: Religion and Indian Cinema*, New York: Routledge.

Dwyer, R. and C. Pinney (2003), *Pleasure and The Nation: The History, Politics and Consumption of Popular Culture in India*, Oxford: Oxford University Press.

Eck, D. L. (1998), *Darśan: Seeing the Divine Image in India*, New York: Columbia University Press.

Edwards, E. (2010), 'From Gujarat to Topshop: South Asian Textiles and Craft', in R. Crill, P. Crang and C. Breward (eds) *Asian Style: Indian Textiles and Fashion in Britain*: 30–44, New Delhi: Bookwise (India) in association with V&A Publishing.

Elias, J. J. (2011), *On Wings of Diesel: Trucks, Indentity and Culture in Pakistan*, Oxford: Oneworld Publications.

Ensler, E. (2000), *The Vagina Monologues*, New York: Dramatists Play Service.

Entwistle, J. (2009), *The Aesthetic Economy of Fashion: Markets and Values in Clothing and Modelling*, Oxford: Berg.

Eriksen, T. H. (2003), 'Introduction', in T. H. Eriksen (ed.) *Globalisation*: 1–14, London: Pluto Press.

Eriksen, T. H. (2005), 'How can the global be local?', in O. Hemer, T. Tufte and T. H. Eriksen (eds) *Media and Glocal Change: Rethinking Communication for Development*: 25–40, Buenos Aires: CLASCO.

Escobar, A. (2011), *Encountering Development: The Making and Unmaking of the Third World*, Princeton, NJ: Princeton University Press.

Express, T. I. (2009), 'Descendents of Nawabs Keep Holi Traditions Alive', *The Indian Express*, Lucknow, 10 March.

Favero, P. (2005), *India Dreams: Cultural Identity Among Young Middle Class Men in New Dehli*, Stockholm: Stockholm Universitet.

Fernandez, J. and M. T. Huber (2001), 'Irony, Practice and the Moral Imagination', in J. Fernandez and M. T. Huber (eds) *Irony in Action: Anthropology, Practice and the Moral Imagination*: 261–264, Chicago, IL: Chicago University Press.

Fernandes, K. (2011), 'JJ Valaya Uncovers Decoded Paradox', *Luxpresso*. Availabe online: http://luxpresso.com/news-couture/jj-valaya-uncovers-decoded-paradox/3452 (accessed 14th September 2015).

Fernandes, L. (2004), 'The Politics of Forgetting: Class Politics, State Power and the Restructuring of Urban Space in India', *Urban Studies*, 41:12, 2415–2430.

Feuerbach, L. (1854), *The Essence of Christianity*, London: J. Chapman.

Fincher, D. (1999), *Fight Club*, 139 min, United States: 20th Century Fox.

Findley, E. B. (1996), 'Nur Jahan's Emroidery Trade and Flowers of the Taj', *Asian Art and Culture*, 9:2, 6–25.

Fisher, M. H. (1985), 'The Imperial Coronation of 1819: Awadh, the British and the Mughals', *Modern Asian Studies*, 19:2, 239–277.

Forth, C. E. (2008), *Masculinity in the Modern West: Gender, Civilization and the Body*, Bazingstoke: Palgrave Macmillan.

Foster, R. J. (2007), 'The Work of the New Economy: Consumers, Brands, and Value Creation', *Cultural Anthropology*, 22:4, 707–731.

Frank, R. H. (2001), *Luxury Fever: Why Money Fails to Satisfy In an Era of Excess*, New York: Free Press.

Fraser, N. and L. Gordon (1994), 'A Genealogy of Dependency: Tracing a Keyword of the US Welfare State', *Signs*, 19:2, 309–336.

Frazer, J. G. (2009), *The Golden Bough: A Study in Magic and Religion*, New York: Cosimo Classsics.

Frederickson, B. L. and T. Roberts (1997), 'Objectification Theory: Toward Understanding Women's Lived Experiences and Mental Health Risks', *Psychology of Women Quarterly*, 21, 173–206.

Freeman, C. (2001), 'Is Local: Global as Feminine: Masculine? Rethinking the Gender of Globalization', *Signs*, 26:4, 1007–1037.

Freud, S., J. Riviere and J. Strachey (1959), *Collected Papers: Papers on Metapsychology. Papers on Applied Psycho-analysis*, London: Basic Books.

Fromm, E. (2013), *Marx's Concept of Man*, online: Open Road Media.

Frøystad, K. (2005), *Blended Boundaries: Caste, Class and Shifting Notions of 'Hinduness' in a North Indian City*, New Delhi: Oxford University Press.

Gagliardi, P. (1990), 'Artifacts as Pathways and Remains of Organizational Life', in P. Gagliardi (ed.) *Symbols and Artifacts: Views of the Corporate Landscape*: 3–38, New York: Aldine de Gruyer.

Geczy, A. (2013), *Fashion and Orientalism: Dress, Textiles and Culture from the 17th to the 21st Century*, London: Bloomsbury.

Geczy, A. and V. Karaminas (2012), *Fashion and Art*. London: Bloomsbury.

Gell, A. (1994), 'The Technology of Enchantment and the Enchantment of Technology', in J. Coote and A. Shelton (eds) *Anthropology, Art and Aesthetics*: 40–63, Oxford: Oxford University Press.

Gilbert, H. and C. Tiffin (2008), 'Burden or Benefit? Imperial Benevolence and its Legacies', Bloomington, IN: Indiana University Press.

Gilman-Opalsky, R. (2011), *Spectacular Capitalism: Guy Debord and the Practice of Radical Philosophy*, New York: Minor Compositions.

Girard, R. (1990), 'Innovation and Repetition', *SubStance*, 19:2/3, 7–20.

Girouard, M. (1981), *The Return to Camelot: Chivalry and the English Gentleman*, New Haven: Yale University Press.

Gonda, J. (1969), *Eye and Gaze in the Veda*, Amsterdam: Elsevier Science.

Goodman, M. K., D. Goodman and M. Redclift (2010), *Consuming Space: Placing Consumption in Perspective*, Farnham: Ashgate.

Gook, B. (2011), 'Being there is everything!', *Memory Studies*, 4:1, 13–22.

Gopalakrishnan, S. (2006), 'Defining, Constructing and Policing "New India": Relationship between Neoliberalism and Hindutva', *Economic and Political Weekly*, 41:26, 2803–2813.

Gordon, B. and M. Feldman (2006), 'Introduction', in B. Gordon and M. Feldman (eds) *The Courtesan's Arts: Cross-Cultural Perspectives*: 3. Oxford: Oxford University Press.

Graff, V., N. Gupta and M. Hasan, (2006), 'Introduction', in V. Graff (ed.) *Lucknow: Memories of a City*: 11. New Delhi: Oxford University Press.

Granovetter, M. (1973), 'The Strength of Weak Ties', *The American Journal of Sociology*, 78:6, 1360–1380.

Granovetter, M. (1983), 'The Strength of Weak Ties: A Network Theory Revisited', *Sociological Theory*, 1, 201–233.

Greenblatt, S. (1991), 'Resonance and Wonder', in I. Karp and S. D. Lavine (eds) *The Poetics and Politics of Museum Display*: 42–56, Washington: Smithsonian Institution Press.

Grimes, R. L. (2011), 'Ritual, Media, and Conflict: An Introduction', in R. L. Grimes, U. Husken, U. Simon and E. Venbrux (eds) *Ritual, Media and Conflict*: 3–34, Oxford: Oxford University Press.

Gude, T. B. (2010), 'Hybrid Visions: The Cultural Landscape of Awadh', in T. B. Gude and S. Markel (eds) *India's Fabled City: The Art of Courtly Lucknow*: 67–102, Los Angeles County Museum of Art: DelMonico Books, Prestel.

Gundle, S. (2009), *Glamour: A History*, Oxford: Oxford University Press.

Gupta, D. (2007), *Mistaken Modernity: India Between Worlds*, New Delhi: HarperCollins Publishers India.

Gupta, D. (2008), 'The Middle Class Myth in India', available online: https://thesouthasianidea.wordpress.com/2008/03/26/the-middle-class-myth-in-india/ (accessed 14th September 2015).

Gupta, S. (2013), *Shootout at Wadala*, 150 mins, India: White Feathers Films.

Hakim, C. (2010), 'Erotic Capital', *European Sociological Review*, 1–20.

Hallam, E. and T. Ingold (2007), *Creativity and Cultural Improvisation*, Oxford: Berg.

Hancock, M. (2002), 'Subjects of Heritage in Urban Southern India', *Environment and Planning D: Society and Space*, 20, 693–717.

Hansen, T. B. (2001), *Wages of Violence: Naming and Identity in Postcolonial Bombay*, Princeton, NJ: Princeton University Press.

Herzfeld, M. (2001), 'Irony and Power: Towards a Politics of Mockery in Greece', in J. Fernandez and M. T. Huber (eds) *Irony in Action: Anthropology, Practice and the Moral Imagination*: 63–81, Chicago, IL: University of Chicago Press.

Hewitt, A. (2005), *Social Choreography: Ideology and Performance in Dance and Everyday*, Durham, NC: Duke University Press.

Hobsbawm, E. J. and T. O. Ranger (2003), *The Invention of Tradition*, Cambridge: Cambridge University Press.

Horkheimer, M. and T. W. Adorno (2002), *Dialectic of Enlightenment: Philosophical Fragments*, Stanford, CA: Stanford University Press.

Horkheimer, M., T. W. Adorno, G. Noeri, and E. Jephcott (2007), *Dialectic of Enlightenment*, Stanford, CA: Stanford University Press.

Howells, R. (2014), 'The Aesthetics of Utopia: Creation, Creativity and a Critical Theory of Design', *Thesis Eleven*, 123:1, 41–61.

Howes, D. (2003), *Sensual Relations: Engaging the Senses in Culture and Social Theory*, Ann Arbor, MI: University of Michigan Press.

Huizinga, J. (1955), *Homo Ludens: A Study of the Play-element in Culture*, London: Beacon Press.

Illouz, E. (2007), *Cold Intimacies: the Making of Emotional Capitalism*, New York: Polity Press.

Inden, R. B. (2000), *Imagining India*, Halesowen: Hurst.

Ingold, T. (2000), *The Perception of the Environment: Essays in Livelihood, Dwelling and Skills*, London: Routledge.

Ingold, T. (2001), 'Beyond Art and Technology: The Anthropology of Skill', in M. B. Schiffer (ed.) *Anthropological Perspectives on Technology*: 17–31, Albuquerque: University of Mexico Press.

Irwin, J. (1973), 'Indian Embroideries', *Historic Textiles of India at the Calico Museum, II*, Ahmedabad: Calico Museum.

Irwin, W., G. A. Dunn and R. Housel (2010), *True Blood and Philosophy: We Wanna Think Bad Things with You*, London: John Wiley & Sons.

Jafri, S. S. A. (2011), 'Chikan Craft as a Subsistance Occupation among the Muslims of Lucknow', *Islam and Muslim Societies: Social Science Journal*, 4:2.

Jain, K. (2001), 'Muscularity and its Ramifications: Mimetic Male Bodies in Indian Mass Culture', *South Asia: Journal of South Asian Studies*, 24:s1, 197–224.

Jain, K. (2007), *Gods in the Bazaar: The Economies of Indian Calender Art*, Durham, NC: Duke University Press.

James, E. L. (2013), *Fifty Shades of Grey*, New York: Knopf Doubleday Publishing Group.

Jameson, F. (1979), 'Reification and Utopia in Mass Culture', *Social Text*, 1, 130–148.

Jani, A. and S. Khosla (2012), *India Fantastique*, London: Thames & Hudson.

Jodhka, S. S. and K. Newman (2007), 'In the Name of Globalization: Meritocracy, Productivity and the Hidden Language of Caste', *Economic and Political Weekly*, 42:41, 4125–4132.

Johar, K. (2006), *Kabhi Alvida na Kehna (Never Say Good Bye)*, 193 min, India: Yash Raj Films.

Jones, C. and A. M. Leshkowich (2003), 'Introduction: The Globalization of Asian Dress: Re-Orienting Fashion or Re-Orientalizing India?', in S. Niessen, A. M. Leshkowich and C. Jone (eds) *Re-Orienting Fashion: The Globalization of Asian Dress*: 31–36, Oxford: Berg.

Joseph, P. and Gilmore, J. H. (2011), *The Experience Economy*, Cambridge, MA: Perseus Books Group.

Jyotirmayananda (1986), *Vivekananda: His Gospel of Man-making with a Garland of Tributes and a Chronicle of his Life and Times with Pictures*, Pondicherry: All India Press.

Kakar, P. (2012), 'No Men Please, We are Models', *The Telegraph*, New Delhi.

Kalyan, R. (2011), 'Fragmentation by Design: Architecture, Finance and Identity', *Grey Room*, 44, 26–53.

Kamdar, M. (2007), *Planet India: How the Fastest Growing Democracy Is Transforming America and the World*, New York: Scribner.

Kapila, S. (2005), 'Masculinity and Madness: Princely Personhood and Colonial Sciences of the Mind in Western India 1871–1940', *Past and Present*, 187, 121–156.

Kapur, A. (1993), 'Deity to Crusader: The Changing Iconography of Ram', in G. Pandey (ed.) *Hindus and Others*: 74–109, New Delhi: Viking.

Kasturi, M. (2010), '"All gifting is sacred": The Sanatana Dharma Sabha Movement, the Reform of *Dana* and Civil Society in Late Colonial India', *The Indian Economic and Social History Review*, 47:1, 107–139.

Keller, K. L. (1999), 'Brand Mantras: Rationale, Criteria and Examples', *Journal of Marketing Management*, 15, 43–51.

Kesavan, M. (1994), 'Urdu, Awadh and the Tawaif: The Islamicate Roots of Hindi Cinema', in Z. Hasan (ed.) *Forging Identities: Gender, Communities and the State*: 244–257, University of California: Westview Press.

Khan, S. R. (2010), *Privilege: The Making of an Adolescent Elite at St. Paul's School*, Princeton, NJ: Princeton University Press.

Khosla, R. and A. Johnston (1996), *Vanguard: Rohit Khosla*, New Delhi: India Book House.

Klein, N. (2002), *No Logo: No Space, No Choice, No Jobs*, New York: Picador.

Knobel, M. and C. Lankshear (2008), 'Remix: The Art and Craft of Endless Hybridization', *Journal of Adolescent and Adult Literacy*, 52:1, 22–33.

Kopytoff, I. (2008), 'The Cultural Biography of Things: Commoditization as Process', in A. Appadurai (ed.) *The Social Life of Things*: 64–94, Cambridge: Cambridge University Press.

Kornblatt, J. D. (1992), *The Cossack Hero in Russian Literature: A Study in Cultural Mythology*, Wisconsin: University of Wisconsin Press.

Korolainen, K. (2012), 'Artification and the Drawing of Distinctions: an Analysis of Categories and Their Uses', *Contemporary Aesthetics*, 10.

Kothari, R. (1986), 'NGOs, the State and World Capitalism', *Economic and Political Weekly*, 21:50, 2177–2182.

Kristeva, J. (1982), *Powers of Horror: An Essay on Abjection*, New York: Columbia University Press.

Kuldova, T. (2009), 'Networks that Make a Difference: The Production of Social Cohesion in Lucknow, North India', dissertation, *Department of Anthropology*, Oslo: University of Oslo.

Kuldova, T. (2010), 'Acting Out Class: On Mimicking, Mocking, Bollywood Stars and the Urban Indian Male', *Journal of The Finnish Anthropological Society*, 35:3, 60–70.

Kuldova, T. (ed.) (2013a), *Fashion India: Spectacular Capitalism*. Oslo: Akademika Publishing.

Kuldova, T. (2013b), 'Laughing at Luxury: Mocking Fashion Designers', in T. Kuldova (ed.) *Fashion India: Spectacular Capitalism*: 167–193. Oslo: Akademika Publishing.

Kuldova, T. (2013c), '"The Maharaja Style": Royal Chic, Heritage Luxury and the Nomadic Elite', in T. Kuldova (ed.) *Fashion India: Spectacular Capitalism*: 51–70. Oslo: Akademika Publishing.

Kuldova, T. (2014), 'Designing an Illusion of India's Future Superpowerdom: Of the Rise of Neo-Aristocracy, Hindutva and Philanthrocapitalism', *The Unfamiliar: An Anthropological Journal*, 4:1, 15–22.

Kuldova, T. (2015), 'Fashion Exhibition as a Critique of Museum Fashion Exhibitions: The Case of "Fashion India: Spectacular Capitalism"', *Critical Studies in Fashion and Beauty*, 5:2, 313–336.

Kumar, R. and C. Muscat (2006) *Costumes and Textiles of Royal India*, New Delhi: Antique Collectors' Club.

Lafargue, P. (1883), *The Right To Be Lazy*, available online: www.marxists.org (first published: Charles Kerr & Co.).

Laidlaw, J. (1995), *Riches and Renunciation: Religion, Economy, and Society Among the Jains*, Oxford: Clarendon Press.

Lal, K. S. 1988), *The Mughal Harem*, New Delhi: Aditya Prakashan.

Lamarche, P. (2007), 'The Use Value of G.A.M.V. Bataille', in S. Winnubst (ed.) *Reading Bataille Now*: 54–73, Bloomington, IN: Indiana University Press.

Lanham, R. A. (2006), *The Economics of Attention: Style and Substance in the Age of Information*, Chicago, IL: University of Chicago Press.

Laporte, D. (2000), *History of Shit*, London: MIT Press.

Larkin, B. (2004), 'Bandiri Music, Globalization, and Urban Experience in Nigeria', *Social Text*, 22:4, 91–112.

Latour, B. (2010), *On the Modern Cult of the Factish Gods*, Durham, NC: Duke University Press.

Lees-Maffei, G. and L. Sandino (2004), 'Dangerous Liaisons: Relationships Between Design, Craft and Art', *Journal of Design History*, 17:3, 207–219.

Lévi-Strauss, C. (1983), *Mythologiques*, Chicago, IL: University of Chicago Press.

Liechty, M. (2003), *Suitably Modern: Making Middle-Class Culture in a New Consumer Society*, Princeton, NJ: Princeton University Press.

Liep, J. (2001), *Locating Cultural Creativity*, London: Pluto Press.

Lindstrom, M. (2009), *Buyology: How Everything we Believe about Why We Buy is Wrong*, London: Random House Business Books.

Linssen, R., L. van Kempen and G. Kraaykamp (2011), 'Subjective Well-being in Rural India: The Curse of Conspicous Consumption', *Social Indicators Research Journal*, 101, 57–72.

Linton, R. (1965), *The Study of Man: An Introduction*, London: Owen.

Lipovetsky, G. (2005), *Hypermodern Times*, Cambridge: Polity Press.

Llewellyn-Jones, R. (1985), *A Fatal Friendship: The Nawabs, the British and the City of Lucknow*, New Delhi: Oxford University Press.

Llewellyn-Jones, R. (2003), 'Off the Tourist Trail: The "Unknown" Lucknow', in R. Llewellyn-Jones (ed.) *Lucknow: Then and Now*: 22–33, Mumbai: Marg Publications.

Lordon, F. (2014), *Willing Slaves of Capital: Spinoza and Marx on Desire*, London: Verso.

MacKenzie, J. M. (1997), *The Empire of Nature: Hunting, Conservation and British Imperialism*, Manchester: Manchester University Press.

Mahbubani, K. (2009), *The New Asian Hemisphere: The Irresistible Shift of Global Power to the East*, Michigan: PublicAffairs.

Malhotra, K. (2012), *Agneepath*, 174 min, India.

Mangalik, M. (2003), 'Lucknow Food, Streets, and Bazaars', in R. Llewellyn-Jones (ed.) *Lucknow: Then and Now*: 34–47, Mumbai: Marg Publications.

Mani, L. (2008), 'The Phantom of Globality and the Delirium of Excess', *Economic and Political Weekly*, 43:39, 41–47.

Mankekar, P. (1998), 'Entangled Spaces of Modernity: The Viewing Family, The Consuming Nation and Television in India', *Visual Anthropology Review*, 14:2, 32–45.

Mann, B. J. and Spradley, J. P. (1975), *The Cocktail Waitress: Woman's Work in a Man's World*, New York: John Wiley & Sons.

Markel, S. and Gude, T. B. (2010), *India's Fabled City: The Art of Courtly Lucknow*, Los Angeles County Museum of Art, Prestel: Del Monico Books.

Markowitz, S. J. (1994), 'The Distinction Between Art and Craft', *Journal of Aesthetic Education*, 28:1, 55–70.

Martin, R. E. (2011), *The College Cost Disease: Higher Cost and Lower Quality*, Cheltenham, UK and Northampton, MA: Edward Elgar.

Marx, K. (1992), *Capital: A Crtique of Political Economy, Volume 1*, London: Penguin Classics.

Maxwell, S. (2012), 'The Changing Luxury Landscape', in S. Jain and G. Atwal (eds) *The Luxury Market in India: Maharajas to Masses*: 29–39, Basingstoke: Palgrave Macmillan.

Mazzarella, W. (2003), '"Very Bombay": Contending with the Global in an Indian Advertising Agency', *Cultural Anthropology*, 18:1, 33–71.

Mazzarella, W. (2006), *Shoveling Smoke: Advertising and Globalization in Contemporary India*, Durham, NC: Duke University Press.

McGoey, L. (2012), 'Philanthrocapitalism and its Critics', *Poetics*, 40, 185–199.

Mead, G. H. (1929), 'The Nature of the Past', in J. Coss (ed.) *Essays in Honor of John Dewey*: 235–242, New York: Holt.

Mehta, P. B. (2011), 'Meritocracy and its Discontents', *NUJS Law Review*, 4:5, 1–13.

Melchior, M. R. and B. Svensson (2014), *Fashion and Museums: Theory and Practice*, New York: Bloomsbury.

Merton, R. K. (1957), *Social Theory and Social Structure*, Glencoe, IL: Free Press.

Michelutti, L. (2008), '"We are Kshatriyas but we behave like Vaishyas": Diet and Muscular Politics Among a Community of Yadavs in North India', *South Asia: Journal of South Asian Studies*, 31:1, 76–95.

Michelutti, L. (2010), 'Wrestling with (Body) Politics: Understanding "Goonda" Political Styles in North India', in P. Price and A. E. Ruud (eds) *Power and Influence in India: Bosses, Lords and Captains*: 44–69, Oxford: Routledge.

Mitchell, T. (2000), 'The Stage of Modernity', in T. Mitchell (ed.) *Questions of Modernity*: 1–34, Minneapolis: University of Minnesota Press.

Mohan, A. R. (2012), *Khiladi 786*, 141 min, India: Eros International.

Mohsini, M. (2011), 'Crafts, Artisans, and the Nation-State in India', in I. Clark-Deces (ed.) *A Companion to the Anthropology of India*: 186–201, Oxford: Blackwell Publishing.

Moskowitz, M. L. (2013), *Go Nation: Chinese Masculinities and the Game of Weiqi in China*, Oakland, CA: University of California Press.

Mukerji, C. (1990), 'Reading and Writing with Nature: Social Claims and the French Formal Garden', *Theory and Society*, 19, 651–679.

Muller, F. (2000), *Art and Fashion*, London: Thames & Hudson.

Nader, L. (1989), 'Orientalism, Occidentalism and Control of Women', *Cultural Dynamics*, 11, 323–355.

Nagrath, S. (2003), '(En)countering Orientalism in High Fashion: A Review of India Fashion Week 2002', *Fashion Theory*, 7:3/4, 361–376.

Nakassis, C. (2013), 'The Quality of a Copy', in T. Kuldova (ed.) *Fashion India: Spectacular Capitalism*: 143–165, Oslo: Akademika Publishing.

Narayan, S. (2012), 'Saris from Paris?', *Financial Times*, India.

Nayar, P. (2010), *Seeing Stars: Spectacle, Society, and Celebrity Culture*, London: Sage.

Nickel, P. M. and A. M. Eikenberry (2009), 'A Critique of the Discourse of Marketized Philanthropy', *American Behavioral Scientist*, 52:7, 974–989.

Nickel, P. M. and A. M. Eikenberry (2010), 'Philanthropy in an Era of Global Governance', in R. Taylor (ed.) *Third Sector Research*: 269–79, New York: Springer.

Nielsen, K. B. and A. Waldrop (2014), *Women, Gender and Everyday Social Transformation in India*, London and New York: Anthem Press.

Nietzsche, F. (2008), *Beyond Good and Evil*, Rockville, MD: Arc Manor.

Nietzsche, F., B. Williams, J. Nauckhoff and A. D. Caro (2001), *Nietzsche: The Gay Science: With a Prelude in German Rhymes and an Appendix of Songs*, Cambridge: Cambridge University Press.

Nowell, I. (2004), *Generation Deluxe: Consumerism and Philanthropy of the New Super-Rich*, Toronto: Dundurn Press.

Nussbaum, M. (2004), *Hiding from Humanity: Disgust, Shame and the Law*, Princeton, NJ: Princeton University Press.

Obeyesekere, G. (1984), *The Cult of the Goddess Pattini*, Chicago, IL: University of Chicago Press.

Oldenburg, V. T. (2006), 'Lifestyle as Resistance: The Case of the Courtesans', in V. Graff (ed.) *Lucknow: Memories of a City*: 136–154, New Delhi: Oxford University Press.

Oldenburg, V. T. (2007), *Shaam-e-Awadh: Writings on Lucknow*, New Delhi: Penguin Books.

Orbach, S. (2009), *Bodies*, London: Profile Books.

Organ, T. (1975), 'Indian Aesthetics: Its Techniques and Assumptions', *Journal of Aesthetic Education*, 9:1, 11–27.

Osella, F. (2012), 'Malabar Secrets: South Indian Muslim Men's (Homo)sociality across the Indian Ocean', *Asian Studies Review*, 36:4, 531–549.

Panofsky, E. (1976), *Gothic Architecture and Scholasticism*, New York: New American Library.

Petievich, C. (2010), 'Innovations Pious and Impious: Expressive Culture in Nawabi Lucknow', in T. B. Gude and S. Markel (eds) *India's Fabled City: The Art of Courtly Lucknow*: 103–121, Los Angeles County Museum of Art: DelMonico Books, Prestel.

Pfaller, R. (2003), 'Little Gestures of Disappearance: Interpassivity and the Theory of Ritual', *European Journal of Psychoanalysis*, 16.

Pfaller, R. (2008), *Das Schmutzige Heilige und die Reine Vernunft: Symptome der Gegenwartskultur*, Berlin: Fischer Taschenbuch Verlag.

Pfaller, R. (2014), *On the Pleasure Principle in Culture: Illusions without Owners*, London: Verso.

Pinney, C. (2002), 'Introduction: Public, Popular, and Other Cultures', in R. Dwyer and C. Pinney (eds) *Pleasure and the Nation: The History, Politics and Consumption of Public Culture in India*: 1–34, New Delhi: Oxford University Press.

Plassman, H., J. O'Doherty, B. Shiv and A. Rangel (2008), 'Marketing Actions Can Modulate Neural Representations of Experienced Pleasantness', *PNAS*, 105:3, 1050–1054.

Plokhy, S. (2012), *The Cossack Myth: History and Nationhood in the Age of Empires*, Cambridge: Cambridge University Press.

Pollock, S. (2001), 'New Intellectuals in Seventeenth-century India', *The Indian Economic and Social History Review*, 38:1, 3–31.

Polsky, S. (2015), 'Feeding into Scarcity', *Jacobin*, available online: www.jacobinmag.com/2015/02/britain-trussell-trust-austerity/ (accessed 2nd May 2015).

Pool, R. (1987), 'Hot and Cold as an Explanatory Model: The Example of Bharuch District in Gujarat, India', *Social Science and Medicine*, 25:4, 389–399.

Prabhavananda, S. and C. Isherwood (transl) (2002), *Bhagavad-Gita: The Song of God*, New York: Signet Classics.

Price, P. G. (1989), 'Kingly Models in Indian Political Behavior: Culture as a Medium of History', *Asian Survey*, 29, 559–572.

Puddick, M. and P. Menon (2012), 'Contemporary Lustre', in S. Jain and G. Atwal (eds) *The Luxury Market in India: Maharajas to Masses*: 48–68, Basingstoke: Palgrave Macmillan.

Puri, J. (1999), *Woman, Body, Desire in Post-colonial India: Narratives of Gender and Sexuality*, New York: Routledge.

Qureshi, O. (2011), 'The Bold, Naughty Bollywood Heroine Comes of Age', *Daily Pioneer*, available online: www.dailypioneer.com/vivacity/21389-the-bold-naughty-bollywood-heroine-comes-of-age.html?tmpl=component&layout=default&page= (accessed 14th September 2015).

Radcliffe-Brown, A. R. (1961), *Structure and Function in Primitive Society: Essays and Addresses*, London: Cohen & West.

Radford, R. (1998), 'Dangerous Liasons: Art, Fashion and Individualism', *Fashion Theory*, 2:2, 151–164.

Rai, A. (1992), *Chikankari Embroidery of Lucknow*, Ahmedabad: National Institute of Design.

Rai, V. and W. Simon (2007), *Think India: The Rise of the World's Next Great Power and What It Means for Every American*, New York: Penguin Group.

Rajan, R. S. (2004), *Real and Imagined Women: Gender, Culture and Postcolonialism*, New Delhi: Taylor & Francis.

Ramaswami, S. (2007), 'Togethering Contra Othering: Male Hindu–Muslim Interrelations in Proletarian Delhi', *South Asian Popular Culture*, 5:2, 117–128.

Ramusack, B. (1995), 'The Indian Princes as Fantasy: Palace Hotels, Palace Museums, and Palace on Wheels', in C. A. Breckenridge (ed.) *Consuming Modernity: Public Culture in South Asian World*: 66–89, Minneapolis: University of Minnesota Press.

Ranciere, J. and S. Corcoran (2010), *Dissensus: On Politics and Aesthetics*, London: Bloomsbury.

Raustiala, K. and Sprigman, C. (2006), 'The Piracy Paradox: Innovation and Intellectual Property in Fashion Design', *Virginia Law Review*, 92:8, 1687–1777.

Ritzer, G. (1998), 'Introduction', in J. Baudrillard (ed.) *The Consumer Society: Myths and Structures*: 1–24, London: Sage.

Roberts, D. (2003), 'Illusion Only is Sacred: From the Culture Industry to the Aesthetic Economy', *Thesis Eleven*, 73: May, 83–95.

Roberts, K. (2004), *Lovemarks: The Future Beyond Brands*, New York: Murdoch Books.

Robinson, S. (2000), *Marked Men: White Masculinity in Crisis*, Columbia: Columbia University Press.

Rodricks, W. (2012), *The Green Room*, New Delhi: Rupa Publications.

Roy, A. (2014), *Capitalism: A Ghost Story*, Chicago IL: Haymarket Books.

Roy, T. and M. Liebl (2004), 'Handmade in India: Traditional Craft Skills in a Changing World', in M. J. Finger and P. Schuler (eds) *Poor People's Knowledge: Promoting Intellectual Property in Developing Countries*: 53–73, New York: Oxford University Press.

Rozin, P. and A. E. Fallon (1987), 'A Perspective on Disgust', *Psychological Review*, 94:1, 23–41.

Rozin, P., L. Millman and C. Nemeroff (1986), 'Operation of the Laws of Sympathetic Magic in Disgust and Other Domains', *Journal of Personality and Social Psychology*, 50:4, 703–712.

Saavala, M. (2012), *Middle-Class Moralities: Everyday Struggle over Belonging and Prestige in India*, Hyderabad: Orient Blackswan.

Sadiq, M. (1960), *Chaudvin ka Chand*, 165 min, India.

Said, E. W. (1979), *Orientalism*, London: Vintage Books.

Sandhya, S. (2009), *Love Will Follow: Why the Indian Marriage is Burning*, India: Random House Publishers.

Sarkar, S. (1998), 'Indian Craft-Technology: Static or Changing – A Case Study of the Kansari's Craft in Bengal, 16th to 18th Centuries', *Indian Journal of History of Science*, 33:2, 131–142.

Sarma, M. S. (2014), 'The Death of the Villain: Neoliberalism and the Hindi Cinema', *Clarion*, 3:1, 84–91.

Sassen, S. (2014), *Expulsions: Brutality and Complexity in the Global Economy*, Cambridge: Harvard University Press.

Saxena, S. (1999), 'Country Profile on Alcohol in India', in L. Riley and M. Marshall (eds) *Alcohol and Public Health in 8 Developing Countries*: 37–60, Geneva: WHO.

Schumpeter, J. A. (1934), *The Theory of Economic Development: an Inquiry into Profits, Capital, Credit, Interest, and the Business Cycle*, New Jersey: Transaction Books.

Scott, D. (2012), 'Cultural Borrowing and Cultural Theft: Why Burberry and Other Luxury Brands Should Take Note of Hermes and its 2011 Sari Collection when Taking Inspiration from Non-Western Cultures', available online: www.inter-disciplinary.net/critical-issues/wp-content/uploads/2012/08/scottfashpaper.pdf (accessed 14th September 2015).

Sell, S. K. (2014), *Private Power, Public Law: The Globalization of Intellectual Property Rights*, Cambridge Books Online: Cambridge University Press.

Sengupta, H. (2009), *Ramp Up: The Business of Indian Fashion*, New Delhi: Dorling Kindersley.

Serazio, M. (2013), *Your Ad Here: The Cool Sell of Guerrilla Marketing*, New York: New York University Press.

Shapiro, R. (2004), 'The Aesthetic of Institutionalization: Breakdancing in France', *Journal of Arts, Managment, Law and Society*, 33:4, 316–335.

Shapiro, R. and Heinich, N. (2012), 'When is Artification?', *Contemporary Aesthetics*, 10.

Sharar, A. H. (2005), *Lucknow: The Last Phase of an Oriental Culture*, New Delhi: Oxford University Press.

Sharma, M. (2011), *Ladies vs. Ricky Bahl*, 140 min, India: Yash Raj Films.

Shetty, R. (2011), *Singham*, 142 min, India: Reliance Entertainment.

Shiner, L. (2012), 'Artification, Fine Art, and the Myth of "the Artist"', *Contemporary Aesthetics*, 10.

Simmel, G. (1957), 'Fashion', *American Journal of Sociology*, 62:6, 541–558.

Singh, G. and B. Lal (1979), 'Alcohol in India', *Indian Journal of Psychiatry*, 21, 39–45.

Singh, M. and S. Dwivedi (2010), *Automobiles of the Maharajas*, New York: Rizzoli.

Singh, V. (2004), *Romancing with Chikankari*, New Delhi: Tushar Publications.

Sinha, D. (2012), 'Renewing India's Relationship with Luxury', in S. Jain and G. Atwal (eds) *The Luxury Market in India: Maharajas to Masses*: 7–13, Basingstoke: Palgrave Macmillan.

Sinha, M. (1999), 'Giving Masculinity a History: Some Contributions from the Historiography of India', *Gender and History*, 11:3, 445–460.

Smith, A. (2000), *The Wealth of Nations: (A Modern Library E-Book)*, London: Random House.

Smith, M. D. (1996), 'The Empire Filters Back: Consumption, Production and the Politics of Starbucks Coffee', *Urban Geography*, 17:6, 502–524.

Sontag, S. (1992), 'Foreword', in M. Leiris (ed.) *Manhood: A Journey from Childhood into the Fierce Order of Virility*: vii–xv, Chicago, IL: University of Chicago Press.

Sramek, J. (2006), '"Face Him Like a Briton": Tiger Hunting, Imperialism, and British Masculinity in Colonial India, 1800–1875', *Victorian Studies*, 48:4, 659–680.

Srinivas, T. (2010), *Winged Faith: Rethinking Globalization and Religious Pluralism Through the Satya Sai Movement*, New York: Columbia University Press.

Srinivasan (2006), 'Royalty's Courtesans and God's Mortal Wives: Keepers of Culture in Precolonial India', in B. Gordon and M. Feldman (eds) *The Courtesan's Arts: Cross-cultural Perspectives*: 161–181, Oxford: Oxford University Press.

Srour, N. (2013), 'Hindi Cinema and Masculinities: From Salman Khan to John Abraham', in T. Kuldova (ed.) *Fashion India: Spectacular Capitalism*: 211–222, Oslo: Akademika Publishing.

Steele, V. (2008), 'Museum Quality: The Rise of the Fashion Exhibition', *Fashion Theory*, 12:1, 7–30.

Stein, H. F. (1984), 'The Vitalization of Symbolic Interactionism', *Social Psychology Quarterly*, 50:1, 83–94.

Sundar, P. (2013), 'Philanthropy in the Building of Modern India', in M. Cantegreil, D. Chanana and R. Kattumuri (eds) *Revealing Indian Philanthropy*: 31–38, London: Alliance Publishing Trust.

Svašek, M. (2009), 'Improvising in a World of Movement: Transit, Transition and Transformation', in H. K. Anheier and Y. R. Isar (eds) *Cultural Expression, Creativity and Innovation*: 62–77, London: Sage.

Tahiliani, T. (2011), 'Press Release: Artisanal – Bringing the Craft to the Fore', retrieved on 14 September 2015 from http://strandofsilk.com/blog/tarun-tahiliani/news/tahiliani-bridal-couture-expo.

Tambiah, S. J. (1968), 'The Magical Power of Words', *Man*, 3:2, 175–208.

Tarlo, E. (1996), *Clothing Matters: Dress and Identity in India*, London: Hurst & Company.

Taylor, M. (2005), 'Culture Transition: Fashion's Cultural Dialogue between Commerce and Art', *Fashion Theory*, 9:4, 445–460.

Thapan, M. (2009), *Living the Body: Embodiment, Womanhood and Identity in Contemporary India*, New Delhi: Sage.

Thussu, D. K. (2013), *Communicating India's Soft Power: Buddha to Bollywood*, London: Palgrave Macmillan.

Tosh, J. (1994), 'What Should Historians do with Masculinity? Reflections on Nineteenth Century Britain', *History Workshop Journal*, 38, 179–202.

Tripathi, A. (2010), *The Immortals of Meluha: The Shiva Trilogy 1*, London: Quercus Publishing.

Tripathi, A. (2011), *The Secret of the Nagas: The Secret of the Nagas–Shiva Trilogy 2 Series*: Westland, MI: Westland Books.

Tripathi, A. (2013), *The Oath of the Vayuputras*, Westland, MI: Westland Books.

Trivedi, M. (2010), *The Making of the Awadh Culture*, New Delhi: Primus Books.

Tronti, M. (1966), 'The Strategy of Refusal', available online: http://libcom.org/library/strategy-refusal-mario-tronti (accessed 10th September 2014).

Tseëlon, E. (2011), 'Introduction: A Critique of the Ethical Fashion Paradigm', *Critical Studies in Fashion and Beauty*, 2:1&2, 3–68.

Tyabji, L. (2007), 'Handcrafting a Culture', *Seminar 575: Between Cultures – A Symposium on the Changing Face of Lucknow*, 32–35.

Tyabji, L. and S. Das (2007), *Threads and Voices: Behind the Indian Textile Tradition*: Published for Marg Publications, Mumbai on behalf of the National Centre for the Performing Arts.

Uberoi, P. (2010), *Freedom and Destiny: Gender, Family, and Popular Culture in India*, New Delhi: Oxford University Press.

UNESCO, C. R. Trust and Artesanias de Colombia (2005), 'Designers Meet Artisans', New Delhi: UNESCO.

Upadhya, C. (2008), 'Rewriting the Code: Professionals and the Reconstruction of the Indian Middle Class Identity', in C. Jaffrelot and P. van der Veer (eds) *Patterns of Middle Class Consumption in India and China*: 55–87, New Delhi: Sage.

Valaya, J. J. (2009), 'Foreword', in H. Sengupta (ed.) *Ramp Up: The Business of Indian Fashion*: viii–xiii, New Delhi: Dorling Kindersley.

Valaya, J. J. (2012), 'Fine Dressmaking', available online: www.explosivefashion.in/blog_post_detail.php?id=787 (accessed 20th March 2013).

Varma, P. K. (1998), *The Great Indian Middle-Class*, London: Penguin Books.

Varshney, A. (1997), 'Postmodernism, Civic Engagement, and Ethnic Conflict: A Passage to India', *Comparative Politics*, 30:1, 1–20.

Vasudev, S. (2012), *Powder Room: The Untold Story of Indian Fashion*, Noida: Random House India.

Vatsyayana, M., W. Doniger and S. Kakar, (2009), *Kamasutra*, Oxford: Oxford University Press.

Veblen, T. (1970), *The Theory of the Leisure Class: An Economic Study of Institutions*, London: Unwin Books.

Venkatesan, S. (2006), 'Shifting Balances in a "Craft Community": The Mat Weavers of Pattamadai, South India', *Contributions to Indian Sociology*, 40:1, 63–89.

Venkatesan, S. (2009), *Craft Matters: Artisans, Development and the Indian Nation*, New Delhi: Orient Blackswan.

Waldrop, A. (2004), 'Gating and Class Relations: the Case of a New Delhi "Colony"', *City and Society*, 16:2, 93–116.

Walker, M. (2010), 'Courtesans and Choreographers: The (Re)Placement of Women in the History of Kathak Dance', in P. Chakravorty and N. Gupta (eds) *Dance Matters: Performing India*: 279–300, New Delhi: Routledge.

Warner, M. (2010), 'Max Warner Global Ambassador for Chivas Regal', *Urban Male Magazine*, Spring 102.

Weber, M. (2005), *The Protestant Ethic and the Spirit of Capitalism*, London: Routledge.

Weeks, K. (2011), *The Problem with Work: Feminism, Marxism, Antiwork Politics, and Postwork Imaginaries*, Durham, NC: Duke University Press.

Werbner, P. (1986), 'The Virgin and the Clown: Ritual Elaboration in Pakistani Migrants' Weddings', *Man*, 21:2, 227–250.

Wilde, O. (2004), *The Soul of Man Under Socialism*, Whitefish, Montana: Kessinger Publishing.

Wilkinson-Weber, C. M. (1999), *Embroidering Lives: Women's Work and Skill in the Lucknow Embroidery Industry*, Albany, NY: State University of New York Press.

Wilkinson-Weber, C. M. (2013), *Fashioning Bollywood: The Making and Meaning of Hindi Film Costume*, London: Bloomsbury.

Willerslev, R. and M. A. Pedersen (2011), 'Proportional Holism: Joking the Cosmos into the Right Shape in North Asia', in T. Otto and N. Bubandt (eds) *Experiments in Holism: Theory and Practice in Contemporary Anthropology*: 262–278, New York: John Wiley & Sons.

Willerslev, R. and C. Suhr (2014) 'Introduction: Montage as an Amplifier of Invisibility', in R. Willerslev and C. Suhr (eds) *Transcultural Montage*: 1–15, London: Berghahn Books.

Williams, R. (1973), 'Base and Superstructure in Marxist Cultural Theory', *New Left Review*, I/82.

Williams, R. (2002), 'Culture is Ordinary', in B. Highmore (ed.) *The Everyday Life Reader*: 91–100, London: Routledge.

Wilson, E. (2007), 'A Note on Glamour', *Fashion Theory*, 11:1, 95–108.

Yoshida, M. (2001), 'Joking, Gender, Power, and Professionalism among Japanese Inn Workers', *Ethnology*, 40:4, 361–369.

Yurchak, A. (2006), *Everything Was Forever, Until It Was No More: The Last Soviet Generation*, Princeton, NJ: Princeton University Press.

Zafar, A. A. (2014), *Gunday*, 152 min, India: Yash Raj Films.

Žižek, S. (1989), *The Sublime Object of Ideology*, London: Verso.

Žižek, S. (2006), 'Nobody has to be Vile: The Philanthropic Enemy', *London Review of Books*, 28:7.

INDEX